The Tongue Set Free

ELIAS CANETTI

THE TONGUE
SET FREE

Remembrance of a European Childhood

Translated from the German by
JOACHIM NEUGROSCHEL

Farrar, Straus and Giroux
New York

Published simultaneously in Canada by
Collins Publishers, Toronto

First Farrar, Straus and Giroux printing, 1983

Library of Congress Cataloguing in Publication Data
Canetti, Elias.
The tongue set free.
Translation of: Die gerettete Zunge.
1. Canetti, Elias—Biography—Youth.
2. Authors, Austrian—20th century—Biography.
I. Title.
PT2605.A58Z4713   1983   833′.912 [B]   83-16363
ISBN 0-374-51802-5
www.fgsbooks.com

P1

For Georges Canetti
1911–1971

Contents

Part One: Ruschuk, 1905–1911
My Earliest Memory   3
Family Pride   4
Kako la Gallinica; Wolves and Werewolves   7
The Armenian's Ax; The Gypsies   11
My Brother's Birth   14
The Turk's House; The Two Grandfathers   16
Purim; The Comet   19
The Magic Language; The Fire   22
Adders and Letters   25
The Murder Attempt   28
A Curse on the Voyage   30

Part Two: Manchester, 1911–1913
Wallpaper and Books; Strolls along the Mersey   37
Little Mary; The Sinking of the *Titanic*; Captain Scott   43
Napoleon; Cannibal Guests; Sunday Fun   50
Father's Death; The Final Version   55
The Heavenly Jerusalem   61
German on Lake Geneva   65

Part Three: Vienna, 1913–1916
The Earthquake of Messina; *Burgtheater* at Home   79
The Indefatigable Man   84
Outbreak of the War   90
Medea and Odysseus   93
A Trip to Bulgaria   96

The Discovery of Evil; Fortress Vienna   105
Alice Asriel   111
The Meadow near Neuwaldwegg   116
Mother's Illness; Herr Professor   119
The Beard in Lake Constance   124

Part Four: Zurich—*Scheuchzerstrasse*, 1916–1919
The Oath   133
A Roomful of Presents   136
Espionage   140
Seduction by the Greeks; The School of Sophistication   143
The Skull; Dispute with an Officer   151
Reading Day and Night; The Life of Gifts   154
Hypnosis and Jealousy; The Seriously Wounded   160
The Gottfried Keller Celebration   166
Vienna in Trouble; The Slave from Milan   169

Part Five: Zurich—Tiefenbrunnen, 1919–1921
The Nice Old Maids of the Yalta Villa; Dr. Wedekind   179
Phylogeny of Spinach; Junius Brutus   191
Among Great Men   195
Shackling the Ogre   198
Making Oneself Hated   202
The Petition   207
Getting Prepared for Prohibitions   214
The Mouse Cure   218
The Marked Man   222
The Arrival of Animals   224
Kannitverstan; The Canary   229
The Enthusiast   233
History and Melancholy   241
The Collection   245
The Appearance of the Sorcerer   248
The Black Spider   250
Michelangelo   255
Paradise Rejected   259

Part One

RUSCHUK
1905–1911

My Earliest Memory

My earliest memory is dipped in red. I come out of a door on the arm of a maid, the floor in front of me is red, and to the left a staircase goes down, equally red. Across from us, at the same height, a door opens, and a smiling man steps forth, walking towards me in a friendly way. He steps right up close to me, halts, and says: "Show me your tongue." I stick out my tongue, he reaches into his pocket, pulls out a jackknife, opens it, and brings the blade all the way to my tongue. He says: "Now we'll cut off his tongue." I don't dare pull back my tongue, he comes closer and closer, the blade will touch me any second. In the last moment, he pulls back the knife, saying: "Not today, tomorrow." He snaps the knife shut again and puts it back in his pocket.

Every morning, we step out of the door and into the red hallway, the door opens, and the smiling man appears. I know what he's going to say and I wait for the command to show my tongue. I know he's going to cut it off, and I get more and more scared each time. That's how the day starts, and it happens very often.

I kept it to myself and asked my mother about it only much later. She could tell by the ubiquitous red that it was the guesthouse in Carlsbad, where she had spent the summer of 1907 with my father and me. To take care of the two-year-old baby, she had brought along a nanny from Bulgaria, a girl who wasn't even fifteen. Every morning at the crack of dawn, the girl went out holding the child on her arm; she spoke only Bulgarian, but got along fine in the lively town, and was always back punctually with the child. Once, she was seen on the street with an unknown young man, she couldn't say anything about him, a chance acquaintance. A few weeks later, it turned out that the young man lived in the room right across from us, on the other side of the corridor. At night, the girl sometimes went to his room quickly. My

parents felt responsible for her and sent her back to Bulgaria immediately.

Both of them, the maid and the young man, had always left the
house very early in the morning, that's how they must have met, that's
the way it must have started. The threat with the knife worked, the
child quite literally held his tongue for ten years.

Family Pride

Ruschuk, on the lower Danube, where I came into the world, was a
marvelous city for a child, and if I say that Ruschuk is in Bulgaria,
then I am giving an inadequate picture of it. For people of the most
varied backgrounds lived there, on any one day you could hear seven
or eight languages. Aside from the Bulgarians, who often came from
the countryside, there were many Turks, who lived in their own neighborhood, and next to it was the neighborhood of the Sephardim, the
Spanish Jews—our neighborhood. There were Greeks, Albanians, Armenians, Gypsies. From the opposite side of the Danube came Rumanians; my wetnurse, whom I no longer remember, was Rumanian.
There were also Russians here and there.

As a child, I had no real grasp of this variety, but I never stopped
feeling its effects. Some people have stuck in my memory only because
they belonged to a particular ethnic group and wore a different costume
from the others. Among the servants that we had in our home during
the course of six years, there was once a Circassian and later on an
Armenian. My mother's best friend was Olga, a Russian woman. Once
every week, Gypsies came into our courtyard, so many that they seemed
like an entire nation; the terrors they struck in me will be discussed
below.

Ruschuk was an old port on the Danube, which made it fairly
significant. As a port, it had attracted people from all over, and the
Danube was a constant topic of discussion. There were stories about
the extraordinary years when the Danube froze over; about sleigh rides
all the way across the ice to Rumania; aboqt starving wolves at the
heels of the sleigh horses.

Wolves were the first wild animals I heard about. In the fairy tales
that the Bulgarian peasant girls told me, there were werewolves, and
one night, my father terrorized me with a wolf mask on his face.

It would be hard to give a full picture of the colorful time of those
early years in Ruschuk, the passions and the terrors. Anything I subsequently experienced had already happened in Ruschuk. There, the

rest of the world was known as "Europe," and if someone sailed up
the Danube to Vienna, people said he was going to Europe. Europe
began where the Turkish Empire had once ended. Most of the Sephardim were still Turkish subjects. Life had always been good for them
under the Turks, better than for the Christian Slavs in the Balkans.
But since many Sephardim were well-to-do merchants, the new Bulgarian regime maintained good relations with them, and King Ferdinand, who ruled for a long time, was said to be a friend of the Jews.

The loyalties of the Sephardim were fairly complicated. They were
pious Jews, for whom the life of their religious community was rather
important. But they considered themselves a special brand of Jews,
and that was because of their Spanish background. Through the cen-
turies since their expulsion from Spain, the Spanish they spoke with
one another had changed little. A few Turkish words had been absorbed, but they were recognizable as Turkish, and there were nearly
always Spanish words for them. The first children's songs I heard were
Spanish, I heard old Spanish *romances*; but the thing that was most
powerful, and irresistible for a child, was a Spanish attitude. With
naive arrogance, the Sephardim looked down on other Jews; a word
always charged with scorn was *Todesco,* meaning a German or Ashkenazi
Jew. It would have been unthinkable to marry a *Todesca,* a Jewish
woman of that background, and among the many families that I heard
about or knew as a child in Ruschuk, I cannot recall a single case of
such a mixed marriage. I wasn't even six years old when my grandfather
warned me against such a misalliance in the future. But this general
discrimination wasn't all. Among the Sephardim themselves, there were
the "good families," which meant the ones that had been rich since
way back. The proudest words one could hear about a person were:
"*Es de buena famiglia*—he's from a good family." How often and *ad
nauseam* did I hear that from my mother. When she enthused about the
Viennese *Burgtheater* and read Shakespeare with me, even later on, when
she spoke about Strindberg, who became her favorite author, she had
no scruples whatsoever about telling that she came from a good family,
there was no better family around. Although the literatures of the
civilized languages she knew became the true substance of her life, she
never felt any contradiction between this passionate universality and
the haughty family pride that she never stopped nourishing.

Even back in the period when I was utterly her thrall (she opened
all the doors of the intellect for me, and I followed her, blind and
enthusiastic), I nevertheless noticed this contradiction, which tormented
and bewildered me, and in countless conversations during that time of
my adolescence I discussed the matter with her and reproached her,

but it didn't make the slightest impression. Her pride had found its channels at an early point, moving through them steadfastly; but while I was still quite young, that narrowmindedness, which I never understood in her, biased me against any arrogance of background. I cannot take people seriously if they have any sort of caste pride, I regard them as exotic but rather ludicrous animals. I catch myself having reverse prejudices against people who plume themselves on their lofty origin. The few times that I was friendly with aristocrats, I had to overlook their talking about it, and had they sensed what efforts this cost me, they would have forgone my friendship. All prejudices are caused by other prejudices, and the most frequent are those deriving from their opposites.

Furthermore, the caste in which my mother ranked herself was a caste of Spanish descent and also of money. In my family, and especially in hers, I saw what money does to people. I felt that those who were most willingly devoted to money were the worst. I got to know all the shades, from money-grubbing to paranoia. I saw brothers whose greed had led them to destroy one another in years of litigation, and who kept on litigating when there was no money left. They came from the same "good" family that my mother was so proud of. She witnessed all those things too, we often spoke about it. Her mind was penetrating; her knowledge of human nature had been schooled in the great works of world literature as well as in the experiences of her own life. She recognized the motives of the lunatic self-butchery her family was involved in; she could easily have penned a novel about it; but her pride in this same family remained unshaken. Had it been love, I could have readily understood it. But she didn't even love many of the protagonists, she was indignant at some, she had scorn for others, yet for the family as a whole, she felt nothing but pride.

Much later, I came to realize that I, translated to the greater dimensions of mankind, am exactly as she was. I have spent the best part of my life figuring out the wiles of man as he appears in the historical civilizations. I have examined and analyzed power as ruthlessly as my mother her family's litigations. There is almost nothing bad that I couldn't say about humans and humankind. And yet my pride in them is so great that there is only one thing I really hate: their enemy, death.

Kako la Gallinica
Wolves and Werewolves

An eager and yet tender word that I often heard was *la butica*. That was what they called the store, the business, where my grandfather and his sons usually spent the day. I was rarely taken there because I was too little. The store was located on a steep road running from the height of the wealthier districts of Ruschuk straight down to the harbor. All the major stores were on this street; my grandfather's *butica* was in a three-story building that struck me as high and stately because the residential houses up on the rise had only one story. The *butica* dealt in wholesale groceries, it was a roomy place and it smelled wonderful. Huge, open sacks stood on the floor, containing various kinds of cereals, there was millet, barley, and rice. If my hands were clean, I was allowed to reach into the sacks and touch the grains. That was a pleasant sensation, I filled my hand, lifted it up, smelled the grains, and let them slowly run back down again; I did this often, and though there were many other strange things in the store, I liked doing that best, and it was hard to get me away from the sacks. There was tea and coffee and especially chocolate. There were huge quantities of everything, and it was always beautifully packed, it wasn't sold in small amounts as in ordinary shops. I also especially liked the open sacks on the floor because they weren't too high for me and because when I reached in, I could feel the many grains, which meant so much to me.

Most of the things in the store were edible, but not all. There were matches, soaps, and candles. There were also knives, scissors, whetstones, sickles, and scythes. The peasants who came from the villages to shop used to stand in front of the instruments for a long time, testing the keenness with their fingers. I watched them, curious and a bit fearful; I was not allowed to touch the blades. Once, a peasant, who was probably amused by my face, took hold of my thumb, put it next to his, and showed me how hard his skin was. But I never received a gift of chocolate; my grandfather, who sat in an office in the back, ruled with an iron hand, and everything was wholesale. At home, he showed me his love because I had his full name, even his first name. But he didn't much care to see me in the store, and I wasn't allowed to stay long. When he gave an order, the employee who got the order dashed off, and sometimes an employee would leave the *butica* with packages. My favorite was a skinny, poorly dressed, middle-aged man, who always smiled absently. He had indefinite movements and jumped when my grandfather said anything. He appeared to be dreaming and was altogether different from the other people I saw in the store. He always had a friendly word for me; he spoke so vaguely that I could never understand him, but I sensed that he was well disposed towards me. His name was Chelebon, and since he was a poor and hopelessly incapable relative, my grandfather hired him out of pity. My grandfather always called to Chelebon as if he were a servant; that was how I remembered him, and I found out only much later that he was a brother of my grandfather's.

The street running past the huge gate of our courtyard was dusty and drowsy. If it rained hard, the street turned into mud, and the droshkeys left deep tracks. I wasn't allowed to play in the street, there was more than enough room in our big courtyard, and it was safe. But sometimes I heard a violent clucking from outside, it would get louder and louder and more excited. Then, before long, a man in black, tattered clothes, clucking and trembling in fear, would burst through the gate, fleeing the street children. They were all after him, shouting "*Kako! Kako!*" and clucking like hens. He was afraid of chickens, and that was why they harrassed him. He was a few steps ahead of them and, right before my eyes, he changed into a hen. He clucked violently, but in desperate fear, and made fluttering motions with his arms. He breathlessly dashed up the steps to my grandfather's house, but never dared to enter; he jumped down on the other side and remained lying motionless. The children halted at the gate, clucking, they weren't allowed into the courtyard. When he lay there as if dead, they were a bit scared and ran away. But then they promptly launched into their victory chant: "*Kako la gallinica! Kako la gallinica!*—Kako the chicken! Kako the chicken!" No sooner were they out of earshot than he got to his feet, felt himself all over, peered about cautiously, listened anxiously for a while, and then stole out of the courtyard, hunched, but utterly silent. Now he was no longer a chicken, he didn't flutter or cluck, and he was once again the exhausted neighborhood idiot.

Sometimes, if the children were lurking not too far away in the street, the sinister game started all over again. Usually, it moved to another street, and I couldn't see anything more. Maybe I felt sorry for Kako, I was always scared when he jumped, but what I couldn't get enough of, what I always watched in the same excitement, was his metamorphosis into a gigantic black hen. I couldn't understand why the children ran after him, and when he lay motionless on the ground after his leap, I was afraid he would never get up again and turn into a chicken again.

The Danube is very wide in its Bulgarian lower reaches. Giurgiu, the city on the other bank, was Rumanian. From there, I was told, my wetnurse came, my wetnurse, who fed me her milk. She had supposedly been a strong, healthy peasant woman and also nursed her own baby, whom she brought along. I always heard her praises, and even though I can't remember her, the word "Rumanian" has always had a warm sound for me because of her.

In rare winters, the Danube froze over, and people told exciting stories about it. In her youth, Mother had often ridden a sleigh all the way over to Rumania, she showed me the warm furs she had been bundled in. When it was very cold, wolves came down from the mountains and ravenously pounced on the horses in front of the sleighs. The coachman tried to drive them away with his whip, but it was useless, and someone had to fire at them. Once, during such a sleigh ride, it turned out that they hadn't taken anything to shoot with. An armed Circassian, who lived in the house as a servant, was supposed to come along, but he had been gone, and the coachman had started without him. They had a terrible time keeping the wolves at bay and were in great danger. If a sleigh with two men hadn't happened to come along from the opposite direction, things might have ended very badly, but the two men shot and killed one wolf and drove the others away. My mother had been terribly afraid; she described the red tongues of the wolves, which had come so close that she still dreamt about them in later years.

I often begged her to tell me this story, and she enjoyed telling it to me. Thus wolves became the first wild beasts to fill my imagination. My terror of them was nourished by the fairy tales I heard from the Bulgarian peasant girls. Five or six of them always lived in our home. They were quite young, perhaps ten or twelve years old, and had been brought by their families from the villages to the city, where they were hired out as serving maids in middle-class homes. They ran around barefoot in the house and were always in a high mettle; they didn't have much to do, they did everything together, and they became my earliest playmates.

In the evening, when my parents went out, I stayed at home with the girls. Low Turkish divans ran all the way along the walls of the huge living room. Aside from the carpets everywhere and a few small tables, they were the only constant furnishing that I can remember in that room. When it grew dark, the girls got scared. We all huddled together on one of the divans, right by the window; they took me into their midst, and now they began their stories about werewolves and vampires. No sooner was one story finished than they began the next; it was scary, and yet, squeezing against the girls on all sides, I felt good. We were so frightened that no one dared to stand up, and when my parents came home, they found us all wobbling in a heap.

Of the fairy tales I heard, only the ones about werewolves and vampires have lodged in my memory. Perhaps no other kinds were told. I can't pick up a book of Balkan fairy tales without instantly recognizing some of them. Every detail of them is present to my mind, but not in the language I heard them in. I heard them in Bulgarian, but I know them in German; this mysterious translation is perhaps the oddest thing that I have to tell about my youth, and since the language history of mosthchildren runs differently, perhaps I ought to say more about it.

To each other, my parents spoke German, which I was not allowed to understand. To us children and to all relatives and friends, they spoke Ladino. That was the true vernacular, albeit an ancient Spanish, I often heard it later on and I've never forgotten it. The peasant girls at home knew only Bulgarian, and I must have learned it with them. But since I never went to a Bulgarian school, leaving Ruschuk at six years of age, I very soon forgot Bulgarian completely. All events of those first few years were in Ladino or Bulgarian. It wasn't until much later that most of them were rendered into German within me. Only especially dramatic events, murder and manslaughter so to speak, and the worst terrors have been retained by me in their Ladino wording, and very precisely and indestructibly at that. Everything else, that is, most things, and especially anything Bulgarian, like the fairy tales, I carry around in German.

I cannot say exactly how this happened. I don't know at what point in time, on what occasion, this or that translated itself. I never probed into the matter; perhaps I was afraid to destroy my most precious memories with a methodical examination based on rigorous principles. I can say only one thing with certainty: The events of those years are present to my mind in all their strength and freshness (I've fed on them for over sixty years), but the vast majority are tied to words that I did not know at that time. It seems natural to me to write them down now; I don't have the feeling that I am changing or warping anything. It is not like the literary translation of a book from one languagz to another, it is a translation that happened of its own accord in my unconscious, and since I ordinarily avoid this word like the plague, a word that has become meaningless from overuse, I apologize for employing it in this one and only case.

The Armenian's Ax
The Gypsies

The delight in topographical drawing, which Stendhal so deftly indulges in throughout his *Henri Brulard*, is beyond me, and, to my sorrow, I was always a poor draftsman. So I have to describe the layout of the residential buildings around our courtyard garden in Ruschuk.

When you stepped through the large gate from the street into the courtyard, Grandfather Canetti's house stood immediately to the right. It looked statelier than the other houses, it was also higher. But I can't say whether it had an upper floor in contrast to the other single-story houses. It appeared taller in any event because there were more steps leading up to it. It was also brighter than the other houses, it may have been painted a light color.

Opposite, to the left of the courtyard gate, stood the house where my father's eldest sister, Aunt Sophie, lived with her husband, Uncle Nathan. His family name was Eliakim, a name I never cared for; perhaps it disturbed me because it didn't sound Spanish like all the other names. They had three children, Régine, Jacques, and Laurica. This last child, the youngest, was four years older than I, an age difference that played a baleful part.

Next to this house, in the same line, also on the left side of the courtyard, stood our house, which looked just like my uncle's. A few steps ran up to the two houses, ending in a porch the width of both together.

The garden courtyard between these three houses was very large; the draw well for water stood facing us, not in the center, but a little off to the side. It didn't yield enough, and most of the water came in gigantic barrels that were drawn by mules from the Danube. The Danube water couldn't be used without first being boiled, and it stood then in huge caldrons, cooling off on the porch in front of the house.

Behind the draw well and separated from the courtyard by a hedge, there was the orchard. It wasn't especially attractive, it was too regular, and perhaps not old enough; my mother's relatives had far more beautiful orchards.

It was through the narrow side of our house that you came in from the large courtyard. The house then stretched out far into the back, and even though it had only that one floor, it is very spacious in my memory. On the further side of the courtyard, you could walk all the way around the house, past the long side, and then enter a smaller yard, into which the kitchen opened. Here there was wood to be chopped, geese and chickens scurried about, there was always a hustle and bustle in the kitchen, the cook carried things out or in, and the half dozen little girls jumped about and were busy.

In this kitchen yard, there was often a servant chopping wood, and the one I remember best was my friend, the sad Armenian. While chopping, he sang songs, which I couldn't understand, but which tore my heart. When I asked my mother why he was so sad, she said bad people had wanted to kill all the Armenians in Istanbul, and he had lost his entire family. He had watched from a hiding place when they had killed his sister. Then he had fled to Bulgaria, and my father had felt sorry for him and taken him into the house. When he chopped wood now, he always had to think of his little sister, and that was why he sang those sad songs.

I developed a deep love for him. Whenever he chopped wood, I stood up on the divan at the end of the long living room, by the window facing the kitchen yard. Then I leaned out the window to watch him, and when he sang, I thought of his sister—and then I would always wish for a little sister myself. He had a long black mustache and pitch-black hair, and he seemed very huge, perhaps because I saw him when he lifted his arm up high with the ax. I loved him even more than the store employee Chelebon, whom I saw very infrequently after all. The Armenian and I exchanged a few words, but very few, and I don't know what the language was. But he waited for me before he started chopping. The instant he saw me, he smiled slightly and raised the ax, and it was terrible to watch his rage as he smashed into the wood. He became gloomy then and sang his songs. When he put the ax down, he smiled at me again, and I waited for his smile just as he waited for me, he, the first refugee in my life.

Every Friday, the Gypsies came. On Friday, the Jewish homes prepared everything for the Sabbath. The house was cleaned from top to bottom, the Bulgarian girls scooted all over the place, the kitchen hummed with activity, no one had time for me. I was all alone and waiting for the Gypsies, my face pressed against the garden window of the gigantic living room. I lived in panic fear of them. I assume it was the girls who also told me about Gypsies during the long evenings in the darkness. I thought about their stealing children and was convinced that they were after me.

But despite my fear, I wouldn't have missed seeing them; it was a splendid sight they offered. The courtyard gate had been opened wide for them, for they needed space. They came like an entire tribe: in the middle, tall and erect, a blind patriarch, the great-grandfather, as I was told, a handsome, white-haired old man; he walked very slowly, leaning on two grown granddaughters right and left and wearing colorful rags. Around him, thronging densely, there were Gypsies of all ages, very few men, almost nothing but women, and countless children, the infants in their mother's arms; the rest sprang about, but never moved very far from the proud old man, who always remained the center. The whole procession had something strangely dense about it, I never otherwise saw so many people huddling so close together as they moved along; and in this very colorful city, they were the most colorful sight. The rags they had pieced together for their clothing shone in all colors, but the one that stood out sharpest was red. Sacks dangled from many of the shoulders, and I couldn't look at those sacks without imagining that they contained stolen children.

The Gypsies struck me as something without number, yet when I now try to estimate their number in my image of them, I would think that they were no more than thirty or forty. But still, I had never seen so many people in the big courtyard, and since they moved so slowly because of the old man, they seemed to fill the courtyard endlessly. They didn't stay there, however, they moved around the house and into the smaller courtyard by the kitchen, where the wood also lay in stacks, and that was where they settled.

I used to wait for the moment when they first appeared at the entrance gate, and no sooner had I spotted the blind old man than I dashed, yelling "*Zinganas! Zinganas!*" through the long living room and the even longer corridor that connected the living room with the kitchen in back. My mother stood there, giving instructions for the Sabbath dishes; certain special delicacies she prepared herself. I ignored the little girls, whom I often met on the way; I kept yelling and yelling, until I stood next to my mother, who said something calming to me. But instead of remaining with her, I ran the whole long way back, glanced through the window at the progress of the Gypsies, who were a bit further by now, and then I promptly reported on them in the kitchen again. I wanted to see them, I was obsessed with them, but the instant I saw them I was again seized with fear that they were after me, and I ran away screaming. For a whole while, I kept dashing back and forth like that, and that's why, I believe, I retained such an intense feeling for the wide range of the house between the two courtyards.

As soon as they had all arrived at their destination by the kitchen, the old man settled down, the others grouped around him, the sacks opened, and the women accepted all the gifts without fighting for them. They got big pieces of wood from the pile, they seemed particularly keen on them; they got many foods. They got something of everything that was already prepared, by no means were leftovers fobbed off on them. I was relieved when I saw that they had no children in the sacks, and under my mother's protection I walked among them, studying them carefully buthmaking sure I didn't get too close to the women, who wanted to caress me. The blind old man ate slowly from a bowl, resting and taking his time. The others didn't touch any of the food stuffs, everything vanished in the big sacks and only the children were allowed to nibble on the sweet things they had been given. I was amazed at how friendly they were to their children, not at all like nasty child-snatchers. But that changed nothing in my terror of them. After what seemed like a very long while, they started off again, the procession moved somewhat faster than upon entering; it went around the house and through the courtyard. I watched them from the same window as they vanished through the gate. Then I ran to the kitchen one last time to announce: "The Gypsies are gone!" Our servant took me by the hand, led me to the gate, and locked it up, saying: "Now they won't come back." The courtyard gate normally stayed open in the daytime, but on Fridays it was locked, so that any further group of Gypsies coming along afterwards would know their people had been here already and would move on.

My Brother's Birth

At a very early time, when I was still in a highchair, the floor seemed very far away, and I was scared of falling out. Uncle Bucco, my father's eldest brother, visited us, picked me up, and placed me on the floor. Then he made a solemn face, put his palm on my head, and spoke: "*Yo ti bendigo, Eliachicu, Amen!*" (I bless thee, little Elias, Amen!) He said it very emphatically, I liked the solemn tone; I believe I felt bigger when he blessed me. But he was a joker and laughed too soon; I sensed he was making fun of me, and the great moment of benediction, which I was always taken in by, ended in embarrassment.

This uncle endlessly repeated everything he did. He taught me lots of ditties, never resting until I could sing them myself. When he came again, he asked about them, patiently training me to perform for the adults. I would wait for his blessing, even though he always promptly destroyed it, and had he been more restrained, he would have been my favorite uncle. He lived in Varna, where he managed a branch of Grandfather's business, and he came to Ruschuk for the holidays and special occasions. The family spoke respectfully about him because he was the *Bucco*, which was the honorary title for the firstborn son in a family. I learned early on how important it was to be a firstborn son, and had I remained in Ruschuk, I would also have become a *Bucco*.

For four years, I remained the only child, and all that time, I wore little dresses like a girl. I wanted to wear trousers like a boy, and was always put off until later. Then my brother Nissim was born, and on this occasion I was allowed to wear my first pants. Everything that happened then I experienced in my trousers with great pride, and that is why I have retained every detail.

There were lots of people in the house, and I saw anxious faces. I was not allowed to go to my mother in the bedroom, where my crib was too; I wandered around by the door, to catch a glimpse of her whenever someone went in. But they always shut the door so quickly that I never laid eyes on her. I heard a wailing voice, which I didn't recognize, and when I asked who that was, I was told: "Go away!" I had never seen the grownups so anxious, and no one paid any attention to me, which I wasn't used to. (As I found out later, it was a long and hard labor, and they feared for my mother's life.) Dr. Menakhemoff was there, the physician with the long, black beard, and he too—who was otherwise so friendly and had me sing little ditties, for which he praised me—he neither looked at me nor spoke to me, and glared when I wouldn't go away from the door. The wailing grew louder, I heard "*Madre mia querida! Madre mia querida!*" I pressed my head against the door; when it opened, the moaning was so loud that I was horror-stricken. Suddenly I realized it came from my mother, and it was so eerie that I didn't want to see her anymore.

Finally, I was allowed into the bedroom, everyone was smiling, my father was laughing, and they showed me a little brother. Mother lay white and motionless in bed. Dr. Menakhemoff said: "She needs rest!" But the place wasn't at all restful. Strange women were going about the room; now I was there again for everyone, I was cheered up, and Grandmother Arditti, who seldom came into the house, said: "She's better." Mother said nothing. I was afraid of her and ran out and didn't hang around the door either. For a long while after that, my mother was alien to me, and it took months for me to regain confidence in her.

The next thing I can see is the Feast of Circumcision. Many more people came into the house. I was allowed to watch during the circumcision. I have the impression that they deliberately let me look. All doors were open, even the house door, a long covered table for the guests stood in the living room, and in another room, facing the bedroom, the circumcision took place. It was witnessed only by men, all standing. My tiny brother was held over a basin, I saw the knife, and particularly I saw a lot of blood dripping into the basin.

My brother was named after my mother's father, Nissim, and they explained that I was the eldest and was therefore named after my paternal grandfather. The position of the eldest son was so greatly emphasized that I remained conscious of it from that moment of the circumcision on and never lost my pride in it.

People then made merry at the table; I paraded around in my pants. I didn't rest until each of the guests had noticed them, and when new visitors came, I ran to greet them at the door and remained expectantly in front of them. There was a lot of coming and going; when everyone was there, they still missed Cousin Jacques from the neighboring house. "He's gone off on his bicycle," somebody said, and his behavior was disapproved of. After the meal, he arrived, covered with dust. I saw him jumping off the bicycle in front of the house; he was eight years older than I and wore the uniform of a Gymnasium student. He explained about the glorious new thing, he had only just been given the bicycle. Then he tried to sneak inconspicuously into the party, but I blurted out that I wanted a bike too. Aunt Sophie, his mother, swooped upon him and hauled him over the coals. He threatened me with his finger and vanished again.

On that day, I also realized that one has to keep one's mouth closed when eating. Régine, the sister of the bicycle owner, put nuts into her mouth, I stood before her spellbound, watching her chew with her mouth closed. It took a long time, and when she was done, she declared that I would have to eat like that too, otherwise they would stick me back into skirts. I must have learned fast, for I would not give up my trousers for anything in the world.

The Turk's House
The Two Grandfathers

Sometimes, when Grandfather Canetti was in the store, I was taken over to his house to pay respects to my grandmother. She sat on the Turkish divan, smoking and drinking strong coffee. She always stayed home, she never went out; I can't recall ever seeing her outside the house. Her name was Laura and, like Grandfather, she came from Adrianople. He called her "*Oro*," which actually means "gold," I never understood her name. Of all the relatives, she was the one that remained most Turkish. She never got up from her divan, I don't even know how she ever got there, for I never saw her walking, and she would sigh from time to time and drink another cup of coffee and smoke. She would greet me with a lamenting tone and, having said nothing to me, she let me go, lamenting. She had a few wailing sentences for whoever brought me. Perhaps she thought she was ill, perhaps she really was, but she was certainly lazy in an Oriental way, and she must have suffered under Grandfather, who was fiendishly lively.

Wherever he appeared, he was always instantly the center, which I didn't realize at the time; he was feared in his family, a tyrant who could weep hot tears if he wanted to. He felt most comfortable with his grandsons, who bore his name. Among friends and acquaintances, indeed throughout the Sephardic community, he was popular for his beautiful voice, which women particularly succumbed to. Whenever he was invited anywhere, he never took Grandmother along; he couldn't stand her stupidity and her continuous wailing. He was instantly surrounded by a big circle of people, told stories in which he played many parts, and on special occasions, he yielded to entreaties to sing.

Aside from Grandmother, there was a lot in Ruschuk that was Turkish. The first children's song I learned— "*Manzanicas coloradas, las que vienen de Stambol*," "Little apples, red, red apples, those that come from Istanbul"—ended with the name of the Turkish capital, and I heard how gigantic it was, and I soon connected it with the Turks we saw in our city. Edirne (Turkish for Adrianople, the city from which both Canetti grandparents came) was often mentioned. Grandfather sang never-ending Turkish songs, the point being to dwell on certain high notes for a very long time; I much preferred the fiercer and faster Spanish songs.

Not far from us, the well-to-do Turks had their homes; you could recognize them by the narrow-set bars on the windows for guarding the women. The first murder I ever heard about was when a Turk killed someone out of jealousy. On the way to Grandfather Arditti's home, my mother took me past one of those houses; she showed me a high grating, saying a Turkish woman had stood there and looked at a Bulgarian passing by. The Turk, her husband, then came and stabbed her. I don't believe that I had previously really grasped what a dead person was. But I learned what it meant during this promenade with my mother. I asked her whether the Turkish woman, who had been found in a pool of blood on the floor, had gotten up again. "Never!" she said. "Never! She was dead, do you understand?" I heard, but I didn't understand, and I asked again, forcing her to repeat her answer several times, until she lost patience and spoke about something else.

It was not just the dead woman in the pool of blood that impressed me in this story, but also the man's jealousy, which had led to the murder. Something about it appealed to me, and much as I balked at the woman's being definitively dead, I accepted the jealousy without resisting.

I experienced jealousy personally when we arrived at Grandfather Arditti's home. We used to visit him once a week, every Saturday. He lived in a spacious, reddish mansion. You entered through a side gate, to the left of the house, into an old garden, which was far more beautiful than ours. A huge mulberry tree stood there, with low branches and easy to climb. I was not allowed to climb it, but Mother never passed it without showing me a branch at the top; it was her hiding-place, where she used to sit as a young girl when she wanted to read undisturbed. She would steal up there with her book and sit there as quiet as a mouse, and she did it so cleverly that they couldn't see her from below, and when they called her, she didn't hear, because she liked the book so much; she read all her books up there. Not far from the mulberry tree, steps led up to the house; the residential rooms were higher than in our house, but the corridors were dark. We would walk through many rooms until the last room, where Grandfather sat in an armchair, a small, pale man, always warmly bundled in scarves and tartans; he was sickly.

"*Li beso las manos, Señor Padre!*" said Mother. "I kiss your hands, Señor Father!" Then she pushed me ahead; I didn't like him and I had to kiss his hand. He was never funny or angry or tender or severe like the other grandfather, whose name I bore; he was always the same, he sat in an armchair and never budged, he never spoke to me, never gave me anything, and merely exchanged a few phrases with my mother. Then came the end of the visit, and I hated it, it was always the same. He would eye me with a sly smirk and ask in a low voice: "Whom do you like better, Grandfather Arditti or Grandfather Canetti?" He knew the answer, everyone, old and young, was bewitched by Grandfather Canetti, and no one liked Grandfather Arditti. But he wanted to force the truth out of me, and he placed me in a horribly embarrassing predicament, which he enjoyed, for it happened again every Saturday. At first I said nothing, gazing at him helplessly, he asked his question again, until I found the strength to lie and said: "Both!" He would then raise his finger threateningly and yell—it was the only loud sound I ever heard from him: "*Fálsu!*" (False child!) And he drawled out the accented *a*; the word sounded both ominous and plaintive, I can still hear it as though I had visited him only yesterday.

Walking out through the many rooms and corridors, I felt guilty for lying and I was very low-spirited. My mother, though unshakably attached to her family and unwilling ever to give up this ritual of a visit, must have also felt a bit guilty for always re-exposing me to this accusation, which was really meant for the other grandfather but struck only me. As a solace, she took me to the *bagtché*, the orchard and rose garden behind the house. There she showed me all her favorite flowers from her girlhood, and inhaled their fragrances deeply, she had wide nostrils which always quivered. She lifted me up so that I too could smell the roses, and if any fruits were ripe, she would pick some, but Grandfather was not supposed to know because it was Sabbath. It was the most wonderful garden that I can remember, not too well kept, a bit overgrown; and the fact that Grandfather was not to know about this Sabbath fruit, the fact that Mother herself did a prohibited thing for my sake, must have relieved my feeling of guilt, for on the way home I was quite cheerful and kept asking questions again.

At home, I learned from Cousin Laurica that this grandfather was jealous because all his grandchildren liked their other grandfather more, and she confided the reason to me in utmost secrecy: He was *mizquin*, avaricious, but I mustn't tell my mother.

Purim; The Comet

The holiday that we children felt most strongly, even though, being very small, we couldn't take part in it, was Purim. It was a joyous festival, commemorating the salvation of the Jews from Haman, the wicked persecutor. Haman was a well-known figure, and his name had entered the language. Before I ever found out that he was a man who had once lived and concocted horrible things, I knew his name as an insult. If I tormented adults with too many questions or didn't want to go to bed or refused to do something they wanted me to do, there would be a deep sigh: "*Hamán!*" Then I knew that they were in no mood for jokes, that I had played out. "*Hamán*" was the final word, a deep sigh, but also a vituperation. I was utterly amazed when I was told later on that Haman had been a wicked man who wanted to kill all the Jews. But thanks to Mordecai and Queen Esther, he failed, and, to show their joy, the Jews celebrated Purim.

The adults disguised themselves and went out, there was noise in the street, masks appeared in the house, I didn't know who they were, it was like a fairy tale; my parents stayed out till late at night. The general excitement affected us children; I lay awake in my crib and listened. Sometimes our parents would show up in masks, which they then took off; that was great fun, but I preferred not knowing it was they.

One night, when I had dozed off, I was awakened by a giant wolf leaning over my bed. A long, red tongue dangled from his mouth, and he snarled fearfully. I screamed as loud as I could: "A wolf! A wolf!" No one heard me, no one came; I shrieked and yelled louder and louder and cried. Then a hand slipped out, grabbed the wolf's ears, and pulled his head down. My father was behind it, laughing. I kept shouting: "A wolf! A wolf!" I wanted my father to drive it away. He showed me the wolf mask in his hand; I didn't believe him, he kept saying: "Don't you see? It was me, that was no real wolf." But I wouldn't calm down, I kept sobbing and crying.

The story of the werewolf had thus come true. My father couldn't have known what the little girls always told me when we huddled together in the dark. Mother reproached herself for her sleigh story but scolded him for his uncontrollable pleasure in masquerading. There was nothing he liked better than play-acting. When he had gone to school in Vienna, he only wanted to be an actor. But in Ruschuk, he was mercilessly thrust into his father's business. The town did have an amateur theater, where he performed with Mother, but what was it measured by his earlier dreams in Vienna? He was truly unleashed, said Mother, during the Purim festival: He would change his masks several times in a row, surprising and terrifying all their friends with the most bizarre scenes.

My wolf panic held on for a long time; night after night I had bad dreams, very often waking my parents, in whose room I slept. Father tried to calm me down until I fell asleep again, but then the wolf reappeared in my dreams; we didn't get rid of him all that soon. From that time on, I was considered a jeapordized child whose imagination must not be overstimulated, and the result was that for many months I heard only dull stories, all of which I've forgotten.

The next event was the big comet, and since I have never thought about one event without the other, there must be some connection between them. I believe that the appearance of the comet freed me from the wolf; my childhood terror merged into the universal terror of those days, for I have never seen people so excited as during the time of the comet. Also, both of them, the wolf and the comet, appeared at night, one more reason why they came together in my memory.

Everyone talked about the comet before I saw it, and I heard that the end of the world was at hand. I couldn't picture what that was, but I did notice that people changed and started whispering whenever I came near, and they gazed at me full of pity. The Bulgarian girls didn't whisper, they said it straight out in their unabashed way: The end of the world had come. It was the general belief in town, and it must have prevailed for quite a while since it left such a deep stamp on me without my fearing anything specific. I can't say to what extent my parents, as educated people, were infected with that belief. But I'm sure they didn't oppose the general view. Otherwise, after our earlier experience, they would have done something to enlighten me, only they didn't.

One night, people said the comet was now here and would now fall upon the earth. I was not sent to bed; I heard someone say it made no sense, the children ought to come into the garden too. A lot of people were standing around in the courtyard. I had never seen so many there; all the children from our houses and the neighboring houses were among them, and everyone, adults and children, kept staring up at the sky, where the comet loomed gigantic and radiant. I can see it spreading across half the heavens. I still feel the tension in the back of my neck as I tried to view its entire length. Maybe it got longer in my memory, maybe it didn't occupy half, but only a smaller part of the sky. I must leave the answer to that question to others, who were grown up then and not afraid. But it was bright outdoors, almost like during the day, and I knew very well that it actually ought to be night, for that was the first time I hadn't been put to bed at that hour, and that was the real event for me. Everyone stood in the garden, peering at the heavens and waiting. The grownups scarcely walked back and forth; it was oddly quiet, voices were low, at most the children moved, but the grownups barely heeded them. In this expectation, I must have felt something of the anxiety filling everyone else, for in order to relieve me, somebody gave me a twig of cherries. I had put one cherry into my mouth and was craning my neck, trying to follow the gigantic comet with my eyes, and the strain, and perhaps also the wondrous beauty of the comet made me forget the cherry, so that I swallowed the pit.

It took a long time; no one grew tired of it, and people kept standing around in a dense throng. I can't see Father or Mother among them, I can't see any of the individual people who made up my life. I only see them all together, and if I hadn't used the word so frequently later on, I would say that I see them as a mass, a crowd: a stagnating crowd of expectation.

The Magic Language
The Fire

The biggest cleaning in the house came before *Pesakh,* Passover. Everything was moved topsy-turvy, nothing stayed in the same place, and since the cleaning began early—lasting about two weeks, I believe—this was the period of the greatest disorder. Nobody had time for you, you were always underfoot and were pushed aside or sent away, and as for the kitchen, where the most interesting things were being prepared, you could at best sneak a glance inside. Most of all, I loved the brown eggs, which were boiled in coffee for days and days.

On the seder evening, the long table was put up and set in the dining room; and perhaps the room had to be so long, for on this occasion the table had to seat very many guests. The whole family gathered for the seder, which was celebrated in our home. It was customary to pull in two or three strangers off the street; they were seated at the feast and participated in everything.

Grandfather sat at the head of the table, reading the Haggadah, the story of the exodus of the Jews from Egypt. It was his proudest moment: Not only was he placed above his sons and sons-in-law, who honored him and followed all his directions, but he, the eldest, with his sharp face like a bird of prey, was also the most fiery of all; nothing eluded him. As he chanted in singsong, he noticed the least motion, the slightest occurrence at the table, and his glance or a light movement of his hand would set it aright. Everything was very warm and close, the atmosphere of an ancient tale in which everything was precisely marked out and had its place. On seder evenings, I greatly admired my grandfather; and even his sons, who didn't have an easy time with him, seemed elevated and cheerful.

As the youngest male, I had my own, not unimportant function; I had to ask the *Ma-nishtanah.* The story of the exodus is presented as a series of questions and answers about the reasons for the holiday. The youngest of the participants asks right at the start what all these preparations signify: the unleavened bread, the bitter herbs, and the other unusual things on the table. The narrator, in this case my grandfather, replies with the detailed story of the exodus from Egypt. Without my question, which I recited by heart, holding the book and pretending to read, the story could not begin. The details were familiar to me, they had been explained often enough; but throughout the reading I never lost the sense that my grandfather was answering me personally. So it was a great evening for me too, I felt important, downright indispensable; I was lucky there was no younger cousin to usurp my place.

But although following every word and every gesture of my grandfather's, I looked forward to the end throughout the narrative. For then came the nicest part: The men suddenly all stood up and jigged around a little, singing together as they danced: "*Had gadya, had gadya!*"—"A kid! A kid!" It was a merry song, and I was already quite familiar with it, but it was part of the ritual for an uncle to call me over when it was done and to translate every line of it into Ladino.

When my father came home from the store, he would instantly speak to my mother. They were very much in love at that time and had their own language, which I didn't understand; they spoke German, the language of their happy schooldays in Vienna. Most of all, they talked about the *Burgtheater*; before ever meeting, they had seen the same plays and the same actors there and they never exhausted their memories of it. Later I found out that they had fallen in love during such conversations, and while neither of them had managed to make their dream of the theater come true—both had passionately wanted to act—they did succeed in getting married despite a great deal of opposition.

Grandfather Arditti, from one of the oldest and most prosperous Sephardic families in Bulgaria, was against letting his youngest, and favorite, daughter marry the son of an upstart from Adrianople. Grandfather Canetti had pulled himself up by his bootstraps; an orphan, cheated, turned out of doors while young, he had worked his way up to prosperity; but in the eyes of the other grandfather, he remained a playactor and a liar. "*Es mentiroso* (He's a liar)," I heard Grandfather Arditti once say when he didn't realize I was listening. Grandfather Canetti, however, was indignant about the pride of the Ardittis, who looked down on him. His son could marry any girl, and it struck him as a superfluous humiliation that he wanted to marry the daughter of that Arditti of all people. So my parents at first kept their love a secret, and it was only gradually, very tenaciously, and with the active help of their older brothers and sisters and well-disposed relatives, that they succeeded in getting closer to making their wish come true. At last, both fathers gave in, but a tension always remained between them, and they couldn't stand each other. In the secret period, the two young people had fed their love incessantly with German conversations, and one can imagine how many loving couples of the stage played their part here.

So I had good reason to feel excluded when my parents began their conversations. They became very lively and merry, and I associated this transformation, which I noted keenly, with the sound of the German language. I would listen with utter intensity and then ask them what this or that meant. They laughed, saying it was too early for me, those were things I would understand only later. It was already a great deal for them to give in on the word "Vienna," the only one they revealed to me. I believed they were talking about wondrous things that could be spoken of only in that language. After begging and begging to no avail, I ran away angrily into another room, which was seldom used, and I repeated to myself the sentences I had heard from them, in their precise intonation, like magic formulas; I practiced them often to myself, and as soon as I was alone, I reeled off all the sentences or individual words I had practiced—reeled them off so rapidly that no one could possibly have understood me. But I made sure never to let my parents notice, responding to their secrecy with my own.

I found out that my father had a name for my mother which he used only when they spoke German. Her name was Mathilde, and he called her Mädi. Once, when I was in the garden, I concealed my voice as well as I could, and called loudly into the house: "Mädi! Mädi!" That was how my father called to her from the courtyard whenever he came home. Then I dashed off around the house and appeared only after a while with an innocent mien. My mother stood there perplexed and asked me whether I had seen Father. It was a triumph for me that she had mistaken my voice for his, and I had the strength to keep my secret, while she told him about the incomprehensible event as soon as he came home.

It never dawned on them to suspect me, but among the many intense wishes of that period, the most intense was my desire to understand their secret language. I cannot explain why I didn't really hold it against my father. I did nurture a deep resentment toward my mother, and it vanished only years later, after his death, when she herself began teaching me German.

One day, the courtyard was filled with smoke; a few of our girls ran out into the street and promptly came back with the excited news that a neighborhood house was on fire. It was already all in flames and about to burn up. Instantly, the three houses around our courtyard emptied, and except for my grandmother, who never rose from her divan, all the tenants ran out towards the blaze. It happened so fast that they forgot all about me. I was a little scared to be all alone like that; also I felt like going out, perhaps to the fire, perhaps even more in the direction I saw them all running in. So I ran through the open courtyard gate out into the street, which I was not allowed to do, and I wound up in the racing torrent of people. Luckily, I soon caught sight of two of our older girls, and since they wouldn't have changed directions for anything in the world, they thrust me between themselves and hastily pulled me along. They halted at some distance from the conflagration, perhaps so as not to endanger me, and thus, for the first time in my life, I saw a burning house. It was already far gone; beams were collapsing and sparks were flying. The evening was gathering, it slowly became dark, and the fire shone brighter and brighter. But what made an even greater impact on me than the blazing house was the people moving around it. They looked small and dark from that distance; there were very many of them, and they were scrambling all over the place. Some remained near the house, some moved off, and the latter were all carrying something on their backs. "Thieves!" said the girls, "Those are thieves! They're carrying things away from the house before anyone can catch them!" They were no less excited about the thieves than about the fire, and as they kept shouting "Thieves!" their excitement infected me. They were indefatigable, those tiny black figures, deeply bowed, they fanned out in all directions. Some had flung bundles on their shoulders, others ran stooped under the burden of angular objects, which I couldn't recognize, and when I asked what they were carrying, the girls merely kept repeating: "Thieves! They're thieves!"

This scene, which has remained unforgettable for me, later merged into the works of a painter, so that I no longer could say what was original and what was added by those paintings. I was nineteen, in Vienna, when I stood before Brueghel's pictures. I instantly recognized the many little people of that fire in my childhood. The pictures were as familiar to me as if I had always moved among them. I felt a tremendous attraction to them and came over every day. That part of my life which had commenced with the fire continued immediately in these paintings, as though fifteen years had not gone by in between. Brueghel became the most important painter for me; but I did not absorb him, as so many later things, by contemplation and reflection. I found him present within me as though, certain that I would have to come to him, he had been awaiting me for a long time.

Adders and Letters

An early memory takes place on a lake. I see the lake, which is vast, I see it through tears. We are standing by a boat on the shore, my parents and a girl who holds me by the hand. My parents say they want to take the boat out on the lake. I try to tear loose and climb into the boat, I want to go along, I want to go along, but my parents say I can't, I have to stay behind with the girl who's holding my hand. I cry, they talk to me, I keep crying. This takes a long time, they are unrelenting, the girl won't let me go, so I bite her hand. My parents are angry and leave me behind with her, but now to punish me. They vanish in the boat, I yell after them at the top of my lungs, now they're far away, the lake grows bigger and bigger, everything melts in tears.

It was Lake Wörther, in Austria; I was three years old, they told me so a long time afterwards. In Kronstadt, Transylvania, where we spent the next summer, I see forests and a mountain, a castle and houses on all sides of the castle hill; I myself do not appear in this picture, but I remember stories my father told me about serpents. Before coming to Vienna, he had been to boarding school in Kronstadt. There were a lot of adders in the area, and the farmers wanted to get rid of them. The boys learned how to catch them, and received two kreuzers for every sack of dead adders. Father showed me how to grab an adder, right behind the head, so that it can't do anything to you, and how to kill it then. It's easy, he said, once you know how, and it's not the least bit dangerous. I greatly admired him and wanted to know if they were really quite dead in the sack. I was scared that they would pretend to be dead and suddenly shoot out of the sack. The sack was tightly bound up, he said, and they had to be dead, otherwise you couldn't have gotten the two kreuzers. I didn't believe that something could be really fully dead.

Thus we spent three summer vacations in a row in parts of the old Austro-Hungarian monarchy: Carlsbad, Lake Wörther, and Kronstadt. A triangle connecting these three remote points contained a good portion of the old empire.

There would be a great deal to say about the Austrian influence on us even in that early Ruschuk period. Not only had both my parents gone to school in Vienna, not only did they speak German to each other, but my father read the liberal Viennese newspaper *Neue Freie Presse* every day; it was a grand moment when he slowly unfolded it. As soon as he began reading it, he no longer had an eye for me, I knew he wouldn't answer anything no matter what; Mother herself wouldn't ask him anything, not even in German. I tried to find out what it was that fascinated him in the newspaper, at first I thought it was the smell; and when I was alone and nobody saw me, I would climb up on the chair and greedily smell the newsprint. But then I noticed he was moving his head along the page, and I imitated that behind his back without having the page in front of me, while he held it in both hands on the table and I played on the floor behind him. Once, a visitor who had entered the room called to him; he turned around and caught me performing my imaginary reading motions. He then spoke to me even before focusing on the visitor and explained that the important thing was the letters, many tiny letters, on which he knocked his fingers. Soon I would learn them myself, he said, arousing within me an unquenchable yearning for letters.

I knew that the newspaper came from Vienna, this city was far away, it took four days to get there on the Danube. They often spoke of relatives who went to Vienna to consult famous physicians. The names of the great specialists of those days were the very first celebrities that I heard about as a child. When I came to Vienna subsequently, I was amazed that all these names—Lorenz, Schlesinger, Schnitzler, Neumann, Hajek, Halban—really existed as people. I had never tried to picture them physically; what they consisted of was their pronouncements, and these pronouncements had such a weight, the journey to them was so long, the changes their pronouncements effected in the people around me were so cataclysmic, that the names took on something of spirits that one fears and appeals to for help. When someone came back from them, he could eat only certain things, while other things were prohibited for him. I imagined the physicians speaking in a language of their own, which nobody else understood and which one had to guess. It never crossed my mind that this was the same language that I heard from my parents and practiced for myself, secretly, without understanding it.

People often talked about languages; seven or eight different tongues were spoken in our city alone, everyone understood something of each language. Only the little girls, who came from villages, spoke just Bulgarian and were therefore considered stupid. Each person counted up the languages he knew; it was important to master several, knowing them could save one's own life or the lives of other people.

In earlier years, when merchants went traveling, they carried all their cash in money belts slung around their abdomens. They wore them on the Danube steamers too, and that was dangerous. Once, when my mother's grandfather got on deck and pretended to sleep, he overheard two men discussing a murder plan in Greek. As soon as the steamer approached the next town, they wanted to mug and kill a merchant in his stateroom, steal his heavy money belt, throw the body into the Danube through a porthole, and then, when the steamer docked, leave the ship immediately. My great-grandfather went to the captain and told him what he had heard in Greek. The merchant was warned, a member of the crew concealed himself in the stateroom, others were stationed outside, and when the two cutthroats went to carry out their plan, they were seized, clapped into chains, and handed over to the police in the very harbor where they had intended to make off with their booty. This happy end came from understanding Greek, and there were many other edifying language stories.

The Murder Attempt

My cousin Laurica and I were inseparable playmates. She was the youngest daughter of Aunt Sophie in the next house, but four years my senior. The courtyard was our domain. Laurica made sure I didn't run out into the street, but the courtyard was big, and there I was allowed to go anywhere, only I couldn't climb up on the edge of the draw well; a child had once fallen in and drowned. We had a lot of games and got on very well; it was as if the age difference between us didn't exist. We had joint hiding places, which we revealed to no one, and we mutually collected little objects there, and whatever one of us had belonged to the other as well. Whenever I got a present, I promptly ran off with it, saying: "I have to show it to Laurica!" We then conferred about what hiding place to put it in, and we never argued. I did whatever she wanted, she did whatever I wanted, we loved each other so much that we always wanted the same thing. I never let her feel that she was only a girl and a youngest child. Since my brother's birth, when I had started wearing pants, I had been keenly aware of my dignity as the eldest son. Perhaps that helped to make up for the age difference between us.

Then Laurica started school and remained away all morning. I missed her terribly. I played all alone, waiting for her, and when she came home, I caught her right at the gate and asked her all about what she had done in school. She told me about it, I pictured it and longed to go to school in order to be with her. After a time, she came back with a notebook; she was learning how to read and write. She solemnly opened the notebook in front of me; it contained letters of the alphabet in blue ink, they fascinated me more than anything I had ever laid eyes on. But when I tried to touch them, she suddenly grew earnest. She said I wasn't allowed to, only she could touch it, she was not permitted to part with it. I was deeply hurt by this first refusal. But all I could get from her with my tender pleading was that I could point my fingers at letters without touching them, and I asked what the letters meant. This one time, she answered, giving me information, but I realized she was shaky and contradicted herself, and since I was hurt about her holding back the notebook, I said: "You don't even know! You're a bad pupil!"

After that, she always kept the notebooks away from me. She soon had lots of them; I envied her for each one of those notebooks. She knew very well that I did, and a terrible game began. She changed altogether towards me, letting me feel how small I was. Day after day, she let me beg for the notebooks; day after day, she refused to give them to me. She knew how to tantalize me and prolong the torture. I am not surprised that things came to a catastrophe, even if no one foresaw the form it took.

On the day that no one in the family ever forgot, I stood at the gate as usual, waiting for her. "Let me see the writing," I begged the instant she appeared. She said nothing; I realized everything was about to happen again, and no one could have separated us at that moment. She slowly put down the schoolbag, slowly took out the notebooks, slowly leafed around in them, and then held them in front of my nose lightning-fast. I grabbed at them, she pulled them back, and leaped away. From afar, she held an open notebook out at me and shouted: "You're too little! You're too little! You can't read yet!"

I tried to catch her, running after her all over the place, I begged, I pleaded for the notebooks. Sometimes she let me come very near so that I thought I had my hands on the notebooks, and then she snatched them away and pulled away in the last moment. Through skillful maneuvers, I succeeded in chasing her into the shadow of a not very high wall, where she could no longer escape me. Now I had her and I screamed in utmost excitement: "Give them to me! Give them to me! Give them to me!"—by which I meant both the notebooks and the writing, they were one and the same for me. She lifted her arms with the notebooks far over her head, she was much bigger than I, and she put the notebooks up on the wall. I couldn't get at them, I was too little, I jumped and jumped and yelped, it was no use, she stood next to the wall, laughing scornfully. All at once, I left her there and walked the long way around the house to the kitchen yard, to get the Armenian's ax and kill her with it.

The wood lay there, chopped up, stacked up, the ax lay next to it, the Armenian wasn't there. I raised the ax high and, holding it straight in front of me, I marched back over the long path into the courtyard with a murderous chant on my lips, repeating incessantly: "*Agora vo matar a Laurica! Agora vo matar a Laurica!*"—"Now I'm going to kill Laurica! Now I'm going to kill Laurica!"

When I came back and she saw me holding the ax out with both hands, she ran off screeching. She screeched at the top of her lungs, as though the ax had already swung and hit her. She screeched without pausing even once, easily drowning my battle chant, which I kept repeating to myself, incessantly, resolutely, but not especially loud: "*Agora vo matar a Laurica!*"

Grandfather dashed out of the house, armed with a cane; he ran towards me, snatched the ax from my hand, and barked at me furiously. Now all three houses around the courtyard came alive, people emerged from all of them; my father was out of town, but my mother was there. They assembled for a family council and discussed the homicidal child. I could plead all I liked that Laurica had tortured me bloody; the fact that I, at the age of five, had reached for the ax to kill her— indeed, the very fact that I had been able to carry the heavy ax in front of me—was incomprehensible to everyone. I think they understood that the "writing," the "script," had been so important to me; they were Jews, and "Scripture" meant a great deal to all of them, but there had to be something very bad and dangerous in me to get me to the point of wanting to murder my playmate.

I was severely punished, but Mother, who was herself very frightened, did comfort me after all, saying: "Soon you'll learn how to read and write yourself. You don't have to wait till you're in school. You can learn before then."

No one recognized the connection between my murderous goal and the fate of the Armenian. I loved him, his sad songs and words. I loved the ax with which he chopped wood.

A Curse on the Voyage

My relationship to Laurica, however, did not break off fully. She distrusted me and avoided me when she came back from school, and she made sure not to unpack her schoolbag in front of me. I was no longer interested in her writing. After the murder attempt, I was perfectly convinced that she was a bad pupil and was ashamed to show her wrong letters. Perhaps I could save my pride only by telling myself that.

She took a terrible revenge on me, although stubbornly denying it then and later. All I could admit in her favor is that she may not have known what she did.

Most of the water used in the houses was brought in gigantic barrels from the Danube. A mule hauled the barrel, which was installed in a special kind of vehicle, and a "water carrier," who, however, carried nothing, trudged alongside in front, holding a whip. The water was sold at the courtyard gate for very little, unloaded, and put in huge caldrons, where it was boiled. The caldrons of boiling water were then placed in front of the house, on a fairly long terrace, where they stood for a good while to cool off.

Laurica and I were getting on again at least well enough to play tag occasionally. Once, the caldrons of hot water were standing there; we ran in between them, much too close, and when Laurica caught me right next to one, she gave me a shove, and I fell into the hot water. I was scalded all over my body, except for my head. Aunt Sophie, upon hearing the shriek, pulled me out and tore off my clothes, my whole skin went along with them, the family feared for my life, and for many weeks I lay abed in awful pains.

My father was in England at the time, and that was the worst thing of all for me. I thought I was going to die and kept calling out for him, I wailed that I would never see him again; that was worse than the pains. I cannot remember the pains, I no longer feel them, but I still feel the desperate longing for my father. I thought he didn't know what had happened to me, and when they assured me he did know, I cried: "Why doesn't he come? Why doesn't he come? I want to see him!" Perhaps they really were hesitant; he had only just arrived in Manchester a few days earlier to prepare for our moving there. Perhaps they thought my condition would improve by itself and he didn't have to return on the spot. But even if he did learn about it immediately and started back without delay, the journey was long, and he couldn't get here all that soon. They put me off from day to day and, when my condition got worse, from hour to hour. One night, when they thought I had finally fallen asleep, I jumped out of bed and yanked everything off me. Instead of moaning in pain, I shouted for him: "*Cuando viene? Cuando viene?*" (When is he coming? When is he coming?) Mother, the doctor, all the others taking care of me, didn't matter; I can't see them, I don't know what they did, they must have done many careful things for me in those days. I didn't register them, I had only one thought, it was more than a thought, it was the wound in which everything went: my father.

Then I heard his voice, he came to me from behind, I was lying on my belly, he softly called my name, he walked around the bed, I saw him, he lightly put his hand on my hair, it was father, and I had no pains.

Everything that happened from then on I know only from what I was told. The wound became a wonder, the recovery began, he promised not to go away any more and he stayed during the next few weeks. The doctor was positive I would have died if my father hadn't come and

remained. The doctor had already given me up but insisted on my
father's return, his only, not very sure hope. He was the physician who
had brought all three of us into the world, and later on he used to say
that of all the births he had ever known this *re*birth had been the
hardest.

A few months earlier, in January 1911, my youngest brother had
come into the world. The delivery had been easy, and my mother felt
strong enough to nurse him herself. It was quite different from the
previous time; little ado was made over this birth, perhaps because it
had gone so easily, and it remained a center of attention only briefly.

I did sense, however, that great events were in the offing. My parents'
conversations had a different tone, they sounded resolute and earnest,
they didn't always speak German in front of me, and they often mentioned England. I learned that my little brother was named George,
after the new king of England. I liked that because it was unexpected,
but my grandfather cared less for it, he wanted a biblical name and
insisted on one, and I heard my parents say they wouldn't give in, it
was their child, and they would give it the name they wanted to give
it.

The rebellion against the grandfather had probably been going on
for a while; the choice of this name was an open declaration of war.
Two brothers of my mother's had started a business in Manchester, it
had flourished quickly, one of them had suddenly died, the other
offered my father a partnership if he came to England. For my parents,
this was a desirable opportunity to free themselves from Ruschuk,
which was too confining and too Oriental for them, and from the far
more confining tyranny of the grandfather. They immediately agreed
to the partnership, but it was easier said than done, for now a fierce
battle commenced between them and my grandfather, who refused to
give up one of his sons for anything in the world. I did not know the
details of this battle, which lasted for six months, but I sensed the
changed atmosphere in the house and especially in the courtyard, where
the members of the family had to meet.

Grandfather grabbed me in the courtyard at every opportunity, hugging and kissing me, and, when someone could see, weeping hot tears.
I didn't care at all for the continual wetness on my cheeks, although
he always proclaimed that I was his dearest grandchild and he could
not live without me. My parents realized he was trying to bias me
against England and, counteracting that, they told me how wonderful
it would be. "There all the people are honest," said my father. "When
a man says something, he does it, he doesn't even have to shake hands

on it." I was on his side, how else could I have been, he didn't have to promise me that I would start school immediately in England and learn how to read and write.

Grandfather behaved differently to him, and especially to my mother—differently than to me. He regarded her as the author of the emigration project, and when she once said to him, "Yes! We can't stand this life in Ruschuk anymore! We both want to get away from here!," he turned his back to her and never spoke to her again; during the remaining months he treated her like air. As for Father, however, who still had to go to the store, he assaulted him with his anger, which was terrible and became more and more terrible from week to week. Then he saw there was nothing he could do, and a few days before the departure, he cursed his son solemnly in the courtyard, in front of the relatives who were present and who listened in horror. I heard them speaking about it: Nothing, they said, was more dreadful than a father cursing his son.

Part Two

MANCHESTER
1911–1913

Wallpaper and Books
Strolls along the Mersey

For a few months after his death, I slept in my father's bed. It was dangerous leaving Mother alone. I don't know who it was who thought of making me the guardian of her life. She wept a great deal, and I listened to her weeping. I couldn't console her, she was inconsolable. But when she got up and stationed herself at the window, I leapt up and stood next to her. I put my arms around her and wouldn't let go. We did not speak, these scenes did not take place with words. I held her very tight, and if she had jumped out the window, she would have had to take me along. She didn't have the strength to kill me along with herself. I felt her body yield when the tension waned, and she turned to me from the despair of her decision. She pressed my head to her body and sobbed louder. She had thought I was asleep, and strove to weep quietly, so that I wouldn't awake. She was so absorbed in her sorrow that she didn't notice that I was secretly awake, and when she got up very quietly and stole to the window, she was certain that I was fast asleep. Years later, when we spoke about that period, she admitted that she was always surprised each time I stood next to her right away and threw my arms around her. She couldn't escape me, I wouldn't give her up. She let me hold her back, but I sensed that my watchfulness was burdensome to her. She never tried it more than once in any night. After the excitement, we both fell asleep, exhausted. Gradually, she developed something like respect for me and she began treating me like an adult in many ways.

After a few months, we moved from the house on Burton Road, where my father had died, to her older brother's home on Palatine Road. This was a large mansion with many people, and the acute danger was past.

However, the period before that in Burton Road was not just made up of those dreadful nightly scenes. The days were calm and subdued. Towards evening, Mother and I dined at a small card table in the yellow salon. The table, brought in specially (it didn't really belong in the salon), was set for the two of us. There was a cold snack consisting of lots of little delicacies, it was always the same: white sheep's cheese, cucumbers, and olives, as in Bulgaria. I was seven, Mother was twenty-seven. We had an earnest, civilized conversation, the house was very still, there was no noise as in the nursery, my mother said to me: "You are my big son," and she inspired me with the responsibility I felt for her at night. All day long, I yearned for these suppers. I served myself, taking very little on my plate, like her; everything proceeded in gentle movements like clockwork, but as much as I recall the motions of my fingers, I no longer know what we talked about; I have forgotten everything but the one, frequently reiterated sentence: "You are my big son." I see my mother's faint smile when she leaned towards me, the movements of her mouth when she spoke, not passionately as usual, but with restraint; I think that I never felt any sorrow in her during these meals, perhaps it was dulled by my sympathetic presence. Once she explained something about olives to me.

Previously, Mother hadn't meant very much to me. I never saw her alone. We were in a governess's care and always played upstairs in the nursery. My brothers were four and five and one-half years my junior. George, the youngest, had a small playpen. Nissim, the middle son, was notorious for his pranks. No sooner was he left by himself than he got into mischief. He turned on the faucet in the bathroom, and water was already running down the stairs to the ground floor by the time anyone noticed; or he unrolled the toilet paper until the upstairs corridor was covered with it. He kept devising new and worse pranks, and since nothing could stop him, he was dubbed "the naughty boy."

I was the only one going to school, to Miss Lancashire's in Barlowmore Road; I will tell about this school later on.

At home in the nursery, I usually played alone. Actually, I seldom played, I spoke to the wallpaper. The many dark circles in the pattern of the wallpaper seemed like people to me. I made up stories in which they appeared, either I told them the stories or they played with me, I never got tired of the wallpaper people and I could talk to them for hours. When the governess went out with my two younger brothers, I made a point of staying alone with the wallpaper. I preferred its company to anyone else's, at least to that of my little brothers; with them there was nothing but silly excitement and trouble, like Nissim's pranks. When my brothers were nearby, I merely whispered to the wallpaper people; if the governess was present, I simply thought out my stories, not even moving my lips to them. But then everyone left the room, I waited a bit, and then started talking undisturbed. Soon my words were loud and agitated; I only remember that I tried to persuade the wallpaper people to do bold deeds, and when they refused, I let them feel my scorn. I heartened them, I railed at them; when alone, I was always a bit scared, and whatever I felt myself, I ascribed to them, *they* were the cowards. But they also performed and uttered their own lines. A circle in a highly conspicuous place opposed me with its own eloquence, and it was no small triumph when I succeeded in convincing it. I was involved in such an argument with it when the governess returned earlier than expected and heard voices in the nursery. She quickly entered and caught me in the act, my secret was out, from then on I was always taken along on strolls; it was considered unhealthy to leave me alone so much. The loud wallpaper fun was over, but I was tenacious and I got used to articulating my stories quietly, even when my little brothers were in the room. I managed to play with them while also dealing with the wallpaper people. Only the governess, who had set herself the task of weaning me fully from these unhealthy tendencies, paralyzed me; in her presence the wallpaper was mute.

However, my finest conversations in that period were with my real-life father. Every morning, before leaving for his office, he came to the nursery and had special, cogent words for each one of us. He was cheery and merry and always hit upon new antics. In the morning they didn't last long; it was before breakfast, which he had with Mother downstairs in the dining room, and he hadn't read the newspaper yet. But in the evening, he arrived with presents; he brought something for everyone, on no day did he come home without bearing gifts for us. Then he stayed in the nursery for a longer time and did gymnastics with us. His main feat was to put all three of us on his outstretched arm. He held the two little brothers fast, I had to learn to stand free, and even though I loved him like no one else in the world, I was always a bit scared of this part of the exercises.

A few months after I started school, a thing solemn and exciting happened, which determined my entire life after that. Father brought home a book for me. He took me alone into a back room, where we children slept, and explained it to me. It was *The Arabian Nights,* in an edition for children. There was a colorful picture on the cover, I think it was Aladdin and his magic lamp. My father spoke very earnestly and encouragingly to me and told me how nice it would be to read. He

read me a story, saying that all the other stories in the book were as
lovely as this one, and that I should try to read them and then in the
evening always tell him what I had read. Once I'd finished the book,
he'd bring me another. I didn't have to be told twice, and even though
I had only just learned how to read in school, I pitched right into the
wondrous book and had something to report to him every evening. He
kept his promise, there was always a new book there; I never had to
skip a single day of reading.

The books were a series for children, all in the same square format.
They differed only in the colorful picture on the cover. The letters
were the same size in all volumes, it was like reading the same book
on and on. But what a series that was, it has never had its peer. I can
remember all the titles. After *The Arabian Nights* came Grimm's fairy
tales, *Robinson Crusoe, Gulliver's Travels, Tales from Shakespeare, Don Quijote,*
Dante, *William Tell.* I wonder how it was possible to adapt Dante for
children. Every volume had several gaudy pictures, but I didn't like
them, the stories were a lot more beautiful; I don't even know whether
I would recognize the pictures today. It would be easy to show that
almost everything that I consisted of later on was already in these
books, which I read for my father in the seventh year of my life. Of
the characters who never stopped haunting me after that, only Odysseus
was missing.

I spoke about each book to my father after reading it. Sometimes I
was so excited that he had to calm me down. But he never told me, as
adults will, that fairy tales are untrue; I am particularly grateful to
him for that, perhaps I still consider them true today. I noticed, of
course, that Robinson Crusoe was different from Sinbad the Sailor, but
it never occurred to me to think less of one of these stories than the
other. However, I did have bad dreams about Dante's Inferno. When
I heard my mother say to him, "Jacques, you shouldn't have given him
that, it's too early for him," I was afraid he wouldn't bring me any
more books, and I learned to keep my dreams a secret. I also believe—
but I'm not quite certain—that my mother connected my frequent
conversations with the wallpaper people to the books. That was the
period when I liked my mother least. I was cunning enough to whiff
danger, and perhaps I wouldn't have given up my loud wallpaper
conversations so willingly and hypocritically if the books and my
conversations about them with my father hadn't become the most important thing in the world for me.

But he stuck to his purpose and tried *William Tell* after Dante. It was
here that I first heard the word "freedom." He said something to me
about it, which I have forgotten. But he added something about Eng-

land: That was why we had moved to England, he said, because people were free here. I knew how much he loved England, while my mother doted on Vienna. He made an effort to learn the language properly, and once each week a woman came by to give him lessons. I noticed that he pronounced his English sentences differently from German, which he was fluent in since his youth and usually spoke with Mother. Sometimes I heard him pronounce and repeat single sentences. He uttered them slowly, like something very beautiful, they gave him pleasure and he uttered them again. He always, spoke English to us children now; Ladino, which had been my language until then, receded into the background, and I only heard it from others, particularly older relatives.

When I reported to him on the books I read, it had to be in English. I think that this passionate reading helped me to make very rapid progress. He was delighted that my reports were so fluent. What *he* had to say, however, had a special weight, for he thought it out very carefully to make absolutely sure there was no error, and he spoke almost as if he were reading to me. I have a solemn memory of these hours, he was altogether different than when he played with us in the nursery and incessantly kept inventing new antics.

The last book I received from him was about Napoleon. It was written from a British point of view, and Napoleon appeared as an evil tyrant, who wanted to gain control of all countries, especially England. I was reading this book when my father died. My distaste for Napoleon has been unshakable ever since. I had started telling my father about the book, but I hadn't gotten very far. He had given it to me right after *William Tell*, and it was a small experiment for him after the conversation on freedom. When I soon talked excitedly to him about Napoleon, he said: "Just wait, it's too soon. You have to keep reading. It's going to turn out quite different." I know for sure that Napoleon hadn't been crowned emperor yet. Maybe it was a test, maybe he wanted to see if I could resist the imperial splendor. I then finished it after his death, I reread it countless times like all the books I'd gotten from him. I had had little experience with power. My first notion of it stemmed from this book, and I have never been able to hear Napoleon's name without connecting it to my father's sudden death. Of all of Napoleon's murders, the greatest and most dreadful was of my father.

On Sundays, he sometimes took me strolling alone. Not far from our house, the little Mersey River flowed by. On the left side, it was edged by a reddish wall; on the other side, a path wound through a luxuriant meadow full of flowers and high grass. He had told me the English word "meadow," and he asked me for it during every stroll. He felt it was an especially beautiful word; it has remained the most beautiful word in the English language for me. Another favorite word of his was "island." It must have been very important to him that England was an island; perhaps he thought of it as an Isle of the Blest. He also explained it to me, much to my astonishment, over and over again, even when I'd known it for a long time. On our last stroll through the meadow by the Mersey River, he spoke altogether differently than I was accustomed to hearing. He asked me very urgently what I wanted to be, and I said without thinking: "A doctor!"

"You will be what you want to be," he said with so much tenderness that both of us stopped in our tracks. "You don't have to become a businessman like me and the uncles. You will go to the university and you will be what you want most."

I always regarded that conversation as his last wish. But at the time, I didn't know why he was so different when he uttered it. It was only when finding out more about his life, that I realized he had been thinking about himself. During his schooldays in Vienna, he had passionately frequented the *Burgtheater*, and his greatest desire was to become an actor. Sonnenthal was his idol, and young as he was, he managed to get in to see him and tell him of his desire. Sonnenthal told him he was too short for the stage, an actor couldn't be so short. From Grandfather, who was an actor in every utterance of his life, Father had inherited a theatrical gift, but Sonnenthal's pronouncement was devastating for him, and he buried his dreams. He was musical, he had a good voice and he loved his violin above everything. Grandfather, who ruled his children as a ruthless patriarch, thrust each of his sons into the business very early; he wanted to have a branch, managed by one of the sons, in every major city in Bulgaria. When Father spent too many hours with his violin, it was taken away from him, and he came right into the business against his will. He didn't like it at all; nothing interested him less than what was to his advantage. But he was a lot weaker than Grandfather and gave in. He was twenty-nine by the time he finally succeeded, with Mother's help, in fleeing Bulgaria and settling in Manchester. By then, he had a family with three children, whom he had to take care of, so he remained a businessman. It was already a victory from him to have escaped his father's tyranny and left Bulgaria. He had, of course, parted with him on bad terms and he bore his father's curse; but he was free in England and he was determined to treat his owns sons differently.

I don't believe my father was very well read. Music and theater meant more to him than books. A piano stood downstairs in the dining room, and every Saturday and Sunday, when Father wasn't in the office, my parents would make music there. He sang, and Mother accompanied him on the keyboard. It was always German lieder, usually Schubert and Loewe. One lied—it was called "The Grave on the Heath," and I don't known who it way by—swept me off my feet. Whenever I heard it, I would open the nursery door upstairs, sneak down the steps, and hide behind the door to the dining room. I didn't understand German at that time, but the song was heart-rending. I was discovered behind the door, and from then on I had the right to listen inside the dining room. I was brought down especially for this lied and I didn't have to steal downstairs anymore. The text was explained to me, I had indeed often heard German in Bulgaria and secretly repeated it to myself without understanding it; but this was the first time something was translated for me, the first German words I mastered came from "The Grave on the Heath." The song was about a deserter who gets caught and is standing in front of his comrades, who are supposed to shoot him. He sings about what enticed him to flee, I think it was a song from his homeland that he heard. The lyrics end with the verse: "Farewell, you brothers, here's my chest!" Then comes a shot, and finally, there are roses on the grave in the heath.

I waited all a-tremble for the shot, it was an excitement that never faded. I wanted to hear it over and over again and I tormented my father, who sang it for me two or three times in a row. Every Saturday, when he came home, I asked him, even before he had unpacked our gifts, whether he would sing "The Grave on the Heath." He said: "Maybe," but he was actually undecided, because my obsession with this song began to trouble him. I refused to believe that the deserter was really dead; I hoped he'd be saved, and when they had sung it several times and he wasn't saved, I was devastated and bewildered. At night in bed, he came to my mind, and I brooded about him. I couldn't grasp that his comrades had shot him. He had explained everything so well, after all; I certainly wouldn't have fired at him. His death was incomprehensible to me, it was the first death that I mourned.

Little Mary
The Sinking of the *Titanic*
Captain Scott

Soon after our arrival in Manchester, I started school. The school was in Barlowmore Road, some ten minutes from our house. The directress was named Miss Lancashire, and since the county in which Manchester was located was also called Lancashire, I was astonished at her name. It was a school for boys and girls, I found myself solely among English children. Miss Lancashire was fair and treated all the children with equal friendliness. She encouraged me when I told a story in English, for initially I couldn't do as well as the other children. But I learned how to read and write very soon, and when I began reading the books my father brought me, I noticed that Miss Lancashire didn't want to hear about them. Her goal was to have all the children feel comfortable; she didn't care about rapid progress. I never once saw her irritated or angry, and she was so good at what she did that she never had any trouble with the children. Her motions were sure but not athletic, her voice was even and never too penetrating. I cannot recall her giving a single order. There were some things we mustn't do; since she didn't keep repeating herself, we gladly yielded. I loved the school from the very first day. Miss Lancashire didn't have the sharpness of our governess, and above all, she didn't have a sharp, pointed nose. She was small and delicate, with a lovely, round face, her brown smock reached to the floor, and since I couldn't see her shoes, I asked my parents whether she had any. I was very sensitive to being made fun of, and when my mother laughed aloud at my question, I resolved to find Miss Lancashire's invisible shoes. I paid strict attention until I eventually discovered them, and, a bit hurt, I reported my find at home.

Everything I witnessed in England at that time fascinated me with its order. Life in Ruschuk had been loud and fierce, and rich in painful accidents. But something about the school must have made me feel at home too. Its rooms were on the ground floor, as in our house in Bulgaria; there was no upper story as in the new Manchester house, and in back the school faced a large garden. The doors and windows of the schoolroom were always open, and we were out in the garden whenever possible. Athletics was the most important subject by far; the other boys had the rules down pat from the very first day, as though they had been born playing cricket. Donald, my friend, admitted after a while that he had originally thought I was stupid because they had to explain and keep repeating the rules until I finally understood them. At first, he spoke to me out of pity, he sat next to me; but then, once when he was showing me stamps and I knew the country of each stamp right away, and I even pulled out stamps from Bulgaria, which he didn't know, and I gave them to him instead of trading them "because I have so many," he started getting interested in me, and we became friends. I don't think I meant to bribe him; I was a very proud child, but I most certainly wanted to impress him, for I perceived his condescension.

Our stamp-collecting friendship developed so fast that during class we stealthily played little games with the stamps under the desk. Nothing was said to us, we were put in different places in the friendliest way, and our games were restricted to the road home.

In his stead, a little girl was put next to me, Mary Handsome. I instantly grew as fond of her as a postage stamp. Her name surprised me, I didn't know that names can mean anything. She was shorter than I and had fair hair, but the nicest thing about her were her red cheeks, "like little apples." We immediately started talking, and she responded to everything; but even when we weren't talking, during lessons, I had to keep looking at her. I was so utterly enchanted by her red cheeks that I no longer paid any attention to Miss Lancashire, not hearing her questions and answering confusedly. I wanted to kiss the red cheeks and had to pull myself together so as not to do it. After school, I walked with her; she lived in the opposite direction from me, and I left Donald standing there with no explanation, even though he had always walked me most of the way home. I accompanied Little Mary, as I called her, until the corner of the street she lived on; I hastily kissed her on the cheek and hurried home without saying a word about it to anyone.

This was repeated several times, and so long as I merely kissed her goodbye on the corner, nothing happened, perhaps she didn't mention it at home either. But my feelings heightened, school no longer interested me, I waited for the moment when I could walk next to her, and soon the distance to the corner was too long, and I tried to kiss her beforehand on the red cheek. She pushed me away, saying: "You may only give me a goodbye kiss at the corner, otherwise I shall tell my mother." The word "goodbye kiss," which she used as she vehemently turned away, made a deep impression on me, and I now walked faster to her corner, she halted as though nothing had happened, and I kissed her as usual. The next day, I lost patience and kissed her the instant we got on the street. To forestall her anger, I became angry myself and said threateningly: "I'm going to kiss you as often as I like, I'm not waiting till we reach the corner." She tried to run away, I held her fast, we walked a few paces, I kissed her again, I kept kissing her until we came to her corner. She didn't say goodbye when I finally let go, she only said: "Now I'm going to tell my mother."

I wasn't afraid of her mother; my passion for her red cheeks was so great now that at home, to our governess's amazement, I sang: "Little Mary is my sweetheart! Little Mary is my sweetheart! Little Mary is my sweetheart!"

I had gotten the word "sweetheart" from the governess herself. She used it only when kissing my little brother Georgie, he was one year old, and she used to take him out in the perambulator. "You are my sweetheart," said the woman with the bony face and the sharp nose and kissed the child over and over again. I asked what the word "sweetheart" meant, and all I found out was that our maid Edith had a "sweetheart," a boyfriend. What did you do with that? You kissed him, the way the governess kissed little Georgie. That had encouraged me, and I was not aware of any wrongdoing when I intoned my chant of triumph in the governess's presence.

The next day, Mrs. Handsome came to school. She suddenly stood there, a stately woman, I liked her even more than her daughter, and that was lucky for me. She spoke to Miss Lancashire, and then she came to me and said very definitely: "You will not escort little Mary home anymore. Your house lies in a different direction. You two will no longer sit next to each other, and you will not speak to her anymore." It didn't sound angry, she didn't seen annoyed, but it was so definite, and yet quite different from the way my mother would have talked. I did not hold it against Mrs. Handsome; she was like her daughter, whom I didn't see behind her, but I liked everything about her, not only her cheeks, I especially liked the way she spoke. At this time, when I was starting to read, English had an irresistible effect on me, and no one had ever used English to deliver such a speech to me in which I played such an important part.

That was the end of this matter, but, as I was told later on, it hadn't gone all that simply. Miss Lancashire had asked my parents to come see her and had discussed whether I should remain in the school. She had never witnessed such a fierce passion in her school, she was a bit confused and wondered if it might have something to do with "Oriental" children maturing much earlier than British children. Father calmed her down, he guaranteed that it was an innocent thing. Perhaps it had something to do with the girl's conspicuously red cheeks. He asked Miss Lancashire to try one more week, and he proved to be right. I don't believe I ever so much as glanced at Little Mary again. Standing behind her mother, she had been absorbed into her, as far as I was concerned. At home, I often spoke admiringly about Mrs. Handsome. But I don't know what Mary did at school later on, how long she attended, or whether she was taken away and sent to another school. My memory is confined to the period in which I kissed her.

My father probably didn't realize how right he was when he surmised that it had something to do with the girl's red cheeks. Subsequently, I thought about this young love, which I never forgot, and one day I recollected the first Ladino children's song that I had heard in Bulgaria.

I was still carried in people's arms, and a female approached me, singing: "*Manzanicas coloradas, las que vienen de Stambol*" (Little apples, red, red apples, those that come from Istanbul). Her forefinger came closer and closer to my cheek, suddenly giving it a solid poke. I squealed pleasurably, she took me in her arms and hugged and kissed me. It happened over and over, until I learned to sing the song myself. Then I sang it along with her, it was my first song, and everyone who wanted me to sing played that game with me. Four years later, I found my own little apples in Mary, she was smaller than I, I always called her "little," and I'm only surprised that I didn't poke my finger in her cheek before kissing it.

George, the youngest brother, was a very lovely child, with dark eyes and pitch-black hair. Father taught him his first words. Every morning, when he came into the nursery, the same dialogue always went on between them, and I listened in suspense: "Georgie?" said Father in an urgent and quizzical tone of voice, to which George replied: "Canetti"; "Two?" said my father, "Three," the child; "Four?" said my father, "Burton," the child, "Road," said my father. Originally, that was all there was. But gradually, our address was completed, it came, with allotted voices: "West," "Didsbury," "Manchester," "England." The last word was mine, I wouldn't give it up, I added "Europe."

Geography, you see, had become very important to me, and my knowledge of it was increased in two ways, I received a jigsaw puzzle: the multicolored map of Europe, pasted on wood, was cut up into the individual countries. You tossed all the pieces into a heap and then put Europe together again lightning-fast. Thus every country had its own shape, with which my fingers grew familiar, and one day I surprised my father by saying: "I can do it blindfolded!"

"You can*not*!" he said. I shut my eyes tight and reassembled Europe blindly.

"You cheated," he said, "you peeked between your fingers." I was hurt and insisted that he keep his hands over my eyes.

"Hold tight! Hold tight!" I shouted excitedly, and Europe was already together.

"You really can do it," he said and praised me, no praise has ever been so dear to me.

The other way of studying the countries was by collecting stamps. Now it wasn't just Europe, it was the whole world, and the most important part was played by the British colonies. The album for the stamps was also a gift from my Father, and when I got it, one stamp was already pasted at the upper left of each page.

I heard a lot about ships and other countries. *Robinson Crusoe*, "Sinbad

the Sailor," *Gulliver's Travels* were my very favorite stories, and I also
had the stamps with the beautiful pictures. The Mauritius stamp, which
was worth so much that I didn't really understand, was reproduced in
the album, and the first question I was asked when trading stamps with
the other boys was: "Do you have a Mauritius stamp to trade?" This
question was always meant seriously, I often asked it myself.

The two catastrophes that occurred in this period, and that I now
realize were the earliest causes of mass public grief in my life, were
connected with ships and geography. The first was the sinking of the
Titanic, the second the death of Captain Scott at the South Pole.

I can't remember who it was who first spoke about the sinking of the
Titanic. But our governess wept during breakfast, I had never seen her
weeping before, and Edith, the housemaid, came to the nursery, where
we normally never saw her, and wept with her together. I learned
about the iceberg, about the terribly many people who had drowned,
and the thing that had the biggest impact on me was the band that
kept playing as the ship sank. I wanted to know what they had played
and I received a gruff answer. I realized I had asked something unsuit-
able and started crying myself. So actually the three of us were weeping
together when Mother called to Edith from downstairs; perhaps she
had only just heard the news herself. Then we went down, the governess
and I, and Mother and Edith were already standing there, crying
together.

But we must have gone out after all, for I can see people on the
street, everything was very different. The people stood in groups, talking
excitedly, others joined them and had something to say; my little
brother in the pram, who usually elicited an admiring word about his
beauty from all passersby, was completely unheeded. We children
were forgotten, and yet people spoke about children who had been on
the ship, and how they and the women were saved first. People kept
talking about the captain, who had refused to leave the vessel. But the
most frequent word I caught was "iceberg." It stamped itself upon me
like "meadow" and "island," although I didn't get it from my father,
it was the third English word that remained charged for me, the fourth
was "captain."

I don't know exactly when the *Titanic* sank. But in the excitement of
those days, an excitement that endured for some time, I vainly looked
for my father. He would have spoken to me about it after all, he would
have found a soothing word for me. He would have protected me from
the catastrophe, which caved into me with all its strength. Each movement of his remained precious to me, but when I think of the *Titanic*,
I don't see him, I don't hear him, and I feel the naked fear that

overcame me when the ship struck the iceberg in the middle of the night and sank into the cold water while the band played on.

Wasn't he in England? He sometimes took a trip. Nor did I go to school during that time. Maybe the disaster occurred during the holidays, maybe they let us off, maybe no one thought of sending children to school. Mother certainly didn't comfort me, she wasn't affected deeply enough by the catastrophe; and as for the English people in our household, Edith and Miss Bray, I felt closer to them than to my real family. I believe that my pro-English attitude, which carried me through the First World War, was created in the grief and agitation of those days.

The other public event of this time was of a totally different nature, even though the word "captain" played a major role here too. But this man wasn't the captain of a ship, he was a South Pole explorer, and instead of a collision with an iceberg, the accident took place in a wasteland of snow and ice; the iceberg had expanded into a whole continent. It was also the opposite of a panic, no desperate mass of people jumping overboard into the sea; Captain Scott and three of his men had frozen to death in the icy desert. It was, one might say, a ritual British event; the men had reached the South Pole, but they weren't the first. Arriving after unspeakable difficulties and exertions, they found the Norwegian flag planted there. Amundsen had come first. On the way home, they perished, and for a while there was no trace of them. Now they had been found, and their last words were read in their diaries.

Miss Lancashire called us together in school. We knew something dreadful had happened, and not a single child laughed. She gave a talk, describing Captain Scott's enterprise. She did not shrink from depicting the sufferings of the men in the icy wastes. A few details have remained with me, but since I afterwards read everything very carefully, I cannot expect to distinguish between what I heard then and what I read later. Miss Lancashire did not lament what had happened to the men, she spoke firmly and proudly, such as I had never heard her. If her aim was to present the polar explorers as a model for us, then she certainly succeeded in one case, mine. I instantly resolved to become an explorer, and I stuck to this plan for several years. Miss Lancashire ended her talk by saying that Scott and his friends had died as true Englishmen, and that was the only time during the years in Manchester that I heard a pride in being English articulated so openly and bluntly. Afterwards, I heard such things said far more frequently in other countries, with an insolence that angered me when I thought of Miss Lancashire's calm and dignity.

Napoleon; Cannibal Guests; Sunday Fun

Life in the mansion on Burton Road was social and cheerful. We always had guests on weekends. Sometimes I was called in, the guests had asked for me, and there were all sorts of ways I could perform. So I got to know them all well, the members of the family and their friends. The Sephardic colony in Manchester had grown rather quickly, all of them settling not far from one another in the outlying residential districts of West Didsbury and Withington. Exporting cotton goods from Lancashire to the Balkans was a profitable business. A few years before us, Mother's eldest brothers, Bucco and Solomon, had come to Manchester and started a firm. Bucco, who was regarded as sagacious, soon died at an early age, and Solomon, the hard man with the ice-cold eyes, remained alone. He looked for a partner, and that was a chance for my father, who had such a lofty notion of England. Father entered the firm and, being charming, conciliant, and understanding of other people's viewpoints, he formed a useful counterpoise to his brother-in-law. I cannot see this uncle as friendly or fair, he was the hated enemy of my youth, the man who stood for everything I despised. He probably didn't care about me one way or another, but for the family he was the picture of success, and success was money. In Manchester I rarely saw him; he took many business trips, but the family spoke about him all the more. By now, he was quite at home in England and greatly respected among the businessmen. His English, which was perfect, was admired by the latecomers in the family, and not only by them. Miss Lancashire sometimes mentioned him at school. "Mr. Arditti is a gentleman," she said. By which she probably meant that he was well-to-do and had nothing of a foreigner in his behavior. He lived in a big mansion, much higher and more spacious than ours, in Palatine Road, which ran parallel to our street, and since, unlike all the reddish houses I saw in the neighborhood, it was white and shimmery bright, and also perhaps because of the name of the road, it seemed like a palace to me. But as for him, even though he didn't look it, I regarded him as an ogre very early on. It was always Mr. Arditti this, and Mr. Arditti that, our governess made a deferential grimace when she spoke his name, supreme shalt-nots were attributed to him, and when my conversations with the wallpaper people were discovered and I tried to defend them by citing my father, who was very lenient with me, I was told Mr. Arditti would find out about them, and that would have the most frightful consequences. At the sheer mention of his name, I gave up on the spot and promised to break off my relations to the wallpaper people. He was the ultimate authority of all the grownups in my milieu. When I read about Napoleon, I pictured him precisely like this uncle, and the atrocities I ascribed to him were credited to Napoleon. On Sunday mornings, we were allowed to visit our parents in their bedroom, and once, when I entered, I heard my father saying in his solemn and dignified English: "He'll stop at nothing. He'd leave a trail of corpses." Mother noticed me and retorted in German, she seemed angry, and the conversation went on for a while without my understanding it.

If my father was talking about my uncle, then he must have meant business corpses; my uncle hardly had any opportunity for others. But I didn't grasp this at the time, and even though I hadn't gotten very far in Napoleon's life, I comprehended enough of his impact to regard corpses (which I only knew about from books, of course) as corpses.

There were also three cousins of my mother's who had come to Manchester, three brothers. Sam, the eldest, really looked like an Englishman, he had also been in England longer than anyone else. With the drooping corners of his mouth, he encouraged me to pronounce difficult words correctly, and when I grimaced in order to emulate him, he took it amiably and laughed heartily, without hurting my feelings. Miss Lancashire's dictum about that other relative, the ogre-uncle, was something I never recognized, and once, in order to demonstrate this, I stood in front of Uncle Sam and said: "*You're* a gentleman, Uncle Sam!" Perhaps he liked hearing it, in any event he understood, *everyone* understood, for the entire company in our dining room went mute.

All these relatives of my mother, except for one, had started families in Manchester and came visiting with their wives. Only Uncle Solomon was missing, his time was too costly, and he had no interest in conversations with women present, much less in making music. He called these things "frivolities," his head was always full of new business dealings, and he was admired for this "mental activity" too.

Other families we were friends with also came on such evenings. There was Mr. Florentin, whom I liked because of his beautiful name; Mr. Calderon, who had the longest moustache and always laughed. The most mysterious one for me, when he first appeared, was Mr. Innie. He was darker than the others, and people said he was an Arab, by which they meant an Arabic Jew, he had only just recently come from Bagdad. I had *The Arabian Nights* in my head, and when I heard "Bagdad," I expected Caliph Haroun in disguise. But the disguise went too far, Mr. Innie had gigantic shoes. I didn't like that, and I asked him why he had such big shoes. "Because I have such big feet," he said, "would you like to see them?" I believed he was really about to take the shoes off, and I was scared. For one of the wallpaper people, who was my special enemy, excluding himself from all enterprises that I wanted to launch, also had enormous feet. I didn't want to see Mr. Innie's feet, and without saying goodbye, I went up to the nursery. I no longer believed that he came from Bagdad with those feet; I told my parents it wasn't true, and said he was a liar.

My parents' guests had a merry time, they chatted and laughed a lot, they played music, they played cards. Usually they stayed in the dining room, perhaps because of the piano. Guests were entertained more seldom in the yellow salon, which was separated from the dining room by the vestibule and the corridor. However, the salon was the setting of my humiliations, which were linked to the French language. It must have been my mother who insisted that I also learn French, to balance English, which was so dear to my father. A teacher came, a Frenchwoman, and she gave me lessons in the yellow salon. She was dark and thin and there was something invidious about her, but her face has been covered by the faces of other Frenchwomen whom I knew afterwards, I can't find it in me anymore. She came and went punctually, but she never made much of an effort and she merely taught me a story about a boy who was alone in the house and wanted to nibble on something. "*Paul était seul à la maison,*" was how it began. I soon knew the story by heart and recited it to my parents. The boy suffered all manner of misfortunes in his nibblings, and I recited the story as dramatically as possible—my parents seemed very amused, before long they were laughing their heads off. I felt odd. I had never heard them laugh so long and so harmoniously, and when I was done, I sensed that their praise was bogus. Offended, I went up to the nursery and kept rehearsing the story for myself to avoid faltering or making any mistakes.

The next time that visitors came, they all placed themselves in the yellow salon as though for a performance, I was brought down and asked to recite the French story. I began "*Paul était seul à la maison,*" and all faces were already twisting in mirth. But I wanted to show them and I stuck to my guns, I told the story to its end. By then, they were rolling in the aisles. Mr. Calderon, who was always the loudest, clapped his hands and shouted: "Bravo! Bravo!" Uncle Sam, the gentleman, couldn't get his mouth shut and bared all his English teeth. Mr. Innie stretched his gigantic shoes out far, leaned his head back, and howled. Even the ladies, who were usually tender to me and liked kissing me on my head, laughed with gaping mouths as though about to devour me. It was a wild company, I got scared, and eventually, I started crying.

This scene was repeated several times; when guests came, I was cajoled into reciting my Paul story, and instead of refusing I agreed each time, hoping to conquer my tormenting spirits. But it always ended in the same way, except that some of them got used to chorusing the story along with me, thereby forcing me to keep on to the end in case I started crying too early and felt like stopping. No one ever explained to me what was so funny; since then, laughter has remained a riddle for me, which I have thought about a great deal; it is still an unsolved riddle for me, even today.

It was only later on, when I heard French in Lausanne, that I understood the effect of my "Paul" on the gathered visitors. The teacher hadn't made the slightest effort to teach me a proper French accent. She was satisfied if I retained her sentences and repeated them in an English way. The guests, all from Ruschuk, had learned French with a perfect accent at home in the school of the Alliance Française, and now, having trouble with their English, they found it irresistibly comical to hear this British French, and, a shameless mob, they enjoyed the reversal of their own problem in a child that was just going on seven.

I associated all my experiences at that time with the books I read. I was not so far off-target in seeing the uninhibitedly laughing mob of adults as cannibals, such as I knew and feared from *The Arabian Nights* and Grimm's fairy tales. Fear thrives strongest; there is no telling how little we would be without having suffered fear. An intrinsic characteristic of humanity is the tendency to give in to fear. No fear is lost, but its hiding places are a riddle. Perhaps, of all things, fear is the one that changes least. When I think back to my early years, the very first things I recognize are the fears, of which there was an inexhaustible wealth. I find many of them only now; others, which I will never find, must be the mystery that makes me want an unending life.

Loveliest of all were the Sunday mornings; we children were allowed into our parents' bedroom, they both still lay in bed, Father closer to the door, Mother by the window. I was allowed to jump right into his bed, the little brothers went to Mother. He tumbled around with me, asked me about school, and told me stories. It all lasted a long time, I looked forward to this in particular, and I always hoped it would never end. Otherwise everything was scheduled in detail, there were rules and rules, which the governess saw to. But I cannot say that these rules tormented me, for every day ended with Father coming home with gifts that he presented to us in the nursery; and every week ended with Sunday morning and our playing and talking in bed. I paid attention only to Father; I was indifferent to, perhaps even a little scornful about, whatever Mother was doing with my two little brothers in her bed. Since I'd started reading the books that Father brought me, I found my brothers boring or a nuisance; and the fact that Mother took them from us and that I had Father all to myself was the greatest luck. He was especially funny when he was still in bed, he made faces and sang comical songs. He mimicked animals for me, which I had to guess, and if I hit on the animal, he promised he'd take me to the zoo again as a reward. There was a chamber pot under his bed, and it contained so much yellow fluid that I was amazed. But that was nothing, for one day, he got up, stood next to the bed, and passed his water. I watched the tremendous gush, I was flabbergasted that so much water could come out of him, my admiration for him reached the highest pinnacle. "Now you're a horse," I said, I had watched horses passing their water in the street, and the gush and their members seemed gigantic. He admitted I was right: "Now I'm a horse," and of all the animals he mimicked, this one had the greatest impact on me.

It was always Mother who put an end to all the fun. "Jacques, it's time," she said, "the children are getting too wild." He never stopped immediately and never sent me away without first telling me a story that I hadn't heard before. "Think about it!" he said as I stood in the doorway; Mother had rung, and the governess had come to fetch us. I felt solemn because I was supposed to think about something; he never neglected—sometimes days had passed—to ask me about it. He would then listen very carefully and finally approved of what I had said. Perhaps he really did approve of it, perhaps he was only trying to encourage me; the feeling I had when he told me to think about something can only be described as an early sense of responsibility.

I have often wondered if things would have continued like that had he lived longer. Would I eventually have rebelled against him as I did against Mother? I cannot imagine it, his image inside me is undimmed, and I want to leave it undimmed. I believe that he suffered so greatly from his father's tyranny, living under his curse throughout that brief time in England, that he aimed at caution, love, and wisdom in everything concerning me. He was not bitter, because he had escaped; had he remained in Bulgaria, in his father's business, which oppressed him, he would have turned into a different man.

Father's Death
The Final Version

We had been in England for about a year when Mother fell ill. Supposedly, the English air didn't agree with her. The doctor prescribed a cure at Bad Reichenhall; in the summertime, it may have been August 1912, she went. I didn't pay much attention, I didn't miss her, but Father asked me about her, and I had to say something. Perhaps he was worried that her absence wouldn't be good for us children, and he wanted to catch the first signs of change in us on the spot. After a couple of weeks, he asked me whether I would mind if Mother stayed away longer. If we were patient, he added, she would keep improving and would come home to us in full health. The first few times, I had pretended to miss her; I sensed that he expected me to. Now, I was all the more honest in agreeing that she should have a longer treatment. Sometimes he came into the nursery with a letter from her, pointing to it and saying she had written. But he wasn't himself in this period, his thoughts were with her, and he was concerned. In the last week of her absence, he spoke little and never mentioned her name to me; he didn't listen to me very long, never laughed, and devised no pranks. When I wanted to tell him about the latest book he had given me, *The Life of Napoleon*, he was absent-minded and impatient, and cut me off; I thought I had said something foolish and I was ashamed. The very next day, he came to us as merry and exuberant as usual and announced that Mother was arriving tomorrow. I was glad because he was glad; and Miss Bray told Edith something I didn't understand: She said it was *proper* for the mistress to come home. "Why is it proper?" I asked, but she shook her head: "You wouldn't understand. It is *proper!*" When I eventually asked Mother about it in detail—there were so many obscure things, leaving me no peace—I learned that she had been gone for six weeks and wanted to stay on. Father had lost patience and wired her to come back immediately.

The day of her arrival, I didn't see him, he didn't come to the nursery that evening. But he reappeared the very next morning and got my little brother to talk. "Georgie," he said; "Canetti," said the boy; "Two," said Father; "Three," said the boy; "Four," said Father; "Burton," said the boy; "Road," said Father; "West," said the boy; "Didsbury," said Father; "Manchester," said the boy; "England," said Father; and I, in the end, very loudly and superfluously, said, "Eu-

rope." So our address was together again. There are no words that I
have retained more sharply, they were my Father's last words.

He went down to breakfast as usual. Before long, we heard loud
yells. The governess dashed down the stairs, I at her heels. By the open
door to the dining room, I saw my father lying on the floor. He was
stretched out full length, between the table and the fireplace, very
close to the fireplace, his face was white, he had foam on his mouth,
Mother knelt at his side, crying: "Jacques, speak to me, speak to me,
Jacques, Jacques, speak to me!" She kept shouting it over and over
again, people came, our neighbors the Brockbanks, a Quaker couple,
strangers walked in off the street. I stood by the door, Mother grabbed
her head, tore hair out, and kept shouting. I took a timid step into the
room, towards my father, I didn't understand, I wanted to ask him,
then I heard someone say: "Take the child away." The Brockbanks
gently took my arm, led me out into the street, and into their front
yard.

Here, their son Alan welcomed me, he was much older than I and
spoke to me as if nothing had happened. He asked me about the latest
cricket match at school, I answered him, he wanted to know every
detail about it and kept asking until I had nothing more to say. Then
he wanted to know if I was a good climber, I said yes, he showed me
a tree standing there, bending somewhat towards our own front yard.
"But I bet you can't climb that one," he said, "I bet you can't. It's too
hard for you. You wouldn't dare." I took the challenge, looked at the
tree, had my doubts, but didn't show them, and said: "I can too. I can
too!" I strode over to the tree, touched the bark, threw my arms around
the trunk, and was about to swing up, when a window in our dining
room opened. Mother leaned way out, saw me standing at the tree with
Alan, and yelled: "My son, you're playing, and your father is dead!
You're playing, you're playing, and your father is dead! Your father
is dead! Your father is dead! You're playing, your father is dead!"

She yelled it out into the street, she kept yelling louder and louder,
they yanked her back into the room by force, she resisted, I heard her
shouting after I no longer saw her, I heard her shouting for a long
time. Her shouts pushed Father's death into me, and it has never left
me since.

I wasn't allowed to see Mother. I was taken to the Florentins, who
lived halfway to school, in Barlowmore Road. Arthur, their son, was
already something of a friend to me, and in the coming days we became
inseparable. Mr. Florentin and Nelly, his wife, two kind-hearted people, never took their eyes off me for an instant, they were afraid I might
run off to my mother. She was very sick, I was told, no one could see

her, she would soon be fully well again, and then I could go back to her. But they were wrong, I didn't want to go to her at all, I wanted to go to my father. They spoke little about him. The day of his funeral, which was not kept from me, I resolutely declared that I wanted to go along to the cemetery. Arthur had picture books about foreign countries, he had stamps and many games. He was occupied with me day and night; I slept in the same room, and he was so friendly and inventive and earnest and funny that I have a warm feeling even now when I think about him. But on the day of the funeral, nothing helped; when I noticed he wanted to keep me from going to the funeral, I lost my temper and struck out at him. The whole family tried to help me, they locked all doors for safety's sake. I raged and threatened to smash them down, which may not have been beyond me on that day. Finally, they had a fortunate idea, which gradually calmed me down. They promised that I could *watch* the funeral procession. It could be seen from the nursery, they said, if I leaned out, but only from afar.

I believed them and didn't think about how far it would be. When the time came, I leaned way out of the nursery window, so far out that I had to be held fast from behind. I was told that the procession was just turning the corner of Burton Road into Barlowmore Road and then moving away from us towards the cemetery. I peered my eyes out and saw nothing. But they so clearly depicted what could be seen that I finally perceived a light fog in the given direction. That was it, they said, that was it. I was exhausted from the long struggle and I accepted the situation.

I was seven years old when my father died, and he wasn't even thirty-one. There was a lot of discussion about it, he was supposed to have been in perfect health, he smoked a lot, but that was really all they could blame his sudden heart attack on. The English physician who examined him after his death found nothing. But the family didn't much care for English doctors. It was the great age of Viennese medicine, and everyone had consulted a Viennese professor at some point or other. I was unaffected by these conversations, I *could* not recognize any cause for his death, and so it was better for me if none were found.

But, as the years went by, I kept questioning my mother about it. What I learned from her changed every few years; as I gradually got older, new things were added, and an earlier version proved to have been "solicitous" of my youth. Since nothing preoccupied me so much as this death, I lived full of trust at various stages. I finally settled into my mother's last version, making myself at home in it, cleaving to every detail as though it came from a Bible, referring anything that happened in my environment to that version, simply everything that I read or thought. My father's death was at the center of every world I found myself in. When I learned something new a few years later, the earlier world collapsed around me like a stage set, nothing held anymore, all conclusions were false, it was as though someone were wrenching me away from a faith, but the lies that this someone demonstrated and demolished were lies that he himself had told me with a clear conscience, in order to protect my youth. My mother always smiled when she suddenly said: "I only told you that at the time because you were too young. You couldn't have understood." I feared that smile, it was different from her usual smile, which I loved for its haughtiness, but also for its intelligence. She realized she was smashing me to bits when she told me anything new about my father's death. She was cruel and she liked doing it, thereby getting back at me for the jealousy with which I made her life difficult.

My memory has stored up all the versions of that account, I can't think of anything I have retained more faithfully. Perhaps some day I can write them all down completely. They would make a book, an entire book, but now I am following other trails.

I want to record what I heard at the time and also the final version, which I still believe today.

The Florentins spoke about a war having broken out, the Balkan War. It may not have been so important for the British; but I lived among people who all came from Balkan countries, for them it was a domestic war. Mr. Florentin, an earnest, thoughtful man, avoided talking about Father with me, but he did say one thing when we were alone. He said it as though it were something very important, I had the feeling he was confiding in me, because the women, there being several in the household, were not present. He told me that Father had been reading the newspaper at his last breakfast, and the headline had said that Montenegro had declared war on Turkey; he realized that this spelled the outbreak of the Balkan War and that many people would now have to die, and this news, said Mr. Florentin, had killed him. I recalled seeing the *Manchester Guardian* next to him on the floor. Whenever I found a newspaper anywhere in the house, he allowed me to read him the headlines, and now and then, if it wasn't too difficult, he explained what they meant.

Mr. Florentin said there was nothing worse than war, and father had shared this opinion, they had often spoken about it. In England, all the people were against war, he went on, and there would never be another war here.

His words sank into me as though Father had spoken them personally. I kept them to myself, just as they had been spoken between us, as though they were a dangerous secret. In later years, whenever people spoke about how Father, who had been very young, in perfect health, with no disease, had suddenly died as though struck by lightning, I knew—and nothing could ever have gotten me to change my mind—that the lightning had been that dreadful news, the news about the outbreak of the war. There has been warfare in the world since then, and each war, wherever it was, and perhaps scarcely present in the consciousness of the people around me, has hit me with the force of that early loss, absorbing me as the most *personal* thing that could happen to me.

For my mother, however, the picture was quite different, and from her final and definitive version, which she revealed to me twenty-three years later under the impact of my first book, I learned that Father had not exchanged a word with her since the previous evening. She had felt very good in Reichenhall, where she had moved among her own kind, people with serious intellectual interests. Her physician spoke with her about Strindberg, and she began reading him too, she never stopped reading Strindberg after that. The physician asked her about these books, their conversations became more and more interesting, she started realizing that life in Manchester, among the semi-educated Sephardim, was not enough for her, perhaps that was her illness. She confessed this to the doctor, and he confessed his love for her. He proposed that she separate from my father and become his wife. Nothing, except in words, happened between them, nothing that she could reproach herself for, and she never for an instant thought seriously of leaving my father. But the conversations with the doctor meant more and more to her, and she did her best to prolong her stay in Reichenhall. She felt her health rapidly improving, which gave her a not dishonest reason for asking my father to let her continue her cure. But since she was very proud and didn't care to lie, her letters also mentioned the fascinating conversations with the physician. Ultimately, she was grateful to Father when he forced her, by telegraph, to return immediately. She herself might not have had the strength to leave Reichenhall. She arrived in Manchester radiant and happy, and in order to placate my father and perhaps also a bit out of vanity, she told him the whole story and about rejecting the doctor's offer to stay with him. Father couldn't understand how the situation could have reached that point, he interrogated her, and every answer he received added to his jealousy. He insisted that she had made herself culpable, he refused to believe her and saw her answers as lies. Finally, he became so furious that he threatened not to speak another word with her until she confessed the whole truth. He spent the entire evening and the night in silence and without sleeping. She felt utterly sorry for him, even though he was tormenting her, but, unlike him, she was convinced that she had proved her love by returning, and she was not aware of having done anything wrong. She hadn't even allowed the doctor to kiss her goodbye. She did all she could to get Father to talk, but since her hours of effort were to no avail, she grew angry and gave up, lapsing into silence herself.

In the morning, coming down to breakfast, he took his place at the table wordlessly and picked up the newspaper. When he collapsed, under the impact of the stroke, he hadn't spoken a single word to her. First she thought he was trying to frighten her and punish her some more. She knelt down next to him on the floor and begged him, pleaded with him, more and more desperately, to talk to her. When she realized he was dead, she thought he had died because of his disappointment in her.

I know that Mother told me the truth that final time, the truth as she saw it. There had been long, heavy struggles between us, and she had often been on the verge of disowning me forever. But now, she said, she understood the struggle that I had waged for my freedom, now she acknowledged my right to this freedom, despite the great unhappiness that this struggle had brought upon her. The book, which she had read, was flesh of her flesh, she said, she recognized herself in me, she had always viewed people the way I depicted them, that was exactly how she would have wanted to write herself. Her forgiveness was not enough, she went on, she was bowing to me, she acknowledged me doubly as her son, I had become what she had most wanted me to be. She lived in Paris at this time, and she had written a similar letter to me in Vienna, before I visited her. I was very frightened by this letter; even in the days of our bitterest enmity, I had admired her most for her pride. The thought of her bowing to me because of this novel— important as the book may have been to me—was unendurable (her not bowing to anything made up my image of her). When I saw her again, she may have felt my shame, embarrassment, and disappointment, and to convince me that she was in earnest, she let herself go and finally told me the whole truth about my father's death.

Despite her earlier versions, I had occasionally sensed the facts, but then always reproached myself that the distrust which I had inherited from her was leading me astray. To put my mind at ease, I had always repeated my father's last words in the nursery. They were not the words of an angry or despairing man. Perhaps one may infer that after a dreadful and sleepless night, he was about to soften, and perhaps he would have spoken to her after all in the dining room, when his shock at the outbreak of war interfered and struck him down.

The Heavenly Jerusalem

After a few weeks, I moved from the Florentin home back to Burton Road with my mother. At night, I slept in my father's bed, next to hers, and watched over her life. As long as I heard her crying, I didn't fall asleep; when she had slept a bit and then awoke, her soft crying woke me up. I grew close to her during this period, our relationship was different, I became the eldest son not just nominally. She called me the eldest son and treated me accordingly, I felt she was relying on me, she spoke to me as to no other person, and although she never said anything to me about it, I sensed her despair and the danger she was in. I took it upon myself to get her through the night, I was the weight that hung to her when she could no longer stand her torment and wanted to cast away her life. It is very odd that in this way, I successively experienced death and then fear for a life menaced by death.

During the day, she kept a hold on herself, there was plenty for her to take care of, things she wasn't accustomed to, and she did them all. In the evening, we had our little ritual meal, treating one another with a quiet sort of chivalry. I followed each of her movements and registered them, she cautiously interpreted for me what went on during the meal. Earlier, I had known her as impatient and autocratic, overbearing, impulsive; the movement I most clearly remembered was her ringing for the governess to get rid of us children. I had let her know in every way that I liked Father better, and when I was asked the question that so cruelly embarrasses children: "Who do you like better, Father or Mother?", I didn't try to wriggle out of it by saying "both the same," I pointed, without fear or hesitation, at my father. Now, however, each of us was for the other what had remained of Father; without realizing it, we both played him, and it was *his* tenderness that we showed one another.

In these hours, I learned the stillness in which one gathers all mental powers. I needed them more at that time than at any other in my life, for the nights following these evenings were filled with terrible danger; I would be satisfied with myself if I had always stood my ground as well as then.

One month after our misfortune, people collected in our home for the memorial service. The male relatives and friends stood along the wall of the dining room, their hats on their heads, the prayerbooks in their hands. On a sofa against the narrow wall, facing the window, sat Grandfather and Grandmother Canetti, who had come from Bulgaria. I didn't realize back then how guilty my grandfather felt. He had solemnly cursed my father when my father left him and Bulgaria; it very seldom happens that a pious Jew curses his son, no curse is more dangerous and no curse more feared. My father had stuck to his guns, and not much more than a year after arriving in England he was dead. I did hear my grandfather sob loudly in his prayers; he didn't stop weeping, he couldn't see me without hugging me with all his might, he scarcely let me go and he bathed me in tears. I took it for grief and found out only much later that it was the sense of his guilt far more than sorrow; he was convinced that his curse had killed my father. The events of this memorial service horrified me because Father was not present. I kept expecting him to suddenly turn up among us and say his prayers like the other men. I was fully aware that he hadn't concealed himself; but wherever he was, his not coming now, when all the men were saying the memorial prayer for him, was something I couldn't grasp. One of the mourners was Mr. Calderon, the man with the longest moustache, who was also known for laughing all the time. I expected the worst from him. Upon arriving, he spoke unabashedly to the men standing at his left and right, and suddenly he did what I had feared most, he laughed. I strode up to him angrily and asked: "Why are you laughing?" He couldn't be put off and he laughed at me. I hated him for that, I wanted him to go away, I felt like hitting him. But I couldn't have reached the smiling face, I was too little, I would have had to climb on a chair; and so I didn't hit him. When it was over, and the men left the room, he tried to stroke my head, I knocked his hand away and turned my back on him, crying in rage.

Grandfather explained that I as the eldest son, would have to recite the kaddish, the prayer for the dead. Every day, on the anniversary, I would have to recite the kaddish. If ever I failed to do so, Father would feel deserted, as though he didn't have a son. It was the greatest sin, said Grandfather, for a Jew not to say kaddish for his father. He explained it to me with sobs and sighs, I never saw him any different throughout the days of that visit. Mother, of course, as was customary among us, kissed his hand and reverentially called him "Señor Padre." But she never mentioned him during our reticent evening talks, and I distinctly sensed that it wouldn't be proper to ask about him. His incessant grief made a deep impression on me. But I had witnessed Mother's dreadful outburst, and now I saw her crying night after night.

I was worried about her, I merely watched him. He spoke to everyone, lamenting his misfortune. He lamented us too and called us "orphans." But he sounded as if he were ashamed to have orphans for grandchildren, and I rebelled against that sense of shame. I was no orphan boy, I had Mother, and she had already entrusted me with the responsibility of my little brothers.

We did not stay in Burton Road for very long. That same winter, we moved in with her brother on Palatine Road. His mansion had many large rooms and more people. Miss Bray, the governess, and Edith, the housemaid, came along. The two households were combined for a couple of months, everything was twofold, there were many visitors. In the evening, I no longer ate with Mother, and at night I no longer slept in her room. Perhaps she felt better, perhaps the others considered it wiser not to entrust her to my oversight alone. They tried diverting her, friends came to the house or invited her over. She had resolved to settle in Vienna with the children; the house in Burton Road was sold, preparations had to be made for the move. Her efficient brother, whom she thought a great deal of, acted as her adviser. Being a child, I was excluded from these useful conversations. I went to school again, and Miss Lancashire did not treat me like an orphan at all. She showed me something like respect, and once she even told me that I was now the man in the family, and that was the best thing a person could be.

At home in Palatine Road, I was in the nursery again, a much bigger one than the earlier room with the live wallpaper. I didn't miss the wallpaper, I had lost all interest in it under the impact of the recent events. Here I was again with my little brothers and the governess; and Edith, who had little to do, was usually also with us. The room was too large, something was lacking, it felt empty somehow, perhaps there should have been more people; Miss Bray, the governess, who came from Wales, populated it with a congregation. She sang English hymns with us, Edith sang along, a whole new period commenced for us, no sooner were we in the nursery than we launched into song. Miss Bray quickly accustomed us to singing, she was a different woman when she sang, no longer thin and sharp, her enthusiasm infected us children. We sang for all we were worth, even the youngest, two-year-old George, squawled along. There was *one* song in particular that we never got enough of. It was about the Heavenly Jerusalem. Miss Bray had convinced us that our father was now in the Heavenly Jerusalem, and if we sang the song properly, he would recognize our voices and delight in us. There was a wonderful line in it: "Jerusalem, Jerusalem, hark how the angels sing!" And when we came to this line, I believed I could see my father and I sang so ardently that I thought I would burst. However, Miss Bray appeared to have qualms, she said we might disturb the other people in the house, and to make sure that no one interrupted our song, she locked the door. Many of the songs mentioned the Lord Jesus, she told us his story, I wanted to hear about him, I couldn't get enough, and I couldn't understand why the Jews had crucified him. I knew all about Judas instantly, he wore a long moustache and laughed rather than being ashamed of his evil.

Miss Bray, in all innocence, must have carefully selected the hours for her missionizing. We were undisturbed, and after listening attentively to the stories about the Lord Jesus, we could sing "Jerusalem" again, which we kept begging her for. It was all so splendid and glorious that we never said a word about it to anyone. These carryings-on went undiscovered for a long time; they must have continued through weeks and weeks, for I got so used to them that I thought about them even in school, there was nothing I looked forward to as much, even reading was no longer so important, and Mother became alien to me again because she kept conferring with the Napoleon uncle, and I, to punish her for the admiring way she spoke about him, withheld the secret of the hours with Jesus.

One day, somebody suddenly rattled the door. Mother had come home unexpectedly and had been listening outside the nursery. It had been so beautiful, she said later on, that she just had to listen, she was amazed that other people had gotten into the nursery, for it couldn't have been we. Eventually, she did want to know who was singing "Jerusalem" and tried to open the door. When she found it locked, she got annoyed at those insolent strangers in our nursery and shook the door harder and harder. Miss Bray, using her hands to conduct a little, refused to interrupt the song, and we sang it through. Then she calmly opened the door and stood before "Madame." She explained that it did the children good to sing, hadn't "Madame" noticed how happy we had felt lately? The terrible events were behind us at last, she said, and now we knew where we would find our father again; she was so inspired by these hours with us that she promptly tried to convince Mother, courageously and freely. She spoke to her about Jesus, saying he had died for us too. I butted in, fully won over by her, Mother got into a dreadful temper and menacingly asked Miss Bray whether she didn't know that we were Jews, and how could she dare lead her children astray behind her back? She was especially furious at Edith, whom she liked, and who helped her dress every day, talking to Mother a lot, even about her sweetheart; yet she had deliberately concealed what we had been doing in these hours. Edith was dismissed on the

spot, Miss Bray was dismissed, the two women wept, we wept, finally
Mother wept too, but in anger.

Miss Bray did remain after all; George, the youngest, was very
attached to her, and Mother had been planning to take her along to
Vienna for his sake. But she had to promise never again to sing religious
songs with us or say a word about Lord Jesus. Because of our imminent
departure, Edith would have been dismissed anyway in the near future;
her notice was not rescinded, and Mother, who was too proud to endure
disappointment in a person she liked, refused to forgive her.

But with me, Mother experienced for the first time something that
was to mark our relationship forever. She took me to her room, and no
sooner were we alone than she asked me, in the tone of our almost
forgotten evenings together, why I had been deceiving her for so long.
"I didn't want to say anything," was my answer. "But why not? Why
not? You're my big son, after all. I relied on you." "You never tell me
anything either," I said, unmoved. "You talk to Uncle Solomon and
you never tell me anything." "But he's my eldest brother. I have to
confer with him." "Why don't you confer with me?" "There are things
you don't understand yet, you'll get to know them later on." Her words
went in one ear and out the other. I was jealous of her brother because
I didn't like him. Had I liked him, I would not have been jealous of
him. But he was a man "who would stop at nothing," like Napoleon,
a man who starts wars, a murderer.

When I think about it today, I consider it possible that I myself
inspired Miss Bray with my enthusiasm for the songs we sang together.
In the rich uncle's mansion, the "Ogre's Palace," as I privately called
it, we had a secret place that no one knew about, and it may very well
have been my deepest wish to shut Mother out because she had surrendered to the ogre. Every lauding word she spoke about him was taken
by me as a sign of her surrender. The groundwork was now laid for
my decision to be different from him in every respect; and it was only
when we left the mansion and finally went away that I won Mother
back for myself and watched over her faithfulness with the incorrup-
tible eyes of a child.

German on Lake Geneva

By May 1913, everything had been prepared for moving to Vienna, and
we left Manchester. The journey took place in stages; for the first time,
I grazed cities that would eventually expand into the measureless

centers of my life. In London, we stayed, I believe, only for a few hours. But we drove through the town from one railroad station to the other, and I stared in sheer delight at the high, red busses and begged my mother to let me ride in one on the upper deck. There wasn't much time, and my excitement at the jammed streets, which I have retained as endlessly long black whirls, merged into my excitement at Victoria Station, where countless people ran around without bumping into one another.

I have no recollection of the voyage across the Channel, but the arrival in Paris was all the more impressive. A newlywed couple was waiting for us at the station, David, my mother's plainest and youngest brother, a gentle mouse, and, at his side, a sparkling young wife with pitch-black hair and rouged cheeks. There they were again, the red cheeks, but so red that Mother warned me they were artificial when I refused to kiss my new aunt on any other spot. Her name was Esther and she was fresh out of Salonika, which had the largest Sephardic community, so that young men who wanted to marry would get their brides from there. In their apartment, the rooms were so small that I impudently called them doll's rooms. Uncle David wasn't offended, he always smiled and said nothing, the exact opposite of his powerful brother in Manchester, who had scornfully rejected him as a business partner. David was at the peak of his young bliss, they had married a week ago. He was proud that I was instantly enamored of my sparkling aunt, and he kept telling me to kiss her. He didn't know, the poor man, what lay ahead; she soon turned out to be a tenacious and insatiable fury.

We stayed a while in the apartment with the tiny rooms, and I was glad. I was curious and my aunt allowed me to watch her put on her makeup. She explained to me that all women in Paris used makeup, otherwise the men wouldn't like them. "But Uncle David likes you," I said; she didn't answer. She applied some perfume and asked whether it smelled good. I was leery of perfumes; Miss Bray, our governess, said they were "wicked." So I evaded Aunt Esther's question, saying: "Your hair smells best!" Then she seated herself, let down her hair, which was even blacker than my brother's much-admired curls; while she dressed I was allowed to sit next to her and admire her. All this took place openly, right in front of Miss Bray, who was unhappy about it, and I heard her tell Mother that this Paris was bad for the children.

Our journey continued into Switzerland, to Lausanne, where Mother planned to spend a few months. She rented an apartment at the top of the city, with a radiant view of the lake and the sailboats sailing on it. We often climbed down to Ouchy, strolling along the shores of the lake and listening to the band that played in the park. Everything was very bright, there was always a soft breeze, I loved the water, the wind, and the sails, and when the band played, I was so happy that I asked Mother: "Why don't we stay here, it's nicest here."

"You have to learn German now," she said, "you'll attend school in Vienna." And although she never spoke the word "Vienna"' without ardor, it never enticed me as long as we were in Lausanne. For when I asked her if Vienna had a lake, she said: "No, but it's got the Danube," and instead of the mountains in Savoy across from us, she added, Vienna had woods and hills. Now I had known the Danube since my infancy, and since the water that had scalded me came from the Danube, I bore a grudge against it. But here there was this wonderful lake, and mountains were something new. I stubbornly resisted Vienna, and that may have been one slight reason why we stayed in Lausanne somewhat longer than planned.

But the real reason was that I had to learn German first. I was eight years old, I was to attend school in Vienna, and my age would put me in the third grade of elementary school there. My mother could not bear the thought of my perhaps not being accepted into this grade because of my ignorance of the language, and she was resolved to teach me German in a jiffy.

Not very long after our arrival, we went to a bookshop; she asked for an English-German grammar, bought the first book they showed her, took me home immediately, and began instruction. How can I depict that instruction believably? I know how it went—how could I forget?—but I still can't believe it myself.

We sat at the big table in the dining room, I on the narrower side, with a view of the lake and the sails. She sat around the corner to my left and held the textbook in such a way that I couldn't look in. She always kept it far from me. "You don't need it," she said, "you can't understand it yet anyway." But despite this explanation, I felt she was withholding the book like a secret. She read a German sentence to me and had me repeat it. Disliking my accent, she made me repeat the sentence several times, until it struck her as tolerable. But this didn't occur often, for she derided me for my accent, and since I couldn't stand her derision for anything in the world, I made an effort and soon pronounced the sentence correctly. Only then did she tell me what the sentence meant in English. But this she never repeated, I had to note it instantly and for all time. Then she quickly went on to the next sentence and followed the same procedure; as soon as I pronounced it correctly, she translated it, eyed me imperiously to make me note it, and was already on the next sentence. I don't know how many sentences she expected to drill me in the first time; let us conservatively say a few; I fear it was many. She let me go, saying: "Repeat it all to yourself. You must not forget a single sentence. Not a single one. Tomorrow, we shall continue." She kept the book, and I was left to myself, perplexed.

I had no help, Miss Bray spoke only English, and during the rest of the day Mother refused to pronounce the sentences for me. The next day, I sat at the same place again, the open window in front of me, the lake and the sails. She took up yesterday's sentences, had me repeat one and asked what it meant. To my misfortune, I had noted the meaning, and she said in satisfaction: "I see this is working!" But then came the catastrophe, and that was all I knew; except for the first, I hadn't retained a single sentence. I repeated them after her, she looked at me expectantly, I stuttered and lapsed into silence. When this happened with several sentences, she grew angry and said: "You remembered the first one, so you must be able to do it right. You don't want to. You want to remain in Lausanne. I'll leave you alone in Lausanne. I'm going to Vienna, and I'll take Miss Bray and the babies along. You can stay in Lausanne by yourself!"

I believe I feared that less than her derision. For when she became particularly impatient, she threw her hands together over her head and shouted: "My son's an idiot! I didn't realize that my son's an idiot!" Or: "Your father knew German too, what would your father say!"

I fell into an awful despair, and to hide it, I looked at the sails, hoping for help from the sails, which couldn't help me. Something happened that I still don't understand today. I became as attentive as the devil and learned how to retain the meanings of the sentences on the spot. If I knew three or four of them correctly, she did not praise me; instead, she wanted the others, she wanted me to retain all the sentences each time. But since this never happened, she never praised me once and was always gloomy and dissatisfied whenever she let me go during those weeks.

I now lived in terror of her derision, and during the day, wherever I was, I kept repeating the sentences. On walks with the governess, I was sullen and untalkative. I no longer felt the wind, I didn't hear the music, I always had my German sentences and their English meanings in my head. Whenever I could, I sneaked off to the side and practiced them aloud by myself, sometimes drilling a mistake as obsessively as the correct sentences. After all, I had no book to check myself in; she stubbornly and mercilessly refused to let me have it, though knowing what friendship I felt for books and how much easier it would all have been for me with a book. But she had the notion that one shouldn't make things easy for oneself; that books are bad for learning languages; that one must learn them orally, and that a book is harmless only when one knows something of the language. She didn't notice that I ate little because of my distress. She regarded the terror I lived in as pedagogical.

On some days, I succeeded in remembering all the sentences and their meanings, aside from one or two. Then I looked for signs of satisfaction in her face. But I never found them, and the most I could attain was her not deriding me. On other days, it went less well, and then I trembled, awaiting the "idiot" she had brought into the world; that affected me the worst. As soon as the "idiot" came, I was demolished, and she failed to hit the target only with her remark about Father. His affection comforted me, never had I gotten an unfriendly word from him, and whatever I said to him, he enjoyed it and let me be.

I hardly spoke to my little brothers now and gruffly pushed them away, like my mother. Miss Bray, whose favorite was the youngest, but who liked all three of us very much, sensed the dangerous state I was in, and when she caught me drilling all my German sentences, she became vexed and said it was enough, I ought to stop, I already knew too much for a boy of my age; she said she had never learned a foreign language and got along just as well in her life. There were people all over the world who understood English. Her sympathy did me a lot of good, but the substance of her words meant nothing to me; my mother had trapped me in a dreadful hypnosis, and she was the only one who could release me.

Of course, I listened when Miss Bray said to Mother: "The boy is unhappy. He says Madame considers him an idiot!"

"But he *is* one!" she was told. "Otherwise I wouldn't say so!" That was very bitter, it was the word on which everything hinged for me. I thought of my cousin Elsie in Palatine Road, she was retarded and couldn't speak properly. The adults had said pityingly: "She's going to remain an idiot."

Miss Bray must have had a good and tenacious heart, for ultimately it was she who saved me. One afternoon, when we had just settled down for the lesson, Mother suddenly said: "Miss Bray says you would like to learn the Gothic script. Is that so?" Perhaps I had said it once, perhaps she had hit upon the idea herself. But since Mother, while saying these words, gazed at the book in her hand, I grabbed the opportunity and said: "Yes, I would like to. I'll need it at school in Vienna." So I finally got the book in order to study the angular letters. But teaching me the script was something for which Mother had no patience at all. She threw her principles overboard, and I kept the book.

The worst sufferings, which may have lasted for a month, were past. "But only for the writing," Mother had said when entrusting me with the book. "We shall still continue drilling the sentences orally." She couldn't prevent me from reading the sentences too. I had learned a great deal from her already, and there *was* something to it, in the emphatic and compelling way she pronounced the sentences for me. Anything new I kept learning from her as before. But whatever I heard I could subsequently strengthen by reading, thus making a better showing in front of her. She had no more grounds for calling me an "idiot" and was relieved about it herself. She had been seriously worried about me, she said afterwards; perhaps I was the only one in the huge clan who was not good at languages. Now she was convinced of the reverse, and our afternoons turned into sheer pleasure. It could even happen that I astounded her, and sometimes, against her will, words of praise escaped her, and she said: "You are my son, after all."

It was a sublime period that commenced. Mother began speaking German to me outside the lessons. I sensed that I was close to her again, as in those weeks after Father's death. It was only later that I realized it hadn't just been for my sake when she instructed me in German with derision and torment. She herself had a profound need to use German with me, it was the language of her intimacy. The dreadful cut into her life, when, at twenty-seven, she lost my father, was expressed most sensitively for her in the fact that their loving conversations in German were stopped. Her true marriage had taken place in that language. She didn't know what to do, she felt lost without him, and tried as fast as possible to put me in his place. She expected a great deal from this and found it hard to bear when I threatened to fail at the start of her enterprise. So, in a very short time, she forced me to achieve something beyond the strength of any child, and the fact that she succeeded determined the deeper nature of my German; it was a belated mother tongue, implanted in true pain. The pain was not all, it was promptly followed by a period of happiness, and that tied me indissolubly to that language. It must have fed my propensity for writing at an early moment, for I had won the book from her in order to learn how to write, and the sudden change for the better actually began with my learning how to write Gothic letters.

She certainly did not tolerate my giving up the other languages; education, for her, was the literature of all the languages she knew, but the language of our love—and what a love it was!—became German.

She now took just me along on visits to friends and family in Lausanne, and it is not surprising that the two visits that have stuck in my memory were connected with her situation as a young widow. One of her brothers had died in Manchester even before we moved there; his widow Linda and her two children were now living in Lausanne. It may have been because of her that my mother stopped over in Lausanne. She was invited to dinner at Linda's and took me along, explaining that Aunt Linda had been born and bred in Vienna and spoke a particularly beautiful German. I had already made enough progress, she said, to show what I knew. I was ecstatic about going; I was burning to wipe out all traces of my recent derision for ever and always. I was so excited that I couldn't sleep the night before, and I talked to myself in long German conversations that always ended in triumph. When the time for the visit came, Mother explained to me that a gentleman would be present, he came to Aunt Linda's for dinner every day. His name was Monsieur Cottier, he was a dignified gentleman, no longer young, and a highly prominent official. I asked whether he was my aunt's husband and I heard my mother saying, hesitant and a bit absent: "He may be someday. Now Aunt Linda is still thinking of her two children. She wouldn't like to hurt their feelings by marrying so quickly, even though it would be a great support for her." I instantly sniffed danger and said: "You've got three children, but I'm your support." She laughed. "What are you thinking!" she said in her arrogant way. "I'm not like Aunt Linda. I have no Monsieur Cottier."

So German became less important and I had to stand my ground in two ways. Monsieur Cottier was a large, corpulent man with a Vandyke and a belly, who greatly enjoyed the meal at my aunt's. He spoke slowly, pondering every sentence, and gazed with delight at my mother. He was already old and he struck me as treating her like a child. He talked only to her, he said nothing to Aunt Linda, but she kept filling up his plate; he acted as if he didn't notice and kept on eating calmly.

"Aunt Linda's beautiful!" I said enthusiastically on the way home. She had a dark skin and wonderfully large, black eyes. "She smells so good," I added; she had kissed me and smelled even better than my aunt in Paris. "Goodness," said Mother, "she has a gigantic nose and elephant's legs. But the way to a man's heart is through his stomach." She had already said that once during the meal, sarcastically eyeing Monsieur Cottier. I was surprised at her repeating it and asked her what it meant. She explained, very harshly, that Monsieur Cottier liked to eat well, and Aunt Linda kept a fine cuisine. That was why he came every day. I asked if that was why she smelled so good. "That's her perfume," said Mother, "she's always used too much perfume." I sensed that Mother disapproved of her, and though she had acted very friendly to Monsieur Cottier and made him laugh, she didn't seem to think very highly of him.

"No one's going to come to our house to eat," I said suddenly, as though grown up, and Mother smiled and encouraged me further: "You won't allow it, will you, you'll watch out."

The second visit, to Monsieur Aftalion, was a very different matter. Of all the Sephardim that Mother knew, he was the richest. "He's a millionaire," she said, "and still young." When I asked if he was a lot richer than Uncle Solomon, and she assured me he was, I was instantly won over to him. He looked very different too, she told me, he was a good dancer and a cavalier. Everyone lionized him, he was so noble, she said, that he could live at a royal court. "We don't have such people among us anymore," she said, "we were like that in the old days, when we lived in Spain." Then she confided that Monsieur Aftalion had once wanted to marry her, but she had already been secretly engaged to my father. "Otherwise, I might have married him," she said. He had been very sad after that, she told me, and had not wanted any other woman for years. He had only gotten married very recently, and was spending his honeymoon in Lausanne with his wife Frieda, a renowned beauty. He lived in the most elegant hotel, she said, and that was where we would visit him.

I was interested in him because she put him above my uncle. I despised my uncle so much that Monsieur Aftalion's marriage proposal had no special effect on me. I was anxious to see him, merely to have that Napoleon shrink down to a wretched nothing next to him. "Too bad Uncle Solomon won't come along!" I said.

"He's in England," she said. "He can't possibly come along."

"But it would be nice if he came along, so he could see what a real Sephardi is like."

My mother did not resent my hatred of her brother. Although admiring his efficiency, she found it right for me to rebel against him. Perhaps she realized how important it was for me not to have him replace Father as my model, perhaps she regarded this early, indelible hatred as "character," and "character" was more important to her than anything else in the world.

We entered a palace of a hotel, I had never seen anything like it, I even believe it was called "Lausanne Palace." Monsieur Aftalion lived in a suite of gigantic, luxuriously appointed rooms; I felt as if I were in *The Arabian Nights*, and I thought scornfully about my uncle's mansion in Palatine Road, which had so deeply impressed me a year ago. A double door opened, and Monsieur Aftalion appeared in a dark-blue suit and white spats; with his face wreathed in smiles, he walked towards my mother and kissed her hand. "You've grown even more beautiful, Mathilde," he said; she was dressed in black.

"And you have the most beautiful wife," said Mother, she was never at a loss for words. "Where is she? Isn't Frieda here? I haven't seen her since the institute in Vienna. I've told my son so much about her, I brought him along because he absolutely wanted to see her."

"She'll be along in a moment. She hasn't quite finished dressing yet. You two will have to put up with something less beautiful for the moment." Everything was very elegant and refined, in accordance with the grand rooms. He asked what Mother's plans were, listening very attentively but still smiling, and he approved of her settling in Vienna, approved it with fairy-tale words: "You belong in Vienna, Mathilde," he said, "the city loves you, you were always most alive and most beautiful in Vienna."

I wasn't the least bit jealous, not of him, not of Vienna. I found out something that I didn't know and that wasn't written in any of my books, the idea that a city can love a human being, and I liked the idea. Then Frieda came in, and she was the greatest surprise. I had never seen such a beautiful woman, she was as radiant as the lake and splendidly attired and she treated Mother as though *she* were the princess. Culling the loveliest roses from the vases, she gave them to Monsieur Aftalion, and he handed them to Mother with a bow. It wasn't a very long visit, nor did I understand everything that was said; the conversation alternated between French and German, and I wasn't all that good yet in either language, especially French. I also felt that some things that I was not supposed to understand were said in French; but whereas I normally was outraged at such a secret tongue of the adults, I would have cheerfully accepted much worse things from this victor over Napoleon and from his marvelously beautiful wife.

When we left the palace, my Mother struck me as slightly confused. "I nearly married him," she said, looking at me suddenly and adding a sentence, that frightened me: "But then you wouldn't exist today!" I couldn't imagine that, how could I not exist; I was walking next to her. "But I *am* your son," I said defiantly. She may have regretted speaking to me like that, for she paused and hugged me tight, together with the roses she was carrying, and then she praised Frieda: "That was noble of her. She has character!" She very rarely said that, and simply never about a woman. I was glad that she too liked Frieda. When we talked about this visit in later years, she said she had left with the feeling that everything we saw, all that splendor, actually belonged to her, and she had been surprised that she didn't resent or envy Frieda, granting her what she would never have granted any other woman.

We spent three months in Lausanne, and I sometimes think that no other time in my life has been as momentous. But one often thinks that when focusing seriously on a period, and it is possible that each period is the most important and each contains everything. Nevertheless, in Lausanne, where I heard French all around me, picking it up casually and without dramatic complications, I was reborn under my mother's influence to the German language, and the spasm of that birth produced the passion tying me to both, the language and my mother. Without these two, basically one and the same, the further course of my life would have been senseless and incomprehensible.

In August, we set out for Vienna, stopping in Zurich for several hours. Mother left the little brothers in Miss Bray's care in the waiting room and took me up Mount Zurich in a cable car. We got out at a place called Rigiblick. It was a radiant day, and I saw the city spread out vast before me, it looked enormous, I couldn't understand how a city could be so big. That was something utterly new for me, and it was a bit eerie. I asked whether Vienna was this big, and upon hearing that it was "a great deal bigger," I wouldn't believe it and thought Mother was joking. The lake and the mountains were off to the side, not as in Lausanne, where I always had them right before my eyes; there they were in the center, the actual substance of any view. There weren't so many houses to be seen in Lausanne, and here it was the huge number of houses that amazed me, they ran up the slopes of Mount Zurich, where we were standing, and I made no attempt whatsoever to count the uncountable, although I usually enjoyed doing it. I was astonished and perhaps frightened too; I said to Mother reproachfully: "We'll never find them again," and I felt we should never have left the "children"—as we called them in private—alone with the governess, who didn't know a word of any other language. So my first grand view of a city was tinged by a sense of being lost, and the memory of that first look at Zurich, which eventually became the paradise of my youth, has never left me.

We must have found the children and Miss Bray again, for I can see us on the next day, the eighteenth of August, traveling through Austria. All the places we rode through were hung with flags, and when the flags took no end, Mother allowed herself a joke, saying the flags were in honor of our arrival. But she herself didn't know what they were for, and Miss Bray, accustomed to her Union Jack, was getting more and more wrought up and gave us no peace until Mother asked some other passengers. It was the Kaiser's birthday. Franz Joseph, whom

Mother had known as the old Kaiser twenty years earlier during her youth in Vienna, was still alive, and all the villages and towns seemed delighted. "Like Queen Victoria," said Miss Bray, and through the many hours of our train ride to Vienna, I heard stories from her about the long-dead queen—stories that bored me a little—and, by way of variety, stories from Mother about Franz Joseph, who was still alive.

Part Three

VIENNA
1913–1916

The Earthquake at Messina
Burgtheater at Home

Outside the Tunnel of Fun, before the ride began, there was the maw of hell. It opened red and huge, baring its teeth. Small devils, with humans beings skewered on pitchforks, were feeding their victims into this maw, which closed slowly and implacably. But it opened again, it was insatiable, it never got tired, it never had enough; there was—as Fanny, our nursemaid, said—enough room in hell to swallow the whole city of Vienna and all its inhabitants. This wasn't a threat, she knew I didn't believe it; the maw of hell was meant more for my little brothers. She held their hands tightly, and much as she may have hoped for their improvement at the sight of hell, she wouldn't have surrendered them for even an instant.

I hurriedly climbed into the train, squeezing hard against her to make room for the little brothers. There were a lot of things in the Tunnel of Fun, but only one thing counted. I certainly looked at the gaudy groups that came first, but I only pretended: Snow White, Red Riding Hood, and Puss in Boots; all fairy tales were nicer to read, in tableaux, they left me cold. But then came the thing I had been waiting for since we left the house. If Fanny didn't instantly head for the *Wurstelprater*, the amusement park, I would pull and tug and shower her with questions until she gave in, saying: "Are you nagging me again! Okay, let's go to the Tunnel of Fun." I would then let go and hop around her, run ahead and wait impatiently, have her show me the kreuzers for the tickets, for once or twice we had arrived at the Tunnel of Fun only to find that she had forgotten the money at home.

But now we were sitting in it and riding past the fairy-tale tableaux; the train halted briefly in front of each one, and I was so annoyed at the superfluous wait that I cracked silly jokes about the fairy tales, spoiling my brothers' fun. They, in contrast, were utterly unmoved when the chief attraction came: the Earthquake at Messina. There was the town on the blue sea, the many white houses on the slopes of a mountain, everything stood there, solid and peaceful, shining brightly in the sun, the train stopped, and now the seaside town was close enough to touch. At this point, I leaped up; Fanny, infected by my panic, held me tight from behind. There was a dreadful peal of thunder, the day turned dark, a horrible whimpering and whistling resounded, the ground rattled, we were shaken, the thunder boomed again, lightning cracked loudly: all the houses of Messina were swamped in glaring flames.

The train got under way again, we left the ruins. Whatever came after that, I didn't see. I staggered away from the Tunnel of Fun, thinking that everything would be destroyed now, the whole amusement park, the booths, and the giant chestnut trees beyond. I grabbed the trunk of a tree and tried to calm down. I punched it, feeling its resistance. It couldn't be moved, the tree stood fast, nothing had changed, I was happy. It must have been back then that I put my hope in trees.

Our building was on the corner of *Josef-Gall-Gasse*, no. 5; we lived on the third floor; to the left, a vacant lot, which wasn't very big, separated our house from *Prinzenallee*, which was part of the Prater. The windows faced either *Josef-Gall-Gasse* or west—the vacant lot and the trees of the Prater. On the corner, there was a round balcony connecting the two sides. From this balcony, we watched the setting of the big, red sun, with which we became very intimate, and which attracted my youngest brother in a very special way. The instant the red color appeared on the balcony, he dashed out, and once, when he was alone for an instant, he quickly urinated and declared he had to put out the sun.

From here, we could see a small door at the opposite corner of the empty lot, a door leading to the studio of Josef Hegenbarth, the sculptor. Next to it, there were all kinds of litter, stone and wood from the studio, and, always, a small, dark girl was wandering around there; she stared at us curiously whenever Fanny took us to the Prater, and she would have liked to play with us. She stood in our path, sticking a finger in her mouth and twisting her face into a smile. Fanny, who was spic and span and couldn't bear dirt on us either, never failed to shoo her off. "Go away, you dirty little girl!" she gruffly said to her, forbidding us to talk, much less play, with her. For my brothers, these words became the child's name; in their conversations, the "dirty little girl," who embodied everything they weren't allowed to do, played an important role. Sometimes they yelled down from the balcony: "Dirty little girl!" They meant it yearningly, but the little girl wept below. When my mother found out, she gave them a good scolding. But the segregation was all right with her, and it could very well be that, for her, even the yells and their effect were too much of a link to the child.

The residential district by the Danube Canal was called the *Schüttel*; you walked along the canal until the bridge, the *Sophienbrücke*, that's where the school was. I came to Vienna with the new language that I had learned under duress. Mother delivered me to the third grade, which was taught by Herr Tegel. He had a fat, red face in which you could read little, almost like a mask. It was a big class, with over forty pupils; I knew nobody. A little American joined the class on the same day with me and was tested at the same time; before the test, we quickly exchanged a few phrases of English. The teacher asked me where I'd learned German. I said from my mother. How long had I been learning it? Three months. I sensed that he found this odd: instead of a teacher, just a mother, and only three months! He shook his head, saying: "Then you won't know enough for us." He dictated a few sentences to me, not very many. But the real point of the test was to catch me by using the word *läuten* (to ring) in one sentence and *Leute* (people) in the other; the vowel is pronounced the same, but spelled differently. I knew the distinction, however, and wrote both sentences correctly, without hesitating. He picked up the notebook and shook his head again (what could he know about my terror instruction in Lausanne!); since I had fluently replied to all his questions beforehand, he said—and it was as expressionless as everything he'd said previously: "I'll try it with you."

However, when I told Mother about it, she was not surprised. She took it for granted that "her son" ought to know German not just as well as, but better than, the Viennese children. The elementary school had five grades; Mother soon learned that you could skip the fifth if you had good marks, and she said: "After fourth grade, that's in two years, you're going to *Gymnasium*, you'll learn Latin there, it won't be as boring for you."

I can scarcely remember my first year in Vienna, so far as school is concerned. It was only at the end of the year that something happened, when the successor to the throne was assassinated. Herr Tegel had an extra edition of the newspaper framed in black on his desk. We all had to stand up, and he announced the event to us. Then we sang the *Kaiserlied*, the imperial anthem, and he sent us home; one can imagine how glad we were.

Paul Kornfeld was the boy I walked home with; he lived on the

Schüttel, too. He was tall and thin and a bit awkward, his legs seemed to want to go in different directions, there was always a friendly grin on his long face. "You walk with him?" Herr Tegel asked me upon seeing us together in front of the school. "You're offending your teacher." Paul Kornfeld was a very bad pupil, he answered every question wrong if he answered at all; and since he always grinned at such times—he couldn't help it—the teacher was hostile to him. On the way home, a boy once scornfully shouted at us: "Yids!" I didn't know what that meant. "You don't know?" said Kornfeld; he heard it all the time, perhaps because of his conspicuous way of walking. I had never been yelled at as a Jew—either in Bulgaria or in England. I told Mother about it, and she waved it off in her arrogant way: "That was meant for Kornfeld. Not for you." It wasn't that she wanted to comfort me. She simply didn't accept the insult. For her, we were something better, namely Sephardim. Unlike the teacher, she didn't want to keep me away from Kornfeld, on the contrary: "You must always walk with him," she said, "so that no one hits him." It was inconceivable for her that anybody could dare to hit *me*. Neither of us was strong, but I was a lot shorter. She said nothing about what the teacher had said to me. Perhaps it was all right with her if he made such a distinction between us. She didn't want to give me any sense of togetherness with Kornfeld, but since, as she thought, the insult had not been meant for me, I ought to protect him chivalrously.

I liked that, for it fitted in with my readings. I was reading the English books I had brought along from Manchester, and I prided myself on going through them over and over again. I knew precisely how often I had read each one, some of them more than forty times, and since I knew them by heart, any rereading was merely to increase the record. Mother sensed this and gave me other books; she felt I was too old for children's books, and she did everything she could to interest me in other things. Since *Robinson Crusoe* was one of my favorites, she gave me Sven Hedin's *From Pole to Pole*. It was three volumes long, and I received each one on a special occasion. The very first volume was a revelation. It told about explorers in all possible lands, Stanley and Livingstone in Africa, Marco Polo in China. With the most adventurous voyages of discovery, I got to know the earth and its nations. What my father had begun, my mother continued in this way. Upon seeing that the explorers displaced all my other interests, she returned to literature, and to make it appealing for me and not just have me read things I wouldn't understand, she started reading Schiller in German with me and Shakespeare in English.

Thus she came back to her old love, the theater, thereby keeping my father's memory alive, for she had once talked about all these things with him. She made an effort not to influence me. After each scene, she asked how I understood it, and before saying anything herself, she always let me speak first. But sometimes, when it was late, and she forgot about the time, we kept reading and reading, and I sensed that she was utterly excited and would never stop. If things got that far, it also hinged a bit on me. The more intelligently I responded and the more I had to say, the more powerfully her old experiences surfaced in her. As soon as she began talking about one of those old enthusiasms, which had become the inmost substance of her life, I knew that it would go on for a long time; it was no longer important now for me to go to bed, she herself could no more part from me than I from her, she spoke to me as to an adult, enthusiastically praised an actor in a certain role, but also criticized another, who had disappointed her, though that was rarer. Most of all, she loved talking about things that she had absorbed without resistance and with total devotion. Her wide nostrils quivered vehemently, her large, gray eyes no longer saw me, her words were no longer directed at me. I felt that she was talking to Father when she was seized in this way, and perhaps I myself, without realizing it, had become my father. I did not break her spell with a child's questions and I knew how to stoke her enthusiasm.

When she fell silent, she became so earnest that I didn't dare come out with another sentence. She ran her hand over her enormous forehead, there was a hush, my breath stopped. She did not close the book, she let it lie open, and it remained open for the rest of the night after we went to bed. She said none of the usual things, such as that it was late, that I should have been in bed long ago, that I had school tomorrow, everything relating to her normal maternal phrases was wiped out. It seemed natural for her to remain the character whom she had spoken about. Of all of Shakespeare's *dramatis personae*, the one she loved the most was Coriolanus.

I don't believe I understood the plays we read together. I certainly absorbed a lot from them, but in my memory she remained the sole character; it was really all one single play that we enacted together. The most dreadful events and conflicts, which she never spared me, were transformed in her words, which began as explanations and turned into radiant ecstasy.

When I read Shakespeare for myself five or six years later, this time in German, everything was new to me; I was amazed at remembering it differently, namely as a single torrent of fire. That may have been because German had now become the more important language for me. But nothing had translated itself in that mysterious way of the early Bulgarian fairy tales, which I promptly recognized at every encounter in a German book and could correctly finish myself.

The Indefatigable Man

Dr. Weinstock, our family physician, was a small man with a monkey face and indefatigably blinking eyes. He looked old, though he wasn't; perhaps it was the monkey creases in his face that made him appear old. We children did not fear him, although he came fairly often, treating us for all the usual childhood diseases. He was not at all severe; the very fact that he was always blinking and grinning prevented any fear of him. But he liked conversing with Mother and always stuck close to her. She would flinch very slightly, but he would promptly move his hand towards her, placing it on her shoulder or her arm as if soothing or courting. He said "my child" to her, which went against my grain, and he never liked leaving her, his viscous eyes clung to her as if touching her. I didn't like his coming, but since he was a good doctor and never did anything bad to anyone else among us, I had no weapon against him. I counted the times he said "my child" to her, announcing the result to my mother the instant he was gone. "Today he said 'my child' to you nine times," or "Today it was fifteen times." She was surprised at these counts, but never rebuked me; being indifferent to him, she didn't find my "supervision" burdensome. Without understanding such matters, I must have seen his form of address as an "advance," which it probably was, and his image stuck ineradicably in my mind. Fifteen years later, long after he had vanished from our lives, I turned him into a very old man: Dr. Bock, family doctor, eighty years old.

At the time, Grandfather Canetti was very old. He often came to Vienna to visit us. Mother herself cooked for him, something she didn't do frequently; he always wanted the same dish, "*Kalibsbraten*," roast veal. Consonant clusters were hard for his Ladino tongue, and he turned *Kalb* (veal) into "*Kalib*." Appearing at lunchtime, he would hug and kiss us, and his warm tears always ran down my cheeks; he wept at the first greeting, for I was named after him, and I was an orphan, and he never saw me without thinking of my father. I secretly wiped the wetness off my face, and, although fascinated by him, I wished each time that he would never kiss me again. The meal began cheerfully, both of them, the old man and the daughter-in-law, were lively people, and there was a lot to talk about. But I knew what this cheeriness concealed, and I knew it would turn into something else. Every time, as soon as the meal was over, the old argument commenced. He sighed and said: "You should never have left Bulgaria, he'd still be alive today! But for *you*, Ruschuk wasn't good enough. It had to be England. And where is he now? The English climate killed him."

His words had a deep impact on my mother, for she had really wanted to leave Bulgaria and given Father the strength to stand his ground against *his* father. "You made it too hard for him, Señor Padre" (she always addressed him in that way, like her own father). "If you had let him go with a clear conscience, he would have gotten used to the English climate. But you cursed him! You *cursed* him! Who ever heard of a father cursing his son, *his very own son!*" All hell broke loose, he leaped up in a fury, they exchanged phrases that made things worse and worse, he stormed out of the room, grabbed his cane, and left the apartment without thanking her for the "*Kalibsbraten*" (which he had so excessively lauded during the meal), and without saying goodbye to us children. But she remained, weeping, and nothing could calm her down. Just as he suffered from the curse, for which he could never forgive himself, so too she could see my father's last hours, for which she bitterly reproached herself.

Grandfather stayed at the Hotel Austria in *Praterstrasse*; sometimes he brought Grandmother along. At home in Ruschuk, she never rose from her divan, and how he managed to get her up, talk her into traveling with him, and bring her to the Danube ship always remained a riddle for me. At the hotel, he took a single room, either alone or with her, always the same room, and aside from the two beds, there was also a sofa, on which I slept on Saturday nights. He had made that condition; for this night and breakfast on Sunday morning, I belonged to him whenever he was in Vienna. I didn't much care about going to the hotel, it was dark and smelled fusty, whereas our home by the Prater was bright and airy. But on the other hand, the Sunday breakfast was a big event, for he would take me to the *Kaffeehaus*, I would get *café au lait* with whipped cream and, most important of all, a crisp *Kipfel* (a Viennese croissant).

At eleven o'clock, the Talmud-Torah School at 27 *Novaragasse* began; it was there that you learned how to read Hebrew. He set great store by my having religious instruction; he didn't expect much zeal in these matters from my mother, and my spending the night in the hotel was meant as a check: he wanted to be sure that I arrived at the school every Sunday morning, the *Kaffeehaus* and the *Kipfel* were supposed to make it more palatable for me. Everything was a bit freer than with

Mother because he wooed me, he wanted my love and my friendly attitude, and besides, there was no one in the world, no matter how small, whom he didn't care to impress.

The school itself was a woeful place; this was because the teacher looked ridiculous, a poor, groaning man who looked as though he were standing on one leg and freezing. He had no control over the pupils, who did whatever they pleased. We did learn how to read Hebrew and reel off the prayers from books. But we didn't know what the words we read meant; no one thought of explaining them to us. Nor were we told any Bible stories. The sole aim of the school was to teach us to read the prayerbooks fluently, so that the fathers or grandfathers could reap honors with us in temple. I complained to my mother about the stupidity of this instruction, and she confirmed my opinion. How different were our reading sessions! But she explained that she only let me go there so that I might properly learn how to say the kaddish (the prayer for the dead) for Father. In the entire religion, that was the most important thing, she said, nothing else mattered except perhaps the Day of Atonement. As a woman, having to sit off to the side, she didn't much care for the worship in temple; praying meant nothing to her, and reading was important only if she understood what she read. For Shakespeare, she could develop the ardor that she had never felt for her creed.

She had already escaped her religious community by attending school in Vienna as a child, and she would have gone through fire and water for the *Burgtheater*. Perhaps she would have spared me all the external duties of a religion that had no more life for her and even the Sunday school, in which I couldn't learn anything, if the deep tension between her and Grandfather hadn't forced her to give in on this point, which was considered a male issue. She never wished to know what went on in this religious school; when I came home for lunch on Sunday, we were already talking about the play we would read that evening. The dark Hotel Austria and dark *Novaragasse* were forgotten as soon as Fanny opened the apartment door, and the only thing that Mother asked, very hesitantly, which was unlike her, was what Grandfather had said, by which she meant whether he had said anything about her. He never did, but she was afraid he might some day try to bias me against her. She needn't have worried for if ever he *had* tried (something he guarded against), I would never again have gone to him at the hotel.

One of Grandfather's most conspicuous traits was his indefatigability; he, who otherwise seemed so Oriental, was always on the move. No sooner did we think he was in Bulgaria than he popped up again in Vienna, soon taking off for Nurenberg (which he pronounced "*Nürim-berg*" instead of *Nürnberg*). But he also traveled to many other cities, which I can't recall, because he never mispronounced their names badly enough for me to notice. How often did I run into him on *Praterstrasse* or some other street in Leopoldstadt; he was always hurrying, always with a silver-tipped cane, without which he never went anywhere, and as hurried as he was, his eyes, which darted every which way, the eyes of an eagle, never missed anything. All the Sephardim who ran into him (and there were quite a few in that part of Vienna, where their temple stood on *Zirkusgasse*) greeted him with respect. He was rich but he was not arrogant, he spoke to everyone he knew, and he always had something new and surprising to tell. His stories made the rounds; since he traveled a great deal, observing everything that interested him, except for people, and since he never told the same stories to the same person, knowing until an advanced age what he had said to each one, he was always amusing to his peers. For women, he was dangerous, he never forgot a single woman whom he had ever set eyes upon, and the compliments which he was skillful at making (he found new and special compliments for every kind of beauty) lodged in their minds and kept working. As old as he grew, barely aging, his passion for all that was new and interesting, his swift reactions, his domineering and yet ingratiating personality, his eye for women—everything remained equally alive.

He tried to speak to all people in *their* language, and since he had only learned these languages on the side, while traveling, his knowledge of them, except of the Balkan languages (which included his Ladino), was highly defective. He liked counting his languages off on his fingers, and the droll self-assurance in totting them up—God knows how, sometimes seventeen, sometimes nineteen languages—was irresistible to most people despite his comical accent. I was ashamed of these scenes when they took place in front of me, for his speech was so bristling with mistakes that he would even have been flunked by Herr Tegel in my elementary school, not to mention our home, where Mother corrected our least errors with ruthless derision. On the other hand, we restricted ourselves to four languages in our home, and when I asked Mother if it was possible to speak seventeen languages, she said, without mentioning Grandfather: "No. For then you know none at all!"

Although the world in which her intellect moved was utterly alien to him, he had great respect for Mother's education and especially for her being so strict and demanding with us. Much as he resented her luring Father away from Bulgaria with the aid of that very education, he nevertheless set great store by her filling us with it. I believe that he was spurred not only by thoughts of usefulness and advancement in the world, but also by the impetus of his own endowment, which had never been fully realized. Within the narrow circle of his own life, he had gotten very far, and he would never have given up one iota of power over his vast family, but he felt there were plenty of things on the outside that were denied him. He knew only the Hebrew alphabet in which Ladino was written, and the only newspapers he read were in that language. They had Spanish names like *El Tiempo* (Time) and *La Voz de la Verdad* (The Voice of Truth). They were printed in Hebrew letters and appeared, I believe, only once a week. He could read the Latin alphabet, but he felt unsure of himself, and so in all his long life—he lived over ninety years—and in all the many countries he traveled, he had never read anything, much less a book in the local language.

Aside from his business, which he sovereignly mastered, his knowledge was exclusively his own observations of other people. He could mimic them and play them like an actor, and some of the people, whom I knew personally, became so interesting to me because of the way he played them that they bitterly disappointed me in the flesh, while fascinating me more and more in his playacting. Yet with me, he held back in his satirical scenes, letting himself go altogether only in a large company of adults, whose center he was, and entertaining them with his stories for hours and hours. (He had been dead for a long time before I found his peers among the storytellers in Marrakesh, and although I didn't understand a word of their language, they were more familiar to me because of my memory of him than all the countless other people whom I met there.)

His curiosity, as I have said, was always active; I never, not once, saw him tired, and even when alone with him I sensed that he was observing me incessantly, never stopping for an instant. In the nights that I spent in his room at the Hotel Austria, my last thought before dropping off was that he wasn't really sleeping, and implausible as it may sound, I never did catch him asleep. In the morning, he was awake long before me, washed and dressed, and usually he had already spoken his morning prayer, which took rather long. But if I awoke at night for any reason, he would be sitting up in his bed as if having known for quite a time that I would now awaken, and merely waiting to hear what I wanted. Yet he was not one of those people who complained about insomnia. On the contrary, he seemed fresh and ready for anything, a devil of constant alertness and preparedness; many people, despite their respect for him, found him a little eerie because of this excessive vitality.

One of his passions was collecting money for poor girls who wanted to marry but had no dowry. I often saw him in *Praterstrasse,* accosting someone for money for this purpose. He was already holding his red-leather notebook, in which the name and contribution of each donor were recorded. He was already accepting the banknotes and stowing them in his wallet. He never got no for an answer; it would have been scandalous saying no to Señor Canetti. Prestige within the community hinged on this, people always had cash on them for the not-so-small contributions; a "no" would have meant that a man was on the verge of being one of the poor himself, and that was something no one wanted to have said about himself. I do believe, however, that there was also true generosity among these businessmen. Often, with restrained pride, I heard that so-and-so was a good person, which meant that he was lavish with donations for the poor. Grandfather was known for the fact that people especially liked giving to him, if for no other reason than because he himself, in his round Hebrew letters, figured at the head of the collection in the notebook. Since *he* had started out so generously, no one cared to make a poor second, and he very quickly got together a respectable dowry.

In this portrayal of my grandfather, I have concentrated a number of things, including some that I did not discover or experience until much later. Thus, in this first Viennese period, he occupies more space than he really ought to.

For the most incomparably important, the most exciting and special events of this period were my evening readings with my mother and the conversations about everything we read. I cannot render these conversations in detail anymore, for a good portion of me consists of them. If there is an intellectual substance that one receives at an early age, to which one refers constantly, which one never escapes, then it was this. I was filled with blind trust for my mother; the characters she quizzed me about have become so much a part of my world that I can no longer take them apart. I am able to follow all later influences in every detail. But those characters form a dense and indivisible unity. Since that time, that is, since I was ten, it has been something of a dogma for me that I consist of many people whom I am not at all aware of. I believe that they determine what attracts or repels me in the people I meet. They were the bread and salt of my early years. They are the true, the hidden life of my intellect.

Outbreak of the War

We spent the summer of 1914 in Baden by Vienna. We lived in a yellow two-story house, I don't know what street it was on, and we shared this house with a retired high-ranking officer, an ordnance master, who lived on the ground floor with his wife. It was a time in which you couldn't help noticing officers.

We spent a good chunk of the day in the health-resort park, where Mother took us. The spa band played in a round kiosk at the center of the park. The band leader, a thin man, was named Konrath; we boys nicknamed him "carrot," using the English word. I still spoke English nonchalantly with my little brothers; they were three and five years old. Their German was somewhat shaky; Miss Bray had only returned to England a few months ago. It would have been an unnatural restraint to speak anything but English among ourselves, and we were known in the park as the little English boys.

There were always lots of people there, if for no other reason than for the music, but in late July, when war was imminent, the mass of people crowding into the park became denser and denser. The mood became more excited without my understanding why, and when Mother told me that we shouldn't yell so loud in English when we were playing, I didn't pay much heed, and the little brothers even less, of course.

One day, I think it was August 1, the declarations of war commenced. Carrot was leading the band, the musicians were playing, someone handed a note up to Carrot, he opened it, interrupted the music, banged his baton, and read aloud: "Germany has declared war on Russia." The band launched into the Austrian imperial anthem, everyone stood up, even the people sitting on the benches got to their feet and sang along: "God preserve them, God protect them, our Emperor, our land." I knew the anthem from school and joined in somewhat hesitantly. No sooner was it over than it was followed by the German anthem: "Hail to Thee in Victor's Laurels." It was the same tune that I had known in England as "God Save the King." I sensed that the mood was anti-British. I don't know whether it was out of old habit, perhaps it was also defiance, I sang the English words along at the top of my lungs, and my little brothers, in their innocence, did the same in their thin little voices. Since we were in the thick of the crowd, no one could miss it. Suddenly, I saw faces warped with rage all about me and arms and hands hitting at me. My brothers, too, even the youngest, George, got some of the punches that were meant for me, the nine-year-old. Before Mother, who had been jostled away from us, realized what was going on, everyone was beating away at us in utter confusion. But the thing that made a much deeper impact on me was the hate-twisted faces. Someone must have told Mother, for she called very loud: "But they're children!" She pushed over to us, grabbed all three boys, and snapped angrily at the people, who didn't do anything to her, because she spoke like a Viennese; and eventually they even let us out of the awful throng.

I didn't quite understand what I had done, but this first experience with a hostile crowd was all the more indelible. As a result, for the rest of the war, in Vienna until 1916 and then in Zurich, I favored the British. But I had learned my lesson from the punches: So long as I stayed in Vienna, I made sure not to let anyone perceive anything of my attitude. English words outside the house were now severely prohibited for us. I observed the taboo and kept on reading my English books all the more fervently.

The fourth grade of elementary school, which was my second year in Vienna, took place during the war, and anything I remember is connected with the war. We were given a yellow pamphlet of songs, which referred to the war in some way or other. The pamphlet began with the imperial anthem, which we sang at the start and end of each day. Two songs in the yellow pamphlet struck a familiar chord in me. "Dawn of day, dawn of day, to early death you light my way"; but my favorite began with the words: "Two jackdaws are perched at the meadow's edge." I think it continued: "If I die in the foeland, if I fall in Poland." We sang too much from this yellow songbook, but the tone of the songs was certainly more bearable than the terse and dreadful little hate slogans, which found their way down to the youngest pupils: "Serbia must die!" "Crush the Russians!" "Kill the French in the trench!" "Stab the slimy Limey!" The first and only time that I brought such an utterance home and said to Fanny: "Crush the Russians!", she complained to Mother. Maybe it was a Czech sensitivity on her part; she wasn't the least bit patriotic and never joined us children in singing the war songs I learned in school. But perhaps she was a sensible person, especially repelled at hearing that crude utterance from the lips of a nine-year-old child. It struck her hard, for she didn't upbraid me directly; she lapsed into silence, went to Mother, and told her she couldn't remain here if she heard such things from us children. Mother spoke to me in private, asking me very earnestly what I meant with that sentence. I said: "Nothing." The boys at school were saying these things all the time and I couldn't stand it, I told her. This wasn't a lie, for, as I have said, I was on England's side. "Then why are you parroting them? Fanny doesn't like to hear those things. She's offended when you say such ugly things. A Russian is a human being like you or me. My best friend in Ruschuk was Russian. You no longer remember Olga." I had forgotten her and now I recalled her. Her name had often been mentioned among us in the past. This single rebuke was enough. I never again repeated such an utterance, and since Mother had so clearly shown her displeasure, I felt hatred for every bestial war slogan that I subsequently heard at school; I heard them daily. By no means did everyone carry on like that, there were only a few, but they kept doing it over and over. Perhaps because they were a minority, they enjoyed standing out.

Fanny came from a Moravian village; she was a strong woman, everything about her was solid, including her opinions. On the Jewish New Year's Day, pious Jews stood on the bank of the Danube Canal, casting their sins into the water. Fanny, walking past them with us, got worked up. She always had something to say, and say it she did. "It would be better if they didn't sin in the first place," she said. "I can throw things away too." She was put off by the word "sin" and didn't care at all for grand gestures. Most of all, she disliked beggars and Gypsies. Beggars and thieves were the same for her. She was nobody's fool and hated playacting. She could detect bad intentions behind excited talking. The worst thing for her was any kind of hullaballoo, and there was too much of that in our home. One single time, she got carried away and made such a cruel scene that I never forgot it.

Someone rang our bell; I was near her when she opened the door. A beggar stood there, neither old nor crippled, threw himself to his knees, and wrung his hands. His wife was on her deathbed, he moaned, he had eight children at home, they were starving, the poor innocent things. "Have pity, Madame! The poor, innocent things aren't to blame!" He remained kneeling and passionately repeated his speech, it was like a song, and he kept calling Fanny "Madame!" She was dumbstruck, she was no Madame and didn't want to be one, and when she said "Madame" to my mother, it never sounded subservient. For a while, she gazed wordlessly at the kneeling man; his chant echoed loud and poignant in the corridor. Suddenly, she fell to her knees and mimicked him. He got every single one of his sentences back from her lips in a Czech accent, and the duet made such an impact that I began speaking the words too. Both Fanny and the beggar stuck to their guns. But eventually, she stood up and slammed the door in his face. He still lay on his knees, chanting through the closed door: "Take pity, Madame, the poor, innocent things are not to blame!"

"Crook!" said Fanny. "He doesn't have a wife and she's not dying. He doesn't have a child, he gobbles everything up himself. He's lazy and he wants to gobble everything himself! A young man! When did he father eight children!" She was so indignant at the liar that she replayed the entire scene for my mother, who soon came home. I assisted her with the kneeling; and sometimes we enacted the scene together. I showed her what she had done and wanted to punish her for her cruelty, but I also wanted to play it better than she. So she got the beggar's lines from me and then the same lines in her accent. She flew into a rage when I started chanting "Take pity, Madame!" and she forced herself not to kneel again, although my own kneeling tempted her to do so. It was a torment for her because she felt derided in her own language, and suddenly this solid, compact woman was helpless. Once, she forgot herself and gave me a slap, which she would so gladly have given the beggar.

Fanny was now properly scared of theatrics. My evening readings with Mother, which she could hear from the kitchen, got on her nerves. If I told her anything about it the next day or merely spoke to myself, she shook her head, saying: "So much excited, how will boy sleep?" The increase of dramatic life in the apartment irritated Fanny, and when she gave notice one day, my mother said: "Fanny thinks we're crazy. She doesn't understand. She'll stay on this time. But I think we'll be losing her soon." I was very attached to her, so were my little brothers. Mother, not without efforts, got her to change her mind. But then Fanny lost her head one day and, honest woman that she was, she gave my mother an ultimatum. She couldn't stand it anymore, the boy wasn't getting enough sleep. If the evening hubbub didn't stop, she'd have to go. So she went, and we were all sad. Postcards often came from her; I, as her tormenting spirit, was allowed to keep them.

Medea and Odysseus

I first encountered Odysseus in Vienna; by sheer chance, the story of the Odyssey was not among those first books that my father had handed me in England. The series of world literature adapted for children must have included the Odyssey; but whether Father hadn't noticed it or was deliberately saving it for later, I never set eyes upon it. So I only found out about it in German when Mother—I was ten at the time—gave me Schwab's *Myths of Classical Antiquity*.

During our drama evenings, we often came upon the names of Greek gods and figures, whom she had to explain to me; she didn't tolerate leaving anything unclear for me, and sometimes that caused a long delay. Perhaps I also asked more than she could answer; she knew these things only second-hand, from English and French plays, and especially German literature. I received the Schwab book more as an aid in understanding, something that I should tackle myself so as to keep constant digressions from interfering with the *élan* of the evenings, which were the real thing.

The very first character I thereby learned about, Prometheus, had a tremendous impact on me: a benefactor of mankind—what could be more alluring; and then that punishment, Zeus's horrible revenge. In the end, however, I encountered Heracles as a liberator before I got to know his other deeds. Then Perseus and the Gorgon, whose gaze turned men into stone; Phaeton, who was burned up in the chariot of the sun; Daedalus and Icarus—the war had begun already, and people often talked about aviators, who would play their part in it; Cadmos and the dragon's teeth, which I also connected to the war.

I kept silent about all these wonderful things; I took them in without telling about them. In the evening, I could let on that I knew something, but only when the opportunity arose. It was as though I could add my bit to the explanations of what we were reading; that was basically the task I had been assigned. I sensed Mother's joy when I said something tersely without getting entangled in further questions. Some unexplained things I kept to myself. Perhaps I felt strengthened in a dialogue in which the other side was preponderant, and if she didn't feel quite sure about something, the fact that I could arouse her interest by mentioning some detail or other filled me with pride.

Before long, I came to the myth of the Argonauts. Medea seized hold of me with a power that I don't quite understand, and I find it even more incomprehensible that I equated her with my mother. Was it the passion I felt in her when she spoke about the great heroines of the *Burgtheater*? Was it the dreadfulness of death, which I darkly felt to be murder? Her wild dialogues with my grandfather, which topped off every visit of his, left her feeble and crying. He did run off as though feeling beaten, his wrath was powerless, not the wrath of a victor; but she couldn't win this fight either. She fell into helpless despair, which was a torment, and which I couldn't stand to see in her. So it may well have been that I wished her to have supernatural strength, the strength of a sorceress. This is a conjecture that thrusts itself upon me only now: I wanted to see her as the stronger, as the strongest of all, an invincible and unswerving strength.

I didn't keep quiet about Medea, I couldn't, and when I brought the conversation to her, a whole evening was lost. She didn't let on how frightened she was at my equation, I learned that only in later years. She told me about Grillparzer's *Golden Fleece*, about the Medea at the *Burgtheater*, and with this virtual double refraction, she managed to soften the violent effect that the original myth had exerted on me. I got her to admit that she too would have wreaked vengeance on Jason for his betrayal, on him and also on his young wife, but not on the children. She would have taken the children along in the magic chariot, but she didn't know where. Even if they had looked like their father, she would have been stronger than Medea and would have managed to endure the sight of them. So in the end, she stood there as the strongest of all, and had overcome Medea within me.

Odysseus may have helped her, for when I found out about him a short time later, he replaced everything that preceded him and he became the true figure of my youth. I took up the *Iliad* reluctantly because it began with the human sacrifice of Iphigenia; Agamemnon's yielding filled me with a violent dislike of him; so from the very start, I didn't side with the Greeks. I doubted Helen of Troy's beauty, the names of Menelaus and Paris were both ludicrous to me. I was generally dependent on names, there were characters whom I despised just for their names, and others whom I loved for their names, before I ever read their stories: these included Ajax and Cassandra. I can't say when this dependency on names first arose. It was insuperable with the Greeks; their gods divided into two groups for me, and they entered these groups because of their names and only more seldom because of their characters. I liked Persephone, Aphrodite, and Hera; nothing that Hera did could sully her name. I liked Poseidon and Hephaistos; Zeus, in contrast, as well as Ares and Hades, were repulsive. What captivated me about Athena was her birth; I never forgave Apollo for flaying Marsyas, his cruelty overshadowed his name, which I secretly clung to against my conviction. The conflict between names and deeds became a crucial tension for me, and the compulson to harmonize them never let me go. I was devoted to both people and characters because of their names, and any disappointment at their behavior caused me to make the most involved efforts to alter them and make them consistent with their names. But for others, I had to concoct disgusting stories to justify their horrible names. I don't know in which way I was more unjust; for someone who sublimely admired justice, this dependence on names, which could not be influenced by anything, had something truly fatal. I regard it and it alone as a destiny.

At that time, I didn't know any people with Greek names, so they were all new to me and overwhelmed me with a concentrated force. I could meet them with a freedom bordering on the miraculous; they sounded like nothing that was familiar to me, they blended with nothing, they appeared as sheer figures and remained figures. Except for Medea, who totally confused me, I decided for or against each single one of them, and they always remained inexhaustibly effective. With them, I began a life that I personally and consciously justified, and in that alone I was dependent on no one else.

Thus, Odysseus, who concentrated everything Greek for me in that period, became a peculiar model, the first I was able to grasp in purity, the first from which I learned more than from any other person, a complete and very substantial model, presenting itself in many forms, each with its own meaning and place. I assimilated him in all details, and as time went on, there was nothing about him that wasn't significant for me. The number of years he influenced me corresponded to the years of his voyages. Ultimately, recognizable to no one else, he entered *Auto-da-Fé*, by which I mean nothing more than an inmost dependence on him. As total as that dependence was, and as easily as I could demonstrate it today in all particulars, I still remember very clearly with what his effect on the ten-year-old *commenced*, what the new thing was that first took hold of him and troubled him. There was the moment at the Phaeacian court when Odysseus, still unrecognized, hears his own story from the lips of the blind singer Demodokos and secretly weeps; the trick by which he saves his and his comrades' lives by telling Polyphemos that his name is No-One; the singing of the sirens, which he refuses to forgo, and the patient way he, as a beggar, endures the insults of the suitors: always metamorphoses in which he *diminishes* himself; and in the case of the sirens, his indomitable curiosity.

A Trip to Bulgaria

In the summer of 1915, we visited Bulgaria. A large part of Mother's family lived there; she wanted to see her native land and the place where she had spent seven happy years with Father. For weeks beforehand, she was filled with an excitement that I didn't comprehend; it was different from any state I had ever seen her in. She spoke on and on about her childhood in Ruschuk, and the town, which I had never thought about, suddenly gained meaning from her stories. The Sephardim I had known in England and Vienna were always scornful of Ruschuk, calling it an uncultured provincial dump, where the people didn't have the foggiest clue of what was going on in "Europe." They all seemed glad to have escaped it and they considered themselves better and more enlightened people because they now lived elsewhere. Only Grandfather, who was never ashamed of anything, spoke the name of the town with fiery emphasis; his business was there, the center of his world; the houses were there that he had acquired with growing prosperity. Yet I had noticed how little he knew about the things that so greatly interested me; once, when I told him about Marco Polo and China, he said it was all fairy tales, I should only believe what I saw with my own eyes, he knew all about those liars; I realized he never read a book, and since he boasted of knowing many languages but could only speak them with ridiculous mistakes, his loyalty to Ruschuk was no recommendation for me, and his travels from there to countries that didn't have to be discovered anymore filled me with scorn. Still, he had an unerring memory, and once he suprised me, when he came for dinner, with a whole lot of questions about Marco Polo for Mother. He not only asked her who the man was and whether he had ever really lived, but he also inquired about every wondrous detail that I had reported to him, never leaving out a single one, and he almost flew off the handle when Mother explained the part that Marco Polo's account played for the later discovery of America. Yet at the mention of Columbus' mistaking America for India, he calmed down again and said triumphantly: "That comes from believing such a liar! They discover America and think it's India!"

He was unable to force any interest out of me in the place of my birth, but Mother succeeded just like that. During one of our evening sessions, she abruptly said, when talking about a book that she particularly loved: "I first read that up in the mulberry tree in my father's garden." Once she showed me an old copy of Victor Hugo's *Les Misérables*; it still had stains from the mulberries she had eaten while reading. "They were already very ripe," she said, "and I climbed up very high to conceal myself more effectively. When I was supposed to come to lunch, they didn't see me. I kept reading all afternoon and then suddenly I got so hungry that I stuffed myself on mulberries. You have an easier time of it, I always let you read."

"But I do have to go to meals," I said, and started getting interested in the mulberry tree.

She would show it to me, she promised; all our conversations now revolved around travel plans. I was against the idea because our evening sessions would have to pause for a while. But then—I was still under the impact of the myth of the Argonauts and the figure of Medea—she said: "We'll also travel to Varna, on the Black Sea." My resistance collapsed. Kolchis may have been at the other end of the Black Sea, but still and all, it was the same sea, and to lay my eyes upon it I was ready to pay even the high price of interrupting our readings.

We traveled by train, past Kronstadt and through Rumania. I had tender feelings for this country because my family greatly praised the Rumanian woman who had wetnursed me. I was told she had liked me as much as her own child and had subsequently not hesitated to sail from Giurgiu across the Danube just to see how I was getting on. Then they had heard that she had drowned after tumbling into a deep well, and Father, as was his way, had tracked down the family and, secretly, without letting Grandfather find out, he had done whatever he could for them.

In Ruschuk, we did not stay in the old mansion; that would have been too close to Grandfather Canetti. We settled in with Aunt Bellina, Mother's eldest sister. She was the most beautiful of the three sisters and enjoyed some renown for this reason alone. The misfortune that haunted her later, until the end of her life, had not yet broken in upon her and her family; but it was already announcing itself. I remember her as she was then, in the prime of her beauty; I subsequently found her again as Titian's *La Bella* and *Venus of Urbino*, and so her image within me can never change.

She lived in a spacious yellow mansion in Turkish style, right across from her father, Grandfather Arditti, who had died during a trip to Vienna two years earlier. She was as kind as she was beautiful; she knew little and was regarded as stupid because she never wanted anything for herself and always gave presents to people. Since everyone so well remembered her avaricious and money-conscious father, Aunt Bellina was anything but a chip off the old block; she was a wonder of generosity, unable to look at a person without reflecting how she could do something special for him. There was nothing else she ever reflected about. When she fell silent and stared into space, heedless of questions from others, somewhat absent, and with an almost strained look on her face—which did not, however, lose its beauty—people knew she was thinking about a present and was dissatisfied with any that had already flashed into her mind. She would give presents in such a way as to overwhelm the recipient, but she was never really glad, for the present always struck her as too meager, and she even managed to excuse herself for it with honest words. It was not the proud manner of giving that I know from Spanish people, a manner with a certain claim to nobility; it was simple and natural, like breathing in and out.

She had married her cousin Josef, a choleric man, who made life hard for her, and she suffered more and more from him, without ever giving the least hint of it. The orchard in back of the house, where the trees were laden with the most marvelous fruit, enchanted us almost as much as my aunt's presents. The rooms in her house were bright and yet cool, there was far more space than in our apartment in Vienna, and there were all sorts of things to discover. I had forgotten what life was like on Turkish divans, and everything impressed me as new and strange, almost as if I had gone on a voyage of discovery after all, to an exotic land—something that had become the most intense desire of my life. The mulberry tree in Grandfather's garden across the way was disappointing; it wasn't all that high, and since I pictured my mother as tall as she was now, I couldn't understand why they hadn't noticed her in her hiding place. But in the yellow mansion, in my aunt's company, I felt fine and didn't insist on leaving for the Black Sea, which was meant to be the highlight of the trip.

Uncle Josef Arditti with his fat red face and squinting eyes kept pumping me; he knew all sorts of things and was so satisfied with my answers to his questions that he patted my cheeks, saying: "Mark my words! He'll go a long way. He'll be a great lawyer like his uncle!" My uncle was a businessman, not a lawyer, but he knew about the laws in many countries, citing them in detail from memory, and in a great variey of languages, which he then instantly translated into German for me. He tried to catch me by quoting the same law again, perhaps ten minutes later, but slightly altered. He would then eye me a bit insidiously and wait. "But that was different before," I would say, "it was like *this*!" I couldn't stand that kind of language, it filled me with a deep disgust for anything connected with "law," but I too was a know-it-all, and besides, I wanted to reap his praise. "So you paid attention," he would then say, "you're not a moron like all the others here," and he pointed towards the rooms where the others were sitting, including his wife. But he didn't mean just her, he found the whole city stupid, the country, the Balkans, Europe, the world, with the exception of a few renowned lawyers, who might just barely be a match for him.

People whispered about his fits of rage. I was warned about them, they said he was absolutely horrible when he lost his temper. But I needn't be scared, he always calmed down again, you only had to sit there very quietly, and not say a word, God forbid, and if he looked at you, just nod humbly. Mother warned me that she and my aunt would also keep still if it happened, that's the way he was, there was nothing you could do. He particularly aimed at my dead grandfather, said

Mother, but also at his surviving widow, my grandmother, and at all my mother's surviving sisters and brothers, including herself and Aunt Bellina.

I heard this warning so often that I anxiously looked forward to it. But when it did come one day, during a meal, it was so terrible that it became the real memory of that trip. "*Ladrones!*" he suddenly shouted, "*Ladrones!* Do you think I don't know that you're all thieves!" The Ladino word *ladrones* sounds much heavier than "thieves," something like "thieves" and "bandits" together. He now accused every single member of the family, first the absent ones, of robbery, and started with my dead grandfather, his father-in-law, who had excluded him from part of the legacy in favor of Grandmother. Then it was my still-living grandmother's turn; powerful Uncle Solomon in Manchester, *he'd* better watch out. He was going to annihilate him, he knew more about the law, he would bring suits against him in all the countries in the world, not a loophole would be left for him to wiggle through!

I felt no sympathy whatsoever for *that* uncle and, I can't deny it, I was delighted that someone dared to stand up to him, who was generally feared. But then it went on, now it was the turn of the three sisters, even my mother, even Aunt Bellina, his own wife, who was such a kind-hearted person—they were secretly conspiring against him with the family. These scoundrels! These criminals! This riffraff! He would crush them all. Tear their false hearts out of their bodies! Feed their hearts to the dogs! They would remember him! They would beg for mercy. But he was merciless! He only knew law. But he knew it well! Let anyone just try and challenge him! These lunatics! These morons! "You think you're so smart, don't you?" he suddenly turned to my mother. "But your little boy is a thousand times smarter. He's like me! Some day he'll drag you into court! You'll have to cough up your last penny! She's educated, they say, but your Schiller won't help you a bit! The law is all that counts," he banged his knuckles on his forehead, "and the law is here! Here! Here! You didn't know that"—he now turned to me—"you didn't know your mother's a thief! It's better that you know it now, before she robs you, her own son!"

I saw Mother's pleading eyes, but it was no use, I leaped up and shouted: "My mother's no thief! Aunt Bellina's no thief either!" and I was so furious that I burst into tears, but that didn't stop him. He twisted his face, which was terribly bloated, into sweetly piteous creases, and came closer to me: "Shut up! I didn't ask you! You stupid brat! You'll see! I'm sitting right here, your Uncle Josef, telling you straight to your face. I pity you with your ten years, that's why I'm telling you in time: Your mother's a thief! All of them, they're all thieves! The whole family! The whole town! Nothing but thieves."

With that final "*ladrones*," he broke off. He didn't hit me, but I was done for, as far as he was concerned. Later on, after calming down, he said: "You don't deserve my teaching you the law. You'll have to learn by experience. You don't deserve any better."

Most of all, I was amazed at my aunt. She took it as though nothing had happened and was already busy with her presents that very same afternoon. In a conversation between the sisters, whom I eavesdropped on without their knowledge, she told my mother: "He's my husband. He wasn't always like that. He's been this way since Señor Padre died. He can't stand any injustice. He's a good man. You mustn't go away. That might hurt his feelings. He's very sensitive. Why are all good people so sensitive?" Mother said it wouldn't do because of the boy, he mustn't hear such things about the family. She had always been proud of the family, she said. It was the best family in town. Why, Josef himself was part of the family. His own father had been the elder brother of Señor Padre, after all.

"But he's never said anything against his own father! He'll never do that, never! He'd rather bite off his tongue than say anything against his father."

"But then why does he want that money? He's a lot richer than we!"

"He can't stand injustice. He's gotten this way since the death of Señor Padre, he wasn't always like this."

We did go to Varna soon, after all. The sea—I can't remember any earlier sea—wasn't the least bit wild or stormy. In honor of Medea, I had expected it to be perilous, but there was no trace of her in these waters; I believe that the agitation in Ruschuk had repressed all thoughts of her. As soon as really awful things began happening among the people closest to me, the classical figures, whom I was otherwise so filled with, lost much of their color. Once I had defended Mother against her brother-in-law's disgusting accusations, she was no longer Medea for me. On the contrary, it seemed important to take her to safety, to be with her and personally keep an eye on her so that nothing disgusting would adhere to her.

We spent a lot of time on the beach; in the harbor, I was preoccupied with the lighthouse. A destroyer anchored in the harbor, and it was rumored that Bulgaria would enter the war on the side of the Central Powers. In my mother's conversations with friends, I often heard people saying that this was impossible. Never would Bulgaria go to war against Russia, Bulgaria owed Russia her liberation from the Turks, the Russians had fought against the Turks in many wars, and whenever things had gone badly for the Bulgarians, they relied on the Russians. The general in Russian service, Dimitryev, was one of the most popular men in the country; he had been the guest of honor at my parents' wedding.

My mother's oldest friend, Olga, was Russian. We had visited her and her husband in Ruschuk; they struck me as warmer and more open than anyone else I knew. The two friends spoke together like young girls, they spoke French in a quick, jubilant tone, their voices rose and sank incessantly. They never paused for an instant; it was like a twittering, but of very large birds. Olga's husband kept respectfully quiet, his high-buttoned blouse made him look a bit martial; he poured Russian tea into our cups and served us tidbits. Most of all, he made sure that the conversation of the two friends went on fluently without their wasting a minute of their precious time, for years had passed since their last meeting, and when would they see each other again? I heard the name Tolstoy, he had only just died a few years ago; the respect with which his name was uttered was such that I asked Mother later on whether Tolstoy was a greater writer than Shakespeare, which she hesitantly and reluctantly denied.

"Now you see why I won't let anyone say anything against Russians," she said, "They're the most marvelous people. Olga reads every chance she gets. One can talk to her."

"What about her husband?"

"Him too. But she's smarter. She knows her literature better. He respects that. He prefers listening to her."

I didn't say anything, but I had my doubts. I knew that my father had considered Mother more intelligent and placed her far above him, and I also knew that she accepted that. She shared his opinion as a matter of course, and when speaking of him—she always said the nicest things—she also quite naively mentioned how greatly he had admired her intellect. "But still, he was more musical than you," I would protest.

"That's so," she said.

"He also acted better than you, everyone says so, he was the best actor."

"True, true, he had a natural gift for acting, he inherited it from Grandfather."

"He was also merrier than you, a lot, lot merrier."

That was something she didn't mind hearing, for she set great store by dignity and earnestness, and the solemn tones of the *Burgtheater* had passed into her flesh and blood. Then came my punchline.

"He also had a better heart. He was the best man in the world."

There was no doubt or hesitation now, she always enthusiastically agreed. "You'll never find a man as good as he anywhere in the world, never, not ever!"

"What about Olga's husband?"

"He's good too, that's so, but you can't compare him to your father."

And then came the many stories about his good heart, stories I had heard a hundred times and kept wanting to hear over and over; how many people he had helped, even behind her back so that no one knew about it, how she found out and sternly asked him: "Jacques, did you really do this? Don't you think you were overdoing it?"

"I don't know," was his answer, "I can't remember."

"And you know," her tally would always end, "he really had forgotten. He was such a good person that he forgot the good things he'd done. You mustn't think that he had a poor memory otherwise. If he did a part in a play, he wouldn't forget it even months later. And he didn't forget what his father had done to him when he took his violin away and forced him to come to the *butica*. He never forgot what I liked and he could surprise me with something that I had once wished for vaguely—even years afterwards. But if he did a good deed, he would keep it a secret, and he was so skillful at keeping it a secret that he forgot it himself."

"I'll never be able to do that," I said, enthusiastic about my father and sad about myself. "I'll always know."

"You're just more like me," she said, "that's not really good." And then she explained that she was too distrustful to be good, she always instantly knew what people were thinking, she could see through them on the spot as though guessing their most secret impulses. On such an occasion, she once mentioned a writer who had been exactly like her in this way; like Tolstoy, he had died recently: Strindberg. She didn't like saying his name, she had read some books of his a few weeks before Father's death, and the physician in Reichenhall, who had so urgently recommended Strindberg to her, had prompted Father's final and, as she sometimes feared, mortal jealousy. As long as we lived in Vienna, she always had tears in her eyes when she uttered Strindberg's name; only in Zurich did she get so accustomed to him and his books that she could pronounce his name without excessive agitation.

We went on outings from Varna to Monastir, near Euxinograd, where the royal castle stood. We only viewed the castle from afar. For a short while now, since the end of the second Balkan War, it had no longer been in Bulgaria, it now belonged to Rumania. Border crossings in the Balkans, where bitter wars had been waged, were not regarded as pleasurable; in many places, they weren't even possible, and one avoided them. But, while riding in the droshkey and later, when we dismounted, we saw the most luxuriant orchards and vegetable gardens, dark-violet eggplants, peppers, tomatoes, cucumbers, gigantic pumpkins and melons; I couldn't get over my amazement at all the different things that grew here. "That's what it's like here," said Mother, "a blessed land. And it's a civilized land, no one need be ashamed of being born here."

But then in Varna, when the vehement downpours began, the steep main road leading down to the harbor was full of deep holes. Our droshkey got stuck; we had to get out, people came to help the coachman, and they pulled with all their might until the droshkey was free again. Mother sighed: "The same roads as before! These are Oriental conditions. These people will never learn!"

So her opinions wavered, and ultimately she was very glad when we started back to Vienna. But since a shortage of food had begun in Vienna right after the first winter of war, she stocked up on dried vegetables before we left Bulgaria. Countless pieces of the widest variety were threaded together, she filled up a whole suitcase, and was then highly vexed when the Rumanian customs inspectors at Predeal, the station at the Hungarian border, emptied the trunk on the station platform. The train began moving, Mother sprang up, but her treasures lay scattered on the platform amid the jeers of the inspectors, and she had lost the suitcase as well. I felt it was beneath her dignity to grieve about such things, which only had to do with food; and instead of comfort, that was what she got to hear from me, to her annoyance.

She blamed the behavior of the Rumanian officials on our Turkish passports. In a sort of hereditary loyalty to Turkey, where they had always been well treated, most Sephardim had remained Turkish subjects. However, Mother's family, who originally came from Livorno, were under Italian protection and traveled with Italian passports. Had she been traveling with her girlhood passport under the name Arditti, then, she felt, the Rumanians would certainly have acted differently. They liked Italians because that's where their language came from. Most of all, they liked the French.

I had come right out of a war that I didn't care to acknowledge, but it was only on this trip that I began understanding, in an immediate way, something of the wide range and universality of national hatreds.

The Discovery of Evil
Fortress Vienna

In fall 1915, after that summer trip to Bulgaria, I started the first year in the *Realgymnasium*, the kind of secondary school that emphasizes modern languages. It was in the same building as the elementary school, right near the *Sophienbrücke*. I liked this school much better; we had Latin, something new, we got several teachers, no longer boring Herr Tegel, who always said the same thing and had struck me as stupid from the beginning. Our class teacher was Herr Professor Twrdy, a broad, bearded dwarf. When he sat on the podium, his beard lay across the table, and from our desks we could only see his head. No one disliked him, as comical as he appeared to us at first—he had a way of stroking his long beard that inspired respect. Maybe he drew patience from this gesture, he was fair and seldom lost his temper. He taught us Latin declinations, had little luck with most of his pupils, and kept reiterating "*silva, silvae*" for them indefatigably.

I now had more classmates who seemed interesting and whom I still recall. There was Stegmar, a boy who drew and painted marvelously; I was a bad draughtsman and couldn't see enough of his works. Before my eyes, he cast birds, flowers, horses, and other animals on the paper and gave me the loveliest ones just as they were created. Most impressive of all was the way he swiftly tore up a drawing that I was amazed at, throwing it away because it wasn't good enough and starting all over again. That happened a couple of times, but eventually he felt he had succeeded, scrutinized it from all angles, and then handed it to me with a modest and yet slightly solemn gesture. I admired his talent and his generosity, but I was disturbed at not being able to see any difference; all the drawings struck me as equally successful, and even more than his talent I admired the lightning-fast execution of his judgment. I was sorry about every drawing that he ripped up, nothing could have gotten me to destroy any paper with writing or printing on it. It was breathtaking to watch how quickly and unhesitatingly, nay, cheerfully he did it. At home I was told that artists are often like that.

Another classmate, fat, dark, and stocky, was named Deutschberger. His mother had a goulash booth in the Prater amusement park, and the fact that he lived right near the Tunnel of Fun, where I had been something like a habitué not so long ago, captivated me in his favor initially. I thought that someone who lived there had to be a different kind of person, far more interesting than the rest of us. But the fact that he was indeed, and in a different way than I could have known (at eleven, he was already a full-grown cynic), soon led to a bitter enmity.

We used to walk home from school along *Prinzenallee* with another classmate, who was really my friend, Max Schiebl, a general's son. Deutschberger did all the talking; he seemed to know everything about the life of adults and gave us an unvarnished account of it. For him, the Prater, as Schiebl and I knew it, had a different face. He would catch conversations between patrons at the goulash booth, and he had a lip-smacking way of repeating them to us. He always added comments by his mother, who hid nothing from him; he appeared to have no father and was her only child. Schiebl and I looked forward to the walk home, but Deutschberger wouldn't start talking right away; it was only when we had passed the playing field of the Vienna Athletic Club that he felt free to launch into his real subject matter. I believe he needed a little time to figure out what he would shock us with. He always ended with the same sentence: "You can never learn about life early enough, my mother says." He had an instinct for effect and heightened his stories every time. So long as he talked about violence, knifings, muggings, and murders, we let him be. He was against the war, which I liked; but Schiebl didn't care for that and asked him questions in order to make him change the topic. I was too embarrassed to repeat these conversations at home, for a while they remained our well-guarded secret, until his victories went to Deutschberger's head and he dared to go to extremes; this caused a great agitation.

"I know where babies come from," he suddenly said one day, "my mother told me." Schiebl was one year my senior; the issue had already begun absorbing him, and I reluctantly went along with his curiosity. "It's very simple," said Deutschberger, "a man plops on a woman the way the rooster plops on a hen." I, full of the Shakespeare and Schiller evenings with my mother, flew into a rage and shouted: "You're lying! It's not true! You're a liar!" It was the first time I turned against him. He remained utterly derisive and repeated his words. Schiebl kept silent and Deutschberger's total scorn was discharged on me. "Your mother doesn't tell you anything. She treats you like a little kid. Didn't you ever watch a rooster? A man and a woman, etc. You can never learn about life early enough, says my mother."

It wouldn't have taken much for me to start punching him. I left the two boys and ran across the empty lot into our building. We always ate together at a round table; I controlled myself in front of the little brothers and said nothing as yet, but I couldn't eat and was close to tears. As soon as I could, I pulled Mother out to the balcony, where we had our serious conversations during the day, and I told her everything. Naturally, she had noticed my agitation long ago, but when she heard the reason, she was dumbstruck. She, who had a clear and perfect answer for everything, she, who always made me feel that I shared the responsibility of raising the little brothers, she fell silent, silent for the first time, and remained silent so long that I grew scared. But then she looked into my eyes and, addressing me as she always did in our grand moments, she solemnly said: "My son, do you trust your mother?"

"Yes! Yes!"

"It's not true! He's lying. His mother never told him that. Children come in a different way, a beautiful way. I will tell you at a later time. You don't even want to know it now!" Her words instantly removed my desire to know. Nor did I really want to. If only that other thing was a lie! Now I knew that it *was* a lie—and a dreadful lie to boot, for he had made it up, his mother had never told him that.

From that moment on, I hated Deutschberger and treated him like the dregs of humanity. At school, where he was a bad pupil, I never whispered answers to him anymore. During recess, when he came over, I turned my back on him. I never said another word to him. We didn't walk home together anymore, I forced Schiebl to choose between him and me. I did something even worse: When the geography teacher asked him to point out Rome on the map, and he pointed to Naples, the teacher didn't notice; I stood up and said: "He pointed to Naples, that's not Rome," and he received a bad mark. Now that was something I would ordinarily have despised, I stood by my classmates and helped them whenever I could, even against teachers that I liked. But my mother's words had filled me with such hatred of him that I felt anything was permissible. It was the first time I experienced what blind devotion is, though not a word had been spoken about it between Mother and myself. I was enraged at him and saw him as a villain, I gave Schiebl a long description of Richard III and convinced him that Deutschberger was no one else, just young as yet, and somebody ought to put a stop to his game while there was still time.

That was how early the discovery of evil began. My tendency haunted me for a long time, even in later years, when I became a devoted slave to Karl Kraus and believed him about the countless villains he attacked. Life in school became unbearable for Deutschberger. He lost his self-confidence, his pleading looks followed me everywhere, he would have done anything to make peace, but I was intransigent, and it was strange to see this hatred increase, rather than diminish, because of its visible effect upon him. Finally, his mother came to school and confronted me during recess. "Why do you persecute my son?" she asked. "He's never done anything to you. You were always friends." She was an energetic woman with quick, powerful words. Unlike him, she had a neck and she didn't smack her lips when speaking. I enjoyed her asking me for something—leniency for her son—and so, as open as she, I told her the reason for my hostility. Unabashed, I repeated the taboo sentence about the rooster and the hen. She turned to him vehemently; he was standing behind her, trembling. "Did you say that?" He woefully nodded his head, but he didn't deny it, and that ended the whole matter for me. Perhaps I couldn't have refused anything to a mother who treated me as seriously as my own, but I sensed how important he was to her, and so Richard III changed back into a schoolboy like me and Schiebl. The controversial sentence, however, had returned to its alleged source, thereby losing its strength. The persecution collapsed; we didn't become friends again, but I left him alone, to such an extent that I have no further memory of him. When I think back to the rest of my schooltime in Vienna, approximately six more months, he remains vanished.

My friendship with Schiebl, however, became closer and closer. Everything had gone well with us from the first, but now he was my only friend. He lived further up the *Schüttel*, in an apartment similar to ours. For his sake, I also played with soldiers, and since he had very many, entire armies with all branches of arms, cavalry and artillery, I often went to his home, where we fought out our battles. He was very keen on winning and couldn't stand defeats. If beaten, he would bite his lips and make an angry face, sometimes he tried denying his defeat, and I got mad. But that never lasted very long; he was well brought-up, tall and proud, and although he was the spitting image of his mother, and I never got over my surprise at this resemblance, he was no mama's boy. She was the loveliest mother that I knew, and also the tallest. I always saw her erect, high above me; she bent down to us when she brought us a snack, placing the tray on the table with a slight bow of her upper body and promptly straightening up again before inviting us to help ourselves. Her dark eyes haunted me, I dreamt of them at home, although never telling Max, her son. I did ask him, however, if all Tyrolean women had beautiful eyes, to which he decisively said "Yes!" adding, "All Tyrolean men too." But the next time, I realized he'd told her, for she seemed amused when she brought us the afternoon snack, watched us play a bit, contrary to her habit, and asked me about my mother. When she left, I sternly asked Max: "Do you tell your mother everything?" He turned blood-red, but absolutely denied it. He told her nothing, he said, what did I think of him anyway, he didn't even tell his father everything.

The father, a small, slight man, made no impression whatsoever on me. He not only was shorter, but seemed older than the mother. He was a retired general, but had been called back for a special assignment in the war. He was inspector of the fortifications around Vienna. In fall 1915, when the Russians had broken through the Carpathian Mountains, and there were rumors that Vienna was in danger, Schiebl's father took us two along on his inspections when we didn't have school. We drove to Neuwaldegg and then tramped through the Vienna woods, coming to various small "forts" that had been dug into the ground. There were no soldiers here, we were allowed to view everything; we went inside, and while Schiebl's father banged his swagger stick here and there on the dense walls, we peeked through the chinks into the deserted forest, where nothing stirred. The general was a man of few words, he had a somewhat grumpy face, but whenever he addressed us to explain something, even during the walks through the forest, he smiled at us as if we were something special. I never felt embarassed with him. Perhaps he saw future soldiers in us; it was he who had given his son those huge tin armies that kept multiplying incessantly, and Max told me that he inquired about our games and wanted to know who had won. But I wasn't used to such quiet people, and I certainly couldn't picture him as a general. Schiebl's mother would have been an absolutely beautiful general, I would even have gone to war for her sake, but I didn't take the inspection tours with the father seriously; and the war, which was talked about so much, seemed furthest away when he banged his stick on the wall of a "fort."

Throughout my schooldays, and later as well, fathers made no impression on me. They had something lifeless or aged for me. My own father was still inside me, he had spoken about so many things to me, and I had heard him sing. His image stayed as young as he had been; he remained the only father. I was, however, receptive to mothers, and it was astonishing how many mothers I liked.

In the winter of 1915–16, the effects of the war could be felt in everyday life. The time of the enthusiastically singing recruits in *Prinzenallee* was gone. When small groups of them now trudged past us on our way home from school, they didn't look as cheerful as before. They still sang "In the homeland, in the homeland we'll meet again!", but home didn't seem so close to them. They were no longer so certain that they'd be coming back. They sang "I had a comrade," but as though they themselves were the fallen comrade they sang about. I sensed this

change and told my friend Schiebl about it. "They're not Tyroleans,"
he said, "you've got to see the Tyroleans." I don't know where he saw
marching Tyroleans at the time, maybe he and his parents visited
friends from their Tyrolean homeland and heard confident words from
them. His faith in victory was unshakable, he would never have dreamt
of doubting it. He didn't get this confidence from his father, a man of
few and never big words. When he took us along on his excursions, he
never once said: "We shall win." Had he been my father, I would have
long since abandoned any hope for victory. It must have been his
mother who kept his faith up. Perhaps she said nothing either, but her
pride, her unyieldingness, her way of looking at you as though nothing
bad could happen under her protection—I too could never have cherished doubts with such a mother.

Once, walking along the *Schüttel*, we came near the railroad bridge
that spanned the Danube Canal. A train was standing there, it was
stuffed with people. Freight cars were joined to passenger cars; they
were all jammed with people staring down at us, mutely, but ques-
tioningly. "Those are Galician—" Schiebl said, holding back the word
"Jews" and replacing it with "refugees." Leopoldstadt was full of
Galician Jews who had fled from the Russians. Their black kaftans,
their earlocks, and their special hats made them stand out conspicuously. Now they were in Vienna, where could they go? They had to eat
too, and things didn't look so good for food in Vienna.

I had never seen so many of them penned together in railroad cars.
It was a dreadful sight because the train was standing. All the time we
kept staring, it never moved from the spot. "Like cattle," I said, "that's
how they're squeezed together, and there are also cattle cars."

"Well, they're so many of them," said Schiebl, tempering his disgust
at them for my sake; he would never had uttered anything that could
offend me. But I stood transfixed, and he, standing with me, felt my
horror. No one waved at us, no one called, they knew how unwelcome
they were and they expected no word of welcome. They were all men
and a lot were old and bearded. "You know," said Schiebl, "our
soldiers are sent to the war in such freight cars. War is war, my father
says." Those were the only words of his father's that he ever quoted to
me, and I realized he was doing it to wrench me out of my terror. But
it didn't help, I stared and stared, and nothing happened. I wanted the
train to start moving, the most horrible thing of all was that the train
still stood on the bridge.

"Aren't you coming?" said Schiebl, tugging at my sleeve. "Don't you
want to anymore?" We were en route to his home to play with soldiers
again. I did leave now, but with a very queasy feeling, which increased

when we entered his apartment and his mother brought us a snack. "Where were you so long?" she asked. Schiebl pointed at me, saying: "We saw a train of Galician refugees. It was standing on *Franzensbrücke.*"

"Oh," said his mother, pushing the snack towards us. "But you must be hungry by now."

She then left, fortunately, for I didn't touch the food, and Schiebl, empathetic as he was, had no appetite either. He let the soldiers alone, we didn't play; when I left, he shook my hand warmly and said: "But tomorrow, when you come, I'll show you something. I got a new artillery."

Alice Asriel

My mother's most interesting friend was Alice Asriel, whose family came from Belgrade. She herself had become a thoroughgoing Viennese, in language and manner, in everything that occupied her, in each of her reactions. A tiny woman, the tiniest of my mother's friends, none of whom was very tall. She had intellectual interests and an ironic way of talking about things with Mother, none of which I understood. She lived in the Viennese literature of the period and lacked Mother's universal interest. She spoke of Bahr and Schnitzler, in a light way, a bit giddy, never insistent, open to any influence; anyone who spoke to her could impress her, but he had to talk about things in that sphere; she barely heeded anything that wasn't part of the literature of the day. It had to be men from whom she learned what counted; she respected men who spoke well, conversation was her life, discussions, differences of opinion. She loved listening most of all when intellectual men disagreed and argued. She was Viennese if for no other reason than because she always knew, without great effort, what was happening in the world of the intellect. But she just as much liked talking about people, their love affairs, their complications and divorces; she regarded anything connected to love as permissible, never condemned as my mother did; she argued with her when she condemned, and always had a ready explanation for the most involved complications. Anything that people did struck her as natural. Just as she viewed life, that was how life treated her, as though an evil genius had aimed at doing to her what she permitted others. She loved bringing people together, especially of different sexes, and watching their effects on each other, for she felt that true happiness was based chiefly on changing partners; and what she wished for herself, she granted equally to others, indeed she often seemed to be trying it out on them.

She played a role in my life, and what I have just said about her actually comes from later experiences. In 1915, when I first met her, I noticed how untouched she was by the war. She never once mentioned the war in my presence, but not like my mother, for instance, who was against the war with all her passion and kept still about it in front of me to prevent my having any trouble at school. Alice couldn't relate to the war; since she didn't know hatred and believed in live-and-let-live for anything and anyone, she couldn't work up any enthusiasm about the war, and merely thought around it.

In those days, when she visited us in *Josef-Gall-Gasse*, she was married to a cousin, who also came from Belgrade and had also become a Viennese, like her. Herr Asriel was a small, bleary-eyed man, who was known for incompetence in all the practical matters of life. He knew just enough about business to lose all his money, including his wife's dowry. They were living in a middle-class apartment with their three children when he made a last stab at getting on his feet. He fell in love with their maid, a pretty, simple, and submissive girl who felt honored by her employer's attentions. They understood one another, their minds ran in the same channels, but unlike him, she was attractive and constant, and what his wife, in her light and fickle way, couldn't give him, he found in the girl: moral support and absolute devotion. She was his mistress for a whole while before he left his family. Alice, who considered anything permissible, never reproached him; she would have lived on in the *ménage à trois* without batting an eyelash. I heard her telling Mother that she didn't begrudge him anything, anything in the world. He should just be happy, he wasn't happy with her, for there was nothing that kept them in limits from each other. He wasn't capable of literary discussions; when books were talked about, he got migraines; everything was all right with him so long as he never set eyes on the other participants in these conversations and didn't have to join in himself. She gave up telling him about them, she was utterly sympathetic about his migraines, nor did she resent him for their rapidly growing impoverishment. "He's just not a businessman," she told Mother, "does everyone have to be a businessman?" When the subject of the maid came up, and Mother was very hard on her, Alice always had a warm and understanding word for the two of them: "Look, she's so good to him, and with her he's not ashamed of losing everything. He feels guilty with me."

"But he *is* guilty," said Mother. "How can a man be so weak? He's not a man, he's nothing, he shouldn't have gotten married."

"But he didn't *want* to marry. Our parents made us marry so that the money would stay in the family. I was too young, and he was too shy. He was too shy to look a woman in the face. Do you realize I had to force him to look me in the eye, and that was after we'd been married for a while."

"And what did he do with the money?"

"He didn't do *anything* with it. He just lost it. Is money that important? Why shouldn't a person lose money? Do you prefer your relatives with all their money? Why, they're monsters, compared with him!"

"You'll never stop defending him, I think you still care for him."

"I feel sorry for him, and now he's finally found his happiness. She thinks he's a grand gentleman. She kneels before him. Now they've been together for such a long time, and you know, she still kisses his hand and calls him 'Sir!' She cleans the whole apartment every day, there's nothing to clean, everything is spotless, but she keeps cleaning and cleaning, and asks me if I need anything. 'You just rest a bit, Marie,' I say, 'you've worked hard enough.' But it's never enough for her, and if they're not together, she cleans."

"Why, that's outrageous. To think that you haven't kicked her out! I would have shown her the door immediately, the very first moment."

"What about him? I can't do that to him. Should I destroy their happiness?"

I wasn't supposed to eavesdrop. When Alice came over with her three children, we played together, and Mother drank tea with her; Alice launched into her reportage, Mother was very anxious to hear the next installment, and the two of them, seeing me with the other children, never dreamt that I could hear everything. Later on, when Mother made reticent hints that things weren't going so well in the Asriel home, I was cunning enough not to let on that no detail had escaped me. But I had no idea what Herr Asriel was really doing with the maid. I understood the words as they were said, I thought they liked standing together and I didn't suspect anything beyond that; and yet I fully realized that all the details I had caught weren't meant for my ears, and I never once blurted out what I knew. I think I also wanted to experience my mother in a different way; every conversation she had was precious to me, I didn't want to let anything of her elude me.

Alice did not feel sorry for her children, who lived in that unusual atmosphere. The eldest, Walter, was backward, he had his father's bleary eyes and pointed nose and walked just like him, leaning slightly to the side. He spoke entire albeit short sentences, never more than one sentence at a time. He expected no answer to his sentences, but understood what people said, and he was stubbornly obedient. He did whatever he was told to do, but he waited a bit before doing it, so that people thought he hadn't understood. Then suddenly, with a jerk, he did it, he *had* understood. He didn't cause any special trouble, but supposedly he sometimes had fits of rage; you never could tell when they would start, he would calm down soon, but you couldn't risk leaving him alone.

Hans, his brother, was a smart boy, it was delightful playing "literary quartet" with him. Nuni, the youngest, kept up with us, even though these quotations couldn't mean anything to her yet, while Hans and I reveled in the game. We just hurled quotations at one another, we knew them by heart; if one of us said the first word, the other instantaneously supplied the rest. Neither of us ever managed to finish his quotation; it was a point of honor for the other to leap in and finish it. "The place—"

"—a good man entered, it is consecrated."

"God helps—"

"—the man who lets God help him."

"A noble—"

"—man draws other noble men."

That was our very own game; since both of us gabbed equally fast, neither won the contest; a friendship commenced, based on respect, and it was only when the literary quartet was behind us that we turned to other quartets and games. Hans was always present when his mother carried on about connoisseurs of literature, and he had gotten in the habit of talking as fast as those people. He knew how to deal with his brother; he was the only one who could sense a fit coming on, and he was so gentle and obliging with him that he sometimes managed to head off a fit in time. "He's smarter than me," said Frau Asriel in his presence; she had no secrets from her children, that was one of her tolerance principles, and when Mother upbraided her, "You're making the boy conceited, don't praise him so much," Frau Asriel would reply, "Why shouldn't I praise him? He's got a hard enough time of it with his father and what not," by which she meant the retarded brother. As for what she thought about this brother, she kept it to herself, her openness never went that far; her indulgence for Walter was fed by her pride in Hans.

He had a very narrow, elongated head and, unlike his brother, he kept his posture very straight. He pointed his finger at everything he explained, and at me too when disagreeing with me; I always feared that a bit, for when his finger went aloft, he was always right. He was so precocious that he had a hard time with other children. But he wasn't fresh, and if his father said something stupid—which I rarely witnessed since I rarely saw him—he held his tongue and withdrew into himself, as though suddenly disappearing. I then knew that he was ashamed of his father, I knew it although he never said anything about him, perhaps that's why I knew it. His little sister, Nuni, was different in this respect; she adored her father and repeated everything he said: "Common, fine, says my father," she suddenly declared, "but *so* common!" Those were *her* quotations, she was made up of them, and especially when we played "literary quartet," she felt prompted to blurt them out. Those were the only quotations that Hans and I never completed, although we knew them as thoroughly as those by the poets. Nuni was allowed to speak till she was done, and any listener would have been surprised by Herr Asriel's judgments in between the stunted lines of poets. Nuni was reserved towards her mother, and it was normally hard to lure her out of her reserve; one sensed that she was accustomed to disapproving of many things, a critical but reticent child, carried along by her single adoring love of her father.

It was a twofold delight for me when Frau Asriel came with her children. I looked forward to playing with Hans, his know-it-all attitude appealed to me because I had to watch out so carefully; I was seemingly absorbed in the game with him in order to save myself a disgrace, which he always pointed out at the tip of his stretching finger. If I managed to drive him against the wall with, say, geographical things, he would doggedly fight to the finish, never giving in; our argument over the biggest island on earth remained undecided. Greenland was "*hors concours*" for him: How could you tell how big it was with all that ice? Instead of pointing at me, he pointed his finger at the map, and said triumphantly: "Where does Greenland stop?" It was harder for me than him, for I constantly had to find pretexts for going to the dining room where Mother and Frau Asriel were taking their tea. I would look for something in the bookcase, and I kept looking in order to catch as much as possible of the conversation between the two friends. Mother knew how intense things were between Hans and me, I ran so decisively towards the bookcase, riffling through one book, then another, emitting grunts of annoyance if I didn't find something, letting out a long whistle if I did find what I was hunting, and she didn't even reproach me for my whistle—how could she have imagined that I was curious about something else, and eavesdropping on them!

So I took in all the phases of the story of that marriage, to the very last. "He wants to go away," said Frau Asriel, "he wants to live with her."

"But he's been doing that all this time," Mother said, "now he's walking out on all of you."

"He says it can't keep on like this in the long run because of the children. He *is* right, you know. Walter has noticed something, he eavesdropped on them. The two others haven't a clue as yet."

"That's what *you* think. Children notice everything," said Mother, while I listened, unnoticed. "What does he plan to live on?"

"He's going to start a bicycle store with her. He's always liked bicycles. It was his childhood dream to live in a bicycle store. You know, she understands him so well. She keeps telling him to make his childhood dream come true. She'll have to do everything herself. All the work's going to be on her shoulders. I couldn't do it. That's what I call true love."

"And you actually admire that woman."

I vanished, and when I came back to Hans and Nuni, she was quoting again: " 'Bad people have no songs,' says my father."

I was bewildered by what I had just heard, I couldn't talk, and this time I realized how deeply it concerned the two children I was silent with. I held the book shut, though I had brought it to triumph over Hans, and I let him think he was right.

The Meadow near Neuwaldegg

Paula came soon after Fanny had gone, her antipode: tall and slender, a graceful creature, very discreet for a Viennese, and yet cheerful. She would have preferred to laugh all the time; since it didn't seem proper to her in her job, only a smile remained. She smiled when she said something, she smiled when she was silent, I imagined that she slept and dreamt with a smile.

She did not act different whether speaking to Mother or to us children, whether answering a stranger's question on the street or greeting a friend; even the dirty little girl, who was always there, had a happy time with her; Paula halted unabashedly upon seeing her, said a friendly word, sometimes unwrapping a piece of candy for her, surprising the little girl so greatly that she didn't dare accept it. Paula would then coax her nicely and put the candy gently into the girl's mouth.

She didn't much care for the Prater amusement park, it was too coarse for her; she never said so, but I did sense it when we were there. She would shake her head in annoyance as soon as she heard something ugly, and she would give me a cautious sidelong glance to see whether I had understood it. I always pretended I hadn't even noticed, and she soon smiled again. I was so used to her smile that I would have done anything to make her smile again.

In our building, the composer Karl Goldmark lived one floor below, right underneath us, a small, frail man with neatly parted white hair on both sides of his dark face. He would go for strolls on his daughter's arm, not very far, for he was very old by then, but always at the same time every day. I associated him with Arabia; the opera that had made him famous was called *The Queen of Sheba*. I thought he came from there himself, he was the most exotic thing in the neighborhood and hence the most attractive. I never ran into him on the stairs or when he left the building; I saw him only when he was coming back from *Prinzenallee*; he had strolled a few steps there, back and forth, on his daughter's arm. I greeted them respectfully, he lowered his head slightly, that was his almost imperceptible way of taking my greeting. I can't recall what his daughter looked like, it was not her face that lodged in my memory. One day, when he didn't come, I heard that he was ill, and then, toward evening, when I was in our nursery, I heard a loud weeping from downstairs, and it wouldn't stop. Paula, who wasn't sure whether I'd heard it, looked at me dubiously and said: "Herr Goldmark has died. He was very feeble, he couldn't have gone for walks anymore." The weeping came in thrusts and imparted itself to me; I had to keep listening and I moved to it, in the same rhythm, but without crying myself, it seemed to be coming from the floor. Paula grew nervous: "Now his daughter can't go out with him anymore. She's in absolute despair, the poor thing." Paula smiled even now, perhaps to calm me down, for I noticed that it affected her deeply; her father was at the front in Galicia, and they hadn't heard from him in a long time.

On the day of the funeral, *Josef-Gall-Gasse* was black with fiacres and people. We gazed down from our window, we thought there couldn't be a free spot left below, but more and more fiacres and people kept coming and finding room after all.

"Where do they all come from?"

"That's the way it is when a famous man dies," said Paula. "They want to pay their last respects, they like his music so much."

I had never heard his music and I felt excluded. I merely perceived the throng below as a spectacle, perhaps also because the people looked so tiny from the third floor; they were squeezed together, but some managed to doff their black hats to one another. That struck us as improper, but Paula had a placating explanation: "They're glad if they know somebody among all those people, it gives them courage again.'' The daughter's weeping got to me, I heard it many days after the funeral, always towards evening; when it eventually began waning and then stopped, I felt a lack, as though I had lost something indispensable.

A short time later, a man plunged from the fourth floor of a nearby house in *Josef-Gall-Gasse*. The emergency squad came to get him, he was dead, a large blood stain remained on the asphalt and wasn't removed for a long time. When we passed by, Paula took my hand and maneuvered me in such a way that she walked between the blood stain and me. I asked her why the man had done it, and she couldn't explain. I wanted to know when the funeral would take place. There wasn't going to be any, she said. He had been alone and had no kin. Maybe that, she said, was why he hadn't wanted to go on living.

She saw how preoccupied I was with this suicide, and to get my mind on something else, she asked Mother if she could take me along on her next Sunday outing to Neuwaldegg. She had a friend, with whom we rode out in the trolley car, a quiet young man, who gazed at her admiringly and barely said a word. He was so quiet that he wouldn't even have been present if Paula hadn't spoken to both of us at once; whatever she said was aimed at the two of us. She talked in such a way as to expect an answer from us, I replied and the friend nodded. Then we walked a bit through the forest to the *Knödelhütte*, and he said something that I didn't understand: "Next week, Fräulein Paula, it's only five days away." We came to a radiant meadow covered with people, it was huge, it looked as if it had enough space for all the people in the world, but we had to walk around for a long time before we found a spot. Families were lying there, made up of women and children, occasionally young couples, but mostly whole groups of people who belonged together and were playing something that kept them all on the move. A few people basked in the sun, they seemed happy too, many laughed; Paula was at home here, this was where she belonged. Her friend, who greatly respected her, now opened his mouth frequently, one admiring word led to another, he was on furlough, but he wasn't in uniform, perhaps he didn't care to remind her of the war; he had to think about her more, he said, when he wasn't with her. Men were rarer on the meadow than women, I saw no man in uniform, and if I hadn't finally realized that Paula's admirer had to return to the front next week, I would have forgotten there was a war.

That is my last memory of Paula, the meadow near Neuwaldegg, among very many people in the sunshine, I do not see her on the ride home. It is as though she had remained on the meadow to hold her friend back. I don't know why she left us, I don't know why she was suddenly gone. If only her smile did not leave her, if only her admirer came back; her father was no longer alive when we rode out in the trolley.

Mother's Illness
Herr Professor

It was the time when bread became yellow and black, with additions of corn and other, less good things. People had to line up at the food shops; we children were also sent, so that we got a little more. Mother began finding life more difficult. In late winter, she collapsed. I don't know what her illness was, but she was laid up in a sanatorium for long weeks and recovered very slowly. In the beginning, I wasn't allowed to visit her, but gradually she got better, and I arrived at her sanatorium on *Elisabethpromenade* with flowers. That was the first time I saw her physician, the director of the institution, in her room; he was a man with a thick, black beard, who had written medical books and taught at the University of Vienna. He gazed at me with honeyed friendliness from half-shut eyes and said: "Well, so this is the great Shakespeare scholar! And he also collects crystals. I've heard a lot about you. Your mama always talks about you. You're quite advanced for your age."

Mother had spoken to him about me! He knew everything about the things we read together. He *praised* me. Mother never praised me. I distrusted his beard and avoided him. I was afraid he might someday *graze* me with his beard, and I would then be instantly transformed into a slave, who would have to fetch and carry for him. His tone of voice, which was slightly nasal, was like cod-liver oil. He wanted to put his hand on my head, perhaps to praise me with it. But I eluded it by ducking swiftly, and he seemed a bit offended: "That's a proud boy you have there, Madame. He won't let anyone but you touch him!" That word, "touch," stuck in my mind, it fixed my hatred for him, a hatred such as I had never experienced before. He didn't do anything to me, but he flattered me and tried to win me over. From now on, he did it with inventive tenacity, he thought up presents to catch me unawares, and how could he have surmised that an eleven-year-old child's will power was not only equal to his, but stronger?

For he was wooing my mother, she had aroused a deep liking in him, as he told her (but I learned this only later), the deepest in his life. He wanted to divorce his wife for her. He would take care of the three children, he said, and help raise them. All three could study at the

University of Vienna, but the eldest should absolutely become a doctor, and if he felt like it, he could take over the sanatorium eventually. Mother was no longer open with me, she avoided telling me all that, she knew it would have *destroyed* me. I had the feeling that she was staying in the sanatorium too long, he wouldn't release her. "Why, you're completely healthy," I told her at every visit. "Come home and I'll take care of you." She smiled; I spoke like a grownup, a man, or even a doctor who knew everything that had to be done. I would have preferred to carry her out of the sanatorium in my own arms. "One night, I'm going to come and abduct you," I said.

"But it's locked downstairs, you can't come in. You'll have to wait until the doctor allows me to go home. It won't take much longer."

When she returned home, there were many changes. Herr Professor did not vanish from our lives; he came to visit her, he came to tea. He always brought me a present, which I instantly threw away the moment he left the apartment. I never kept a single present of his longer than the extent of his visit, and some of them were books that I would have given anything to read, and wonderful crystals that were missing from my collection. He was quite clever about his presents, for no sooner had I started talking about a book that lured me than it was there, coming from his hands to the table in our nursery, and it was as if a mildew had fallen on the book: Not only did I throw it away, having to find the right places, which was not so easy, but I also never read the book of that title at any time afterwards.

At this point, the jealousy that tortured me all my life commenced, and the force with which it came over me marked me forever. It became my true passion, utterly heedless of any attempts at convincing me or pointing out a better way.

"Today, Herr Professor is coming to tea," said my mother at lunch. For ourselves, we always used the Viennese word *Jause*, but for him it was "tea." Her tea, he had convinced her, was the best in Vienna, she knew how to brew it from her days in England, and while all her supplies had melted down to nothing during the war, she still had enough tea in the house, by some miracle. I asked her what she would do when the tea ran out; she said it wouldn't run out for a long time.

"How much longer? How much longer?"

"It will hold out for another year or two."

She knew what I felt, but she couldn't bear being supervised; perhaps she was exaggerating in order to cure me of asking, for she gruffly refused to *show* me the supplies of tea.

Herr Professor insisted on greeting me upon his arrival, and no sooner had he kissed Mother's hand than she let him enter the nursery, where I was expecting him. He always greeted me with a flattering remark and pulled out his present. I looked hard at it in order to sufficiently hate it on the spot and I insidiously said: "Thank you." We never got into a conversation, the tea, which was served on the balcony of the next room, was waiting, nor did he wish to disturb me in my perusal of the gift. He was convinced he had brought the right thing, every hair in his black beard shone. He asked: "What would you like me to bring you the next time I come?" Since I kept silent, he supplied the answer himself, saying: "I'll find out, I've got my methods." I knew what he meant, he would ask Mother, and although it was my greatest sorrow that she would tell him, I had more important things to worry about; the time for action had come. Scarcely had he closed the door behind him when I hurriedly grabbed the present and stuck it under the table, out of sight. Then I got a chair, dragged it over to the window, knelt on the woven straw of the seat, and leaned out the window as far as I could.

For to my left, not so far away, I could watch Herr Professor taking a seat on the balcony with all sorts of cordialities. He had his back to me; Mother sat on the other, the further side of the balcony, which formed an arc. I only *knew* she was there, I couldn't see her, any more than the tea table standing between them. From his movements, I had to guess everything happening on the balcony. He had a beseeching way of leaning forward, turning slightly left because of the curve in the balcony; I would then see his beard, the object I hated most in the world, and I could also see him raising his left hand and spreading his fingers in elegant affirmation. I could tell whenever he took a sip of tea and I thought in disgust that he was now praising it—he praised everything connected with Mother. I was worried that, although she was very hard to win, his flatteries would turn her head because of her condition, which was weakened by illness. I now applied many things to him and her, things that I had read about and that didn't fit into my life, and I had words like an adult for everything I feared.

I didn't know what goes on between a man and a woman, but I watched to make sure nothing happened. If he leaned over too far, I thought he was about to kiss her, even though that would have been quite impossible, at least because of the tea table between them. I understood nothing of his words and sentences; the only thing I thought I heard, seldom enough, was: "But dear Madame!" It sounded persistent and protesting, as though she had done him an injustice, and I was delighted. The worst thing of all was when he didn't speak for a long time; then I knew that she was talking on and on, and I assumed they were discussing me. I then wished the balcony would collapse and he would be smashed on the sidewalk below. It never occurred to me—perhaps because I didn't see her—that she would have plunged down along with him. Only what I could see, only he, was to plunge down. I pictured him lying below and the police coming to question me. "I threw him down," I would say, "he kissed my mother's hand."

He would remain to tea for something like an hour; it seemed much longer to me, I crouched stubbornly on my chair, never taking my eyes off him for an instant. As soon as he stood up, I jumped off the chair, moved it back to the table, got the present from underneath, placed it exactly where he had originally produced it, and opened the door to the vestibule. He was already standing there, he kissed Mother's hand, took his gloves, cane, and hat, waved to me, more pensive and less eager than upon his arrival. After all, he had plunged down in the meantime and he was lucky to be walking on his legs. He disappeared and I ran to my window: I watched after him as he walked to the end of *Josef-Gall-Gasse*, a short street, turned the corner to the *Schüttel*, and vanished from my sight.

Mother still needed to recuperate, and our reading sessions were less frequent. She no longer acted anything out for me and only had *me* read aloud; I made an effort to think up questions that could arouse her interest. If she gave me a long reply, if she really explained something as in the past, I drew hope and was happy again. But she was often reflective, sometimes lapsing into silence, as though I wasn't there. "You're not listening," I would then say, she started and felt caught. I knew her mind had drifted to other books, which she didn't speak to me about.

She read books that Herr Professor gave her, and she sternly impressed upon me that they weren't for me. Earlier, the key to the bookcase was always in the keyhole so that I could rummage inside to my heart's content, but now she took the key away. A present from him that particularly absorbed her was Baudelaire's *Les Fleurs du Mal*. It was the first time I had ever known her to read poetry. She would never have dreamt of doing that before, she despised poetry. Plays had always been her passion, and she had infected me too. Now she no longer picked up *Don Carlos* or *Wallenstein* and she made a wry face when I mentioned them. Shakespeare still counted, he even counted a lot, but instead of reading him, she merely looked for certain passages, annoyedly shaking her head when she couldn't find them right away, or else her entire face would light up with laughter, her nostrils quivering first, and she never told me what she was laughing about. Novels had interested her earlier, but she now read some that I hadn't noticed before. I saw books by Schnitzler, and when she happened to tell me not only that he lived in Vienna and was really a physician, but also that Herr Professor knew him and that his wife was Sephardic like us, my despair was complete.

"What would you like me to be when I grow up?" I once asked her, in great fear, as if knowing what terrible answer would come. "The best thing is to be both a writer and a doctor," she said.

"You're only saying that because of Schnitzler!"

"A doctor does good, a doctor really helps people."

"Like Dr. Weinstock, huh?" That was a malicious reply. I knew she couldn't stand our family physician because he always tried to put his arm around her.

"No, not exactly like Dr. Weinstock. Do you think he's a writer? He doesn't think about anything. He only thinks about his pleasure. A good doctor understands something about people. Then he can also be a writer and he won't write nonsense."

"Like Herr Professor?" I asked, knowing how dangerous things were now getting. He was no writer, and I wanted to get that in at him.

"He doesn't have to be like Herr Professor," she said, "but he ought to be like Schnitzler."

"Then why can't I read him?" She didn't answer, but she said something that agitated me even more.

"Your father would have liked you to be a doctor."

"Did he tell you that? Did he tell you that?"

"Yes, often. He often told me that. That would have made him so happy."

She had never mentioned it, never once since his death had she mentioned it. I did recall what he had said to me during that stroll along the Mersey. "You ought to be what you want to be. You don't have to be a businessman like me. You'll go to the university, and you'll be what you like best." But I had kept that to myself, never telling anyone, not even her. The fact that she now brought it up for the first time only because she liked Schnitzler and Herr Professor had ingratiated himself with her—that infuriated me. I leapt up from my easy chair, stood angrily in front of her, and shouted: "I don't want to be a doctor! I don't want to be a writer! I'm going to become an explorer! I'm going to travel far away, where no one can ever find me."

"Livingstone was a doctor too," she said derisively, "and Stanley found him!"

"But *you* won't find me!"

War had broken out between us and it got more horrible from week to week.

The Beard in Lake Constance

The two of us were living alone at that time, without my little brothers. During my mother's illness, both had been brought to Switzerland by Grandfather. Relatives had received them and put them in a boys' boarding school at Lausanne. Their absence in the apartment could be felt in different ways. I had the nursery, where the three of us used to spend our time, all to myself. I could concoct anything I wanted to in peace and quiet, and the space for my fight against Herr Professor was not challenged by anyone. He courted only me and brought gifts only for me. While observing his visit from the chair at the window, I didn't have to worry about anything going on in back of me.

I was free in regard to my disquiet and could talk to Mother at any time without having to consider the little bothers, from whom such friction would certainly have had to be hidden. This made everything more open and more savage. The balcony, which had once been the place of all earnest conversations during the day, utterly changed character: I no longer liked it. With my hatred for the tea-drinking Herr Professor linked to this place, I expected it to collapse. When no one could see, I crept out on the balcony, testing the solidity of the stone, albeit only on the side where he used to sit. I hoped for brittleness and was bitterly disappointed that nothing budged. Everything seemed as solid as ever, and my leaps did not cause any shaking, not even the slightest.

The absence of my brothers strengthened my position. It was inconceivable that we should be separated from them forever, and a removal to Switzerland was now frequently considered. I did everything to speed up this trip and made Mother's life in Vienna as hard as possible. The resoluteness and fierceness of my struggle still tortures me in memory. I wasn't at all certain of my victory. The irruption of strange books into Mother's life frightened me far more than Herr Professor personally. Behind him, whom I despised because I knew him and was disgusted by his glib, flattering speech, stood the figure of a writer, of whom I was not allowed to read a single line, whom I didn't even know; and never have I feared any writer so much as Schnitzler at that period.

Getting permission to leave Austria wasn't all that easy in those days. Perhaps Mother had an exaggerated notion of the difficulties to be overcome. She still wasn't fully healthy and was supposed to take a follow-up treatment. She had fond memories of Reichenhall, where she had quickly recuperated four years ago. Now she weighed going with me and spending a few weeks there. She thought it might be easier to obtain an exit visa for Switzerland in Munich. Herr Professor was willing to come to Munich and assist with the formalities. His academic connections and his beard would not fail to impress the officials. I was keen as mustard about the plan upon grasping how earnest it was, and I now suddenly supported my mother in every way. After the implacable enmity that she had gotten from me and that had paralyzed her at every step, she now felt great relief. We made plans for the weeks we would be spending alone in Reichenhall. I secretly hoped we would resume our drama readings. These sessions had grown more and more infrequent, finally vanishing because she was so absent-minded and feeble. I looked forward to wonders from Coriolanus if only I succeeded in reawakening him. But I was too proud to tell her how much hope I was pinning on the return of our evenings. In any event, we would go on excursions from Reichenhall and take a lot of walks.

I can't recall the final days in Vienna. I don't know how we left the familiar apartment and the fateful balcony. I have no memory of the trip either, I only see us again in Reichenhall. A short daily stroll took us to Nonn. There was a small churchyard in Nonn, very hushed, with which she had been smitten back then, four years ago. We wandered among the gravestones, reading the names of the dead, which we soon knew, and nevertheless rereading them. That was where she would like to be buried, she said. She was thirty-one, but I wasn't surprised by her funereal cravings. When we were alone, everything she thought, said, or did entered into me like the most natural thing in the world. I came into being from the sentences she uttered to me at such times.

We went on excursions to the far surroundings, Berchtesgaden and Lake König. But those were trips under the influence of the usual praises, nothing was so intimate and personal as Nonn, that was her place, and perhaps it made such an impact on me because, of all her whims and notions, this was the most withdrawn, as though she had suddenly given up her enormous expectations for her three sons and gone into retirement fifty years ahead of time. I believe that her real after-treatment consisted in these regular brief walks to Nonn. When she stood in the tiny churchyard, uttering her wish again, I sensed that she was improving. She suddenly looked healthy, she had color, she breathed deeply, her nostrils quivered, and she finally spoke again as in the *Burgtheater*, although in an unwonted role.

Thus I didn't miss the unresumed drama sessions after all. Instead, at the same time every evening, we took the precisely demarcated stroll to Nonn, and the things she said to me on the way there and back were again as full and earnest as in the time before her illness. I always felt now as if she were telling me everything, as if she held back nothing; it never seemed to occur to her that I was only eleven years old. Something expansive was in her then, spreading out unrestrained to all sides, and I alone witnessed it, and I alone moved in it.

But as Munich approached, I began worrying. Still, I didn't ask how long we would be staying. To keep me from feeling anxious, she said, of her own accord, that it wouldn't take that much time. After all, that was why Herr Professor was coming. With his help, we might be done with everything in a week. Without him, she said, there was no telling whether the exit visa would even be granted. I believed her, for we were still alone.

At our arrival in Munich, the calamity broke in upon me again. He had arrived *before* us and was waiting for us at the railroad station. The two of us looked out the train window with the same thought, but it was I who first discovered the black beard on the platform. He greeted us with some solemnity, explaining that he would instantly take us to the Hotel Deutscher Kaiser, where, as Mother had wished, a room had been reserved for her and me. He had already notified a few good friends, who would be honored to give us recommendations and otherwise be of assistance in any way. At the hotel, it turned out that he was staying there too. That would make things simpler, he said, so as not to waste any time; with all the running around we would have to do, that was important. Unfortunately, he added, he would have to return to Vienna in six days, the sanatorium didn't allow him to absent himself any longer. I saw through him immediately; the six days were meant to weaken the effect of staying in the same hotel, a piece of news that struck me like the blow of a club, but didn't paralyze me by any means.

I wasn't told where his room was; I assumed it had to be on the same floor, and I was afraid it might be too close to ours. I wanted to find out where that room was and I lurked nearby when he asked for his key. He didn't give his room number; the clerk, as though fully aware of my intention, discreetly handed him the key; I vanished before he noticed me. I swiftly took the elevator up before him to our floor and hid off to the side until he came himself. Very soon, the elevator door opened, he stepped out with the room key in his hand, and walked past without seeing me. I had made myself even smaller than I was; his own beard was what concealed me from his gaze. Squeezing against the wall, I skulked after him, it was a big hotel with long corridors; I was relieved to see that he was going far, far away from our room. No one came in our direction, I was alone with him, I hurried to remain near him. He turned a corner and finally stood outside his door; I heard him sigh before he inserted the key into the lock. It was a loud sigh, and I was amazed—never would I have expected such a man to sigh, I was accustomed to sighs only from Mother and I knew that from her they meant something. Most recently, they had been caused by her weakness; she sighed when feeling badly, and I would try to comfort her and promise her that her strength would soon be restored. Now he stood there—physician and flatterer, owner of a sanatorium, author of a magnificent three-volume medical opus, which had been standing in our Vienna library for several months now and which I wasn't allowed to open—and he was sighing wretchedly. Then he unlocked the door, entered the room, shut the door behind him, and left the key in the lock outside. I put my ear to the keyhole and listened. I heard his voice, he was alone, I had left Mother in our room, where she was supposed to rest and was napping. He spoke quite loudly, but I didn't understand him. I was afraid he might utter Mother's name, and I listened strenuously for him to do that. In my presence, she was "dear Madame" or "honored Madame," but I didn't trust this mode of address and I was determined to challenge him for an unpermissible use of her name. I saw myself tearing the door open, leaping at him, and yelling: "How dare you?" I tore off his glasses and trampled them to very tiny bits: "You're no doctor, you're a quack! I've exposed you! Leave this hotel instantly or I'll turn you over to the police."

But he took care not to do me this favor, no name came over his lips. He was, as I finally realized, speaking French, it sounded like a poem; the Baudelaire he had given her flashed into my mind. So, when alone, he remained what he was in her presence, a wretched flatterer, impalpable, a jellyfish. I shook with disgust.

I dashed all the way back to our room and found my mother still asleep. I sat down by the sofa and watched over her slumber. I was familiar with all changes in her face and I knew when she dreamt.

Perhaps it was good for those six days that I knew the rooms of all the people involved. I was calmer only when I knew they were both separated. *He* was in my power as soon as I heard him in his room. Maybe he was rehearsing the poems he recited to Mother when he was with her. Countless times, I stood at his door, he sensed nothing of my secret activities; I knew when he left the hotel, I knew when he was back again. At any time, I could have said whether he was in his room, and I was quite certain that Mother never entered it. Once, when he left it for an instant and the door was open, I hurriedly stepped inside and glanced around swiftly to see whether there was any picture of Mother anywhere. But there was none, and I vanished as fast as I had come, and I even had the gall to tell Mother: "You ought to give Herr Professor a nice picture of *us* when we go away."

"Both of us, yes," she said, slightly bewildered, "he's helped us so much, he deserves it."

He did what he could in all the agencies, which were often staffed by women because of the war; he accompanied Mother, explaining that his presence was due to her morbid feebleness—he *was* her doctor, after all—and so she was treated politely and considerately everywhere. I was always along; I could thus observe him *in flagrante* so to speak, as he flashed his calling card, handing it to the lady official in an elegantly casual sweep and saying: "Permit me to introduce myself." Then came everything that was spelled out on the card, the sanatorium he directed, the connection to the University of Vienna, etc., and I was surprised that he didn't add his punchline: "I kiss your hand, dear Madame."

We had lunch together in the hotel. I acted polite and well mannered and asked him about his studies. He was astonished at my insatiable questions and thought that I now really wanted to be what he was—he as my model—and he managed to turn that into flattery also. "You haven't told me too much, dear Madame, your son's intellectual curiosity is amazing. I may greet in him a future light of the Vienna Medical Faculty." But I had no intention whatsoever of emulating him, I merely wanted to *unmask* him! I watched out for contradictions in his answers and, while he supplied thorough and somewhat pompous information, I had only one thought in my mind: "He never really studied. He's a quack."

His time came in the evening. He would then win easily, and just as he knew nothing about my secret activities against him, so too he didn't know how great his victory over me was. For Mother went to the theater with him every night, she was starving for the theater, what we had been doing together in its stead could no longer be enough for her, it had died for her, she needed new and real theater. I remained alone in the hotel room when the two of them went out, but beforehand I watched her preparing herself for the evening. She didn't hide how much she was looking forward to it. She spoke about it, radiant and open; even two hours earlier, when all her thoughts were on the coming evening, I watched her with amazement and admiration. All her feebleness had dropped away; right before my eyes, she became powerful, witty, and beautiful, as before, she developed new ideas about the glory of the theater, spoke scornfully about dramas that didn't get to the stage; plays that were merely read were dead, a woeful surrogate, and when I, in order to test her and deepen my misery, asked "Even if they're read aloud?" she would say unabashedly and without the least consideration: "Even if they're read aloud! What good is *our* reading aloud anyway! You don't know what real actors are like!" Then she carried on about the great dramatists who were actors, counted them all up, starting with Shakespeare and Molière, and even went so far as to claim that other playwrights weren't dramatists at all, they ought to be called "play*wrongs*." Thus it went on, until, fragrant and wonderfully dressed, as I thought, she left the room, with the final cruel instruction that I should go to bed soon so that I wouldn't feel too lonely in this strange hotel.

I remained behind, devoid of hope, cut off from what had been our greatest intimacy. A few small maneuvers that followed gave me assurance, but did little else. I first ran down the long corridor to the other side of the hotel, where Herr Professor's room was located. I knocked politely several times, tried the door, and it was only when I was positive that he hadn't concealed himself there that I returned to my room. Every half hour, I checked anew. I didn't think anything special about it. I knew he was in the theater with Mother, but I couldn't confirm it often enough. It fortified the torment that I felt at her defection, but it also set a limit to it. In Vienna, they had gone to a play now and then, but that couldn't be compared with this incessant festival, evening after evening in a row.

I had found out when the final curtain was and I remained dressed until then. I tried to picture what they saw, but my efforts were futile. She never told me about the plays they attended, it made no sense telling me, she said, they were all modern plays that I wouldn't understand. Just before they were bound to show up, I undressed and got into bed. I turned to the wall, pretending to be asleep. I left the lamps shining on her night table, where a peach lay ready for her. She came very soon, I could feel her excitement, I smelled her perfume. The beds were not side by side but along the wall, so that she moved at some distance from me. She sat down on the bed, but not for long. Then she walked up and down the room, not very softly. I couldn't see her because I was facing away, but I heard each of her steps. I wasn't relieved that she was back; I didn't trust in the six days. I saw an eternity of theater evenings ahead, I regarded Herr Professor as capable of any lie.

But I was wrong, the six days passed, and everything was ready for the journey. He accompanied us until Lindau—to the ship. I sensed the solemnity of the parting. At the wharf, he kissed Mother's hand, it took somewhat longer than usual, but no one wept. Then we boarded the ship and stood at the railing, the ropes were untied; Herr Professor stood there, his hat in his hand and moving his lips. Slowly the ship eased away, but I could still see his lips moving. In my hatred, I thought I could make out the words he was saying: "I kiss your hand, dear Madame." Then Herr Professor got smaller, his hat went up and down in an elegant curve, his beard stayed pitch-black, it didn't shrink, now the hat solemnly remained at the level of his head, though a bit away from him, hovering aloft. I didn't look around, I only saw the hat, and I saw the beard, and more and more water separating us from them. I kept staring motionlessly until the beard had grown so small that only I could have recognized it. Then suddenly, he vanished, Herr Professor, the hat and the beard, and I saw the towers of Lindau, which I hadn't noticed before. Now I turned to Mother, I was afraid she would cry, but she didn't cry, we fell into each other's arms, we lay in each other's arms, she ran her fingers through my hair, something she normally didn't do, and she said more mellowly than I had ever heard her speak: "Now, everything's fine. Now, everything's fine." She said it so often that I did start crying after all, even though I didn't have the least desire to cry. For the bane of our life, the black beard, was gone and gone under. I suddenly tore away from her and began dancing around on the deck, running back to her and tearing away once more, and how gladly would I have launched into a chant of triumph, but I knew only the war songs and victory songs, which I didn't like.

That was my mood when I stepped upon Swiss soil.

Part Four

Zurich—
Scheuchzerstrasse
1916–1919

The Oath

In Zurich, we moved into two rooms on the third floor at 68 *Scheuchzerstrasse*, a house belonging to an elderly spinster who took in roomers.

She had a large, bony face, and her name was Helene Vogler. She liked saying her name; even when we knew it quite well, she often told us children what her name was. She always added that she came from a good family, her father having been a music director. She had several brothers; one, who was utterly impoverished and had nothing to eat, came to clean her home. He was older than she, a quiet, slender man, who, much to our surprise, did her housework; we saw him kneeling on the floor or standing with the floor polisher. This was an important instrument, we made its acquaintance here, and the parquet floors were so shiny that we could see our reflections in them. Fräulein Vogler was no less proud of their condition than of her name. She often gave orders to her impoverished brother; sometimes he had to break off what he had only just started because something more important occurred to her. She always thought about what else he could do and was constantly worried that she had neglected something important. He did everything as she told him to do, he never uttered a word of protest. We had taken over Mother's opinion that it was undignified for a man to do such housework, and at his age to boot. "When I see that," she said, shaking her head, "I'd almost rather do it myself. That old man!"

But once, when Mother alluded to it, Fräulein Vogler waxed indignant. "It's his own fault! He's done everything badly in his life. Now his own sister has to be ashamed of him." He was paid nothing by her, but when he had finished his work, he got food. He showed up once a week, and Fräulein Vogler said: "He has a meal once a week." She had a hard time herself, she added, and was forced to take in roomers. That was true, she really had no easy life. But she did have *one* brother she was proud of. He was a head conductor like their father. Whenever he came to Zurich, he stayed at the Hotel Krone on Limmat Quai. She felt very honored when he visited her, often he didn't come for a long time, but she read his name in the papers and knew he was doing well. Once, when I came home from school, she received me with a red face, saying: "My brother is here, the head conductor." He sat quiet and corpulent at the table in the kitchen, as well fed as his brother was shrunken; she had cooked liver with home fries for him, and he too ate alone, while Fräulein Vogler served him. The poor brother would murmur if ever he uttered anything, the corpulent brother didn't talk much either, but whatever he did say came loud and clear; he was quite cognizant of the honor he was paying his sister with his visit and he didn't stay long. The instant he was done eating, he stood up, nodded at us children almost imperceptibly, gave his sister a very terse goodbye, and left her home.

She was a good-natured creature, although crotchety. She watched her furniture with Argus' eyes. Several times a day, she would lament to us in her Swiss German: "Don't make any scratches on my chairs!" If she went out, which seldom happened, we would reiterate her lament in chorus, but we were careful with her chairs, which she checked for new scratches the very instant she came home.

She had a soft spot for artists and mentioned with satisfaction that our rooms had previously been occupied by a Danish writer and his wife and child. She pronounced his name, Aage Madelung, as emphatically as her own. He had written, she said, out on the balcony, which faced *Scheuchzerstrasse*, and he had observed the coming and going below: he had noticed each person and quizzed her about him or her. Within a week, he had known more about the people than she in all the many years she'd been living here. He had given her a novel she said, *Circus Man*, with a dedication; she hadn't understood it, alas. Too bad she hadn't known Herr Aage Madelung when she was younger, her head had been so much better then.

For two or three months, while Mother was looking for a bigger apartment, we stayed with Fräulein Vogler. Grandmother Arditti and her daughter Ernestine, an elder sister of Mother's, lived a few minutes away from us on *Ottikerstrasse*. Every evening, when we children had gone to bed, they came by. One night, seeing the shimmer of light from the living room as I lay in bed, I heard a conversation in Ladino between the three of them; they were fairly intense, and Mother sounded agitated. I got up, sneaked over to the door, and peered through the keyhole: indeed, Grandmother and Aunt Ernestine were still sitting there and talking fast; they, especially Aunt Ernestine, were trying to talk my mother into something. They were advising her to do something that would be best for her, and she seemed totally uninterested in this best. I couldn't understand what it was all about, but some disquiet told me that it could well be the very thing that I feared most, but had thought averted since our arrival in Switzerland. When mother vehemently cried out: "*Ma no lo quiero casar!* But I don't want to marry him!" I knew that my fears had not deceived me. I flung open the door and suddenly stood among the women in my nightshirt. "*I* don't want it!" I angrily shrieked, facing my grandmother. "*I* don't want it! I hurled myself towards Mother and grabbed her so violently that she said, very softly: "You're hurting me." But I wouldn't let go. Grandmother, whom I had always known as mild and feeble—I had never heard anything of any impact from her—said angrily: "Why aren't you asleep? Aren't you ashamed to be eavesdropping at the door?"

"No, I'm not ashamed! You're trying to talk Mother into something! I'm not asleep. I know what you people want. I'll *never* sleep!"

My aunt, who was most at fault, having talked away so obstinately at my mother, kept silent and looked daggers at me. Mother said tenderly: "You've come to protect me. You're my knight. Now I hope you two understand," she turned to them: "*He* doesn't want me to. And I don't want to either."

I wouldn't budge from the spot until the two enemies stood up and left. I still wasn't pacified, for I threatened: "If they come again, I'll never go to sleep. I'll stay up all night so that you won't let them in. If you get married, I'll jump off the balcony!" It was a terrible threat, it was meant in earnest; I know with absolute certainty that I would have done it.

Mother couldn't manage to quiet me down that night. I didn't go back to my bed, neither of us slept. She tried to distract me with stories. My aunt had had a very unhappy marriage and had soon separated from her husband. He suffered from a horrible disease and had gone mad. He had sometimes come to visit us in Vienna. An attendant had brought him to *Josef-Gall-Gasse*. "Here's some candy for the kids," he said to Mother, handing her a large bag of bonbons. When he wanted to speak to us, he always looked in another direction, his eyes gaped and were fixed on the door. His voice kept cracking and sounded like a donkey's braying. He only stayed briefly; the attendant took his arm and pulled him out into the vestibule and then out of the apartment.

"She would like me not to be as unhappy as she is. She means well. She doesn't know any better."

"So she wants you to marry too and be unhappy! *She* saved herself from her husband, and you're supposed to *marry*!" That last word was like a stab, and I pushed the dagger deeper and deeper into me. It hadn't been such a felicitous idea telling me *that* story. But there was no story whatsoever that could have calmed me down; Mother tried so many. Finally, she *swore* that she wouldn't allow the two women to discuss the matter anymore, and if they didn't stop she wouldn't see them again. She had to swear that not just once, but over and over. It was only when she swore by my father's memory that something inside me relaxed, and I started to believe her.

A Roomful of Presents

School was a terrible problem. It was all different from Vienna; the school year didn't begin in the fall, it began in spring. Elementary school, which was called primary school here, had six grades; in Vienna, I had entered the *Realgymnasium* directly from the fourth grade, and since I had already done one year there I really belonged in the second year of the higher school. But all attempts at getting me into it failed. The authorities rigorously stuck to my age; wherever I appeared with Mother, who asked them to accept me on that level, we received the same answer. The thought of my losing a year or more by moving to Switzerland went strongly against her grain, she just wouldn't put up with it. We tried everywhere, once we even traveled to Bern. The answer was terse and most likely the same; since it was given without a "dear Madame" or other Viennese cordialities, it struck us as gross, and when we left such a school principal again Mother was in despair: "Won't you at least test him?" she had pleaded. "He's advanced for his age." But that was the very thing they didn't like to hear: "We make no exceptions."

So she had to make the most difficult decision. Swallowing her pride, she entered me in the sixth grade of the primary school at Oberstrass. It would be over in six months and then they would see whether I was ready for the canton school. Once again, I found myself in a big elementary-school class, and I felt I'd been demoted back to Herr Tegel in Vienna, only here his name was Herr Bachmann. There was nothing to learn—in Vienna I had been two years further. But I experienced something more important, although its significance didn't strike me until later on.

The other pupils were called on by the teacher in Swiss German, and one of these names sounded so enigmatic, that I always looked forward to hearing it again. "Sägerich," with a drawled-out *ä* appeared to be a formation like *Gänserich* (gander) or *Enterich* (drake), but there couldn't be a male for *Säge*, a saw; I couldn't account for the word. Herr Bachmann was enchanted with this name; the boy excelled in neither intelligence nor stupidity, but he called on him far more frequently than all the others. That was just about the only thing I heeded in class, and since my mania for counting was now increasing again, I counted up the number of times Sägerich was called on. Herr Bachmann had a lot of trouble with the pupils, who were dense and mulish, and after getting no answer from five or six of them in a row, he turned expectantly to Sägerich. This boy would stand up, and usually knew nothing either. But he stood broad and powerful, with an encouraging grin and tousled hair; the color of his face was slightly reddish, like that of Herr Bachmann, who enjoyed drinking, and if Sägerich so much as answered, Herr Bachmann would breathe a sigh of relief as though having taken a good draught, and pulled the class along some more.

It took a while for me to realize that the boy's name was *Segenreich*, rich in blessings, and that increased the impact of *Sägerich*, for the prayers I had learned in Vienna all began "*gesegnet seist du, Herr*" (blessed art thou, Lord), and although they had meant little to me, the fact that a boy had "blessing" (*Segen*) in his name and was "rich" in blessings to boot had something wondrous about it. Herr Bachmann, who had a hard life both in school and at home, clung to this and kept calling upon the boy for assistance.

The other pupils spoke only the Zurich dialect of Swiss German among themselves; the instruction in this highest grade of the primary school was in standard German, but Herr Bachmann—and not only when calling names—lapsed into the dialect, in which he, like all the pupils, was fluent, and so it was par for the course that I gradually learned it too. I felt no resistance towards it whatsoever, although I was amazed by it. Perhaps that was because the war hardly ever came up during classroom discussions. In Vienna, my best friend Max Schiebl played with soldiers every day. I had played along because I liked him, but especially because that way I could see his beautiful mother every afternoon. I went into the tin-soldier war every day for Schiebl's mother; for her I would have gone into the real war. At school, however, the war had pretty much covered everything. I had learned how to ward off the thoughtless gross words of some of the other pupils; but I joined in every day when the songs about the Kaiser and the war were sung, despite my growing resistance; there were only two of them, very sad ones, that I like singing. In Zurich, the many words referring to war had not penetrated the language of my fellow pupils. Boring as the classes may have been for me, since I learned nothing new, I nevertheless liked the energetic and unadorned sentences of the Swiss boys. I myself rarely spoke to them, but I listened eagerly, venturing to throw in a sentence only every so often, so long as it was a sentence that I could already pronounce like them, without it striking them as too odd. I soon gave up producing such sentences at home. Mother, watching over the purity of our language and tolerating only languages with a literature, was concerned that I might corrupt my "pure" German, and when, in my eagerness, I tried to defend the dialect, which I liked, she grew angry and said: "I didn't bring you to Switzerland so that you'd forget what I told you about the *Burgtheater!* Do you want to end up talking like Fräulein Vogler?" That was a sharp stab, for we found Fräulein Vogler comical. But I also felt how unfair that was, for my fellow pupils spoke altogether differently from Fräulein Vogler. I practiced Zurich German for myself alone, against my mother's will, concealing from her the progress I was making. That, so far as language went, was my first independent move from her, and although still subjugated to her in all opinions and influences, I began feeling like a "man" in this one thing.

But I was still too rocky in the new language to really make friends with Swiss boys. I hung out with a boy who had come from Vienna, like myself, and a second one whose mother was Viennese. On her birthday, Rudi invited me over, and I came into a circle of rollicking people, who were far more alien to me than anything I had ever heard in Swiss German. Rudi's mother, a young blond woman, lived alone with him, but many men of different ages were present at the birthday party, all of them flattering the mother, clinking glasses to her health, gazing tenderly into her eyes; it was as though Rudi had lots of fathers, but the mother, slightly tipsy, had lamented upon my arrival that I too had no father. She turned now to one guest, now to another, she turned to all sides like a flower in the wind. She alternately laughed and got weepy, and while wiping her tears away she was already laughing again. The company was loud, comical speeches were given in her honor, but I didn't understand them. I was very dazed when such a speech was interrupted by uproarious mirth, and Rudi's mother— groundlessly, I thought—gazed at her son and dismally said: "Poor boy, he has no father."

There was not a single woman at the party; never had I seen so many men alone with one woman, and all of them were thankful for something and paid homage to her, but she didn't seem all that happy about it, for she wept more than she laughed. She spoke with a Viennese intonation. Some of the men, as I soon realized, were Swiss, but none of them lapsed into the dialect; all speeches were given in standard German. One or the other of the men got up, strode over to her with his glass, clinked it, uttering a poignant line, and gave her a kiss for her birthday. Rudi took me to another room and showed me the presents his mother had gotten. The whole room was filled with presents; I didn't have the nerve to really look at them because I hadn't brought anything myself. When I rejoined the guests, she called me over and said: "How do you like my presents?" Stuttering, I apologized for not bringing her a present. But she laughed, pulled me over and kissed me, and said: "You're a darling boy. You don't need a present. When you're big, you'll visit me and bring me a present. Then nobody will visit me anymore." And she started crying again.

At home, I was questioned about this party. It didn't soften Mother any that the woman was Viennese and that everyone at the party had spoken a "good" German. She struck a very earnest tone, even using the weighty form of address "my son," and explained that the guests were nothing but "silly" people, who were not worthy of me. I was never to go to that place again. She pitied Rudi, she said, having a mother like that. Not every woman was capable of bringing up a child alone, and what could I think of a woman who laughed and cried at once.

"Maybe she's sick," I said.

"Sick?" was the prompt and angry retort.

"Maybe she's crazy?"

"What about all those presents? The room full of presents?"

At the time, I didn't know what Mother meant, but for me too, the room with the gifts had been the most unpleasant thing of all. You couldn't move around in it freely, there were too many gifts, and if Rudi's mother hadn't gotten me through my embarrassment so helpfully and tenderly, I wouldn't have tried to defend her, for I didn't care for her one bit.

"She's not sick. She has no character. That's all." That was the final verdict, for character was all that mattered, anything else was negligible compared to that. "You mustn't let Rudi catch on. He's a poor boy. No father and a mother with no character! What's to become of him?"

I suggested bringing him home occasionally, so that she could do something for him. "That won't do any good," she said, "he'll only make fun of our modest way of living."

We already had our own apartment by then, and it really was modest. It was in this Zurich period that Mother kept making it clear to me that we had to live very simply in order to make both ends meet. Maybe it was an educational principle for her, because, as I know today, she certainly wasn't poor. On the contrary, her money was well placed with her brother, his business in Manchester was as flourishing as ever; he was getting richer and richer. He regarded her as his protégée, she admired him, and he would never have dreamt of taking advantage of her. But the difficulties of wartime in Vienna, when direct communication with England was impossible, had left traces in her. She wanted to give all three of us a good education, and this included not getting accustomed to the availability of money. She kept us very short, the cooking was plain. She had no maid, after an experience that unsettled her. She did the housework herself, remarking from time to time that she was making a sacrifice for us, since she had been raised in different circumstances; and when I thought of the life we had led in Vienna, the difference seemed so great that I had to believe in the necessity of such restrictions.

However, I also preferred this kind of puritanical life. It fitted in better with my notions of the Swiss. In Vienna, everything revolved around the imperial family, and from there it went down to the nobility and the other grand families. Switzerland had neither an emperor nor an imperial aristocracy, I imagined—I don't know what prompted me— that wealth wasn't popular either. But I *was* quite certain that every human being mattered, that each one counted. I had made this conception my own with all my heart and soul, and thus only a simple life-style was possible. At that time, I didn't admit to myself the advantages this life-style brought me. For actually, we now had Mother all to ourselves, everything in the new apartment was entwined with her, no one stood between us, and she was never out of our sight. It was an intimate togetherness of wonderful warmth and density. All intellectual matters were preponderant, books and conversations about books were the heart of our existence. Whenever Mother went to plays or lectures or concerts, I participated as fully as if I had attended them myself. Now and then, not very often, she took me along, but I was usually disappointed, for her accounts of such experiences were always a lot more interesting.

Espionage

The apartment we lived in was a small place on the third floor of 73 *Scheuchzerstrasse*. I can only recall three rooms in which we moved; but there must have been a fourth and smaller room, since we once briefly had a maid.

We had a hard time with maids, however. Mother couldn't get used to there not being maids here as in Vienna. A maid was called a "house daughter" and ate at the same table with her employers. That was the first condition that a girl stated upon coming in. Mother, in her high-handed way, found that unbearable. She had always treated her maids well in Vienna, she said, but they lived in their own room, which we never entered, and they ate by themselves in the kitchen. "Dear Madame" was the normal way to address one's employer in Vienna. Here, in Zurich, that was gone, and Mother, who liked Switzerland because of its attitude, could not resign herself to the democratic ways, which reached to the very heart of her household. She tried speaking English at the table, rationalizing it to Hedi, the "house daughter," by saying that the two little brothers were gradually forgetting it. It was necessary, Mother said, to at least refresh their knowledge during meals. That *was* true, but it was also a pretext for leaving the "house daughter" out of our conversations. She was silent upon hearing the reason, but she didn't seem offended. She was silent for a couple of days, but how amazed was Mother when, at lunchtime, Hedi corrected a mistake that George, the youngest, had made in an English sentence. Mother had let the mistake pass, but Hedi *corrected* it with an innocent expression.

"How do you know that?" Mother asked, almost indignant. "Do you know English?"

Hedi had had it at school and understood everything we said.

"She's a spy!" Mother said to me, later on. "She's infiltrated our home! There's no such thing as a maid knowing English! Why didn't she tell us earlier? She's been eavesdropping on us, that awful creature! I will not let my children sit at the same table as a spy!"

And now she remembered that Hedi hadn't come to us alone. She had shown up with a gentleman, who had introduced himself as her father and had scrutinized us and the apartment, inquiring very thoroughly about his daughter's working conditions. "I could tell right away he wasn't her father. He seemed like someone from a good family. He interrogated me as though *I* were looking for work! *I* couldn't have asked more rigorous questions in his place. But he was no housemaid's father. They've planted a spy in our home."

Now there was absolutely nothing to spy on in our apartment, but that didn't bother her, she ascribed an importance to us that would have justified espionage. Cautiously, she took counter-measures. "We can't dismiss her right away, that would look funny. We have to endure her for two more weeks. But we've got to be on our guard. We mustn't say anything against Switzerland, otherwise she'll have us deported."

It didn't occur to Mother that none of us ever said anything against Switzerland. On the contrary: When I told her about school, she was always full of praise, and the only thing she resented in Switzerland was the institution of the "house daughter." I liked Hedi because she wasn't toadyish; she came from Glarus, which had beaten the Haps-

burgs in battle, and she sometimes read my Swiss history book by
Öchsli. And though I was always won over whenever Mother said
"we"—"we have to do this" or "we have to do that," as though I were
drawn into her decisions with equal rights—I made a stab at saving the
situation, and a very cunning stab at that, for I knew how to bribe
Mother: only with intellectual things. "But you know," I said, "she
really likes to read my books. She always asks me what I'm reading.
She also borrows books from me and discusses them with me."

Thereupon, Mother made a very serious face. "My poor boy! Why
didn't you tell me that? You're just not very sophisticated yet. But you
will be." She lapsed into silence and let me writhe a bit. I was alarmed
and nagged: "What is it? What is it?" It had to be something quite
horrible, I couldn't hit upon it. Perhaps it was so bad that she would
never tell me at all. But now she gave me a superior and pitying look,
and I sensed it was about to come out. "She's simply supposed to
discover what I give you to read. Don't you understand? That's why
she was sent into our home. A genuine spy! She's got secrets with a
twelve-year-old and pokes her nose around in his books. She doesn't
let on that she knows English, and she's probably read all our letters
from England!"

Now, to my terror, I recalled seeing Hedi with an English letter in
her hand in the middle of house-cleaning; she had quickly put it away
when I approached. I reported this conscientiously now and was solemnly exhorted. I could tell Mother's solemn intent by the fact that
she began with "my son": "My son, you must tell me everything. You
may think something's not important, but everything is important."

That was the final verdict. For fourteen more days, the poor girl sat
at our table, practicing her English with us. "How innocent she acts!"
Mother told me after each meal. "But *I* saw through her! You can't
pull the wool over *my* eyes!" Hedi kept reading my Öchsli and even
asked what I thought about this or that. Now and then, she had me
explain something and then said, earnest and friendly: "My, you're
smart." I would have liked to warn her, I would have liked to say:
"Please, don't be a spy!" But it wouldn't have helped, Mother was
firmly resolved to dismiss her, and rationalized it after fourteen days
by saying that our material situation had unexpectedly worsened, she
could no longer afford to keep a house daughter. Could she please
write to her father and explain, so that he would come and fetch her.
He did and was no less stern and said, upon leaving: "Now you'll have
to work a bit yourself, Frau Canetti."

Maybe he was gleeful that we were worse off now. Maybe he disapproved of women who don't do their own housekeeping. Mother saw

it differently. "I certainly upset *his* apple-cart! Was he ever furious! As if there were anything to spy on in our home! Naturally, there's a war on and they read the mail. They've noticed we get a lot of letters from England. Bang, they saddle us with a spy. You know, I do understand. They're all alone in the world and they have to protect themselves against the murderers."

She often spoke of how difficult it was to be all alone in the world with three children. How attentive one must be to everything! Now that she had gotten rid of the house daughter and spy at one swoop and felt greatly relieved, she projected that militant sense of loneliness, which has to be defended in such difficulties, onto Switzerland, encircled by belligerent countries and fiercely determined not to be dragged into the war.

Now, the loveliest time began for us: We were alone with Mother. She was ready to pay the price for her arrogance and she did something she had never done in her life: the housework. She cleaned, she cooked, the little brothers helped with drying the dishes. I took over the chore of shoe-shining, and since my brothers watched in the kitchen in order to make fun of me ("Shoeshine boy! Shoeshine boy!" they wooped and danced around me like Indians), I retreated to the kitchen balcony with the dirty shoes, closed the door, and leaned my back against it as I polished the family's shoes. I was thus alone at this occupation and didn't see the war dance of the two devils, but their chanting could be heard even through the closed door of the balcony.

Seduction by the Greeks
The School of Sophistication

In spring 1917, I began the canton school on *Rämistrasse*. The daily walk to and fro became very important. At the start, right after crossing *Ottikerstrasse*, I always ran into the same gentleman strolling there, and the regular encounters lodged in my mind. He had a very lovely white head of hair, walked erect and absent-mindedly; he walked a short piece, halted, looked around for something, and changed his direction. He had a St. Bernard dog, which he often called to: "Dschoddo, come to Papa!" Sometimes the St. Bernard came, sometimes it ran further away; that was what Papa was looking for. But no sooner had he found it than he forgot it again and was as absent-minded as before. His appearance in this fairly ordinary street had something exotic about it, his frequent call made children laugh, but they didn't laugh in his presence for he had something commanding respect as he peered straight ahead, tall and proud and not noticing anyone; they laughed only when they came home, telling about him, or when they played with each other in the street and he was gone. It was Busoni, who lived right there in a corner house; and his dog, as I found out only much later, was named Giotto. All the children in the neighborhood talked about him, but not as Busoni, for they knew nothing about him, they called him "Dschoddo-come-to-Papa!" They were entranced with the St. Bernard, and even more with the fact that the handsome old gentle-man referred to himself as the dog's Papa.

During the twenty-minute walk to and from school, I made up long stories, which were continued from day to day and went on for weeks. I told them to myself, not too loud, but still in an audible murmur, which I suppressed only when I ran into people who made an unpleas-ant impression on me. I knew the way so well that I paid no attention to anything around me, neither right nor left was there anything special to see, but there *was* something special in my story. The action was very exciting, and if the adventures were so suspenseful and unexpected that I couldn't keep them to myself, I would subsequently tell them to my little brothers, who nagged me for the next installment. All these stories were about the war, or more precisely: about overcoming war. The countries that wanted war had to be taught a lesson: namely, they had to be conquered over and over again until they gave up war. Goaded by heroes of peace, the other countries, the good ones, formed an alliance, and they were so much better that they ultimately won. But it wasn't easy, there were endless hard, bitter struggles, with more and more new inventions, unheard-of cunning. The most important thing about these battles was that the dead always came back to life. There were special charms that were invented and employed for that, and it made no small impact on my brothers—who were six and eight years old—when suddenly, all the corpses, even those of the bad party, which refused to stop the warfare, arose from the battle field and were alive once more. That ending was the point of all the stories, and whatever happened during the adventurous weeks of fighting—the triumph and the glory, the actual reward of the storyteller, was the moment when all, without exception, stood up again and had their lives back.

The first class in my school was big; I didn't know anyone, and it was natural that my thoughts initially gravitated to the few school-mates whose interests were related to mine. And if they actually mas-tered anything that I lacked, I admired them and never let them out of sight. Ganzhorn excelled in Latin, and although I had a big head start from Vienna, he was able to compete with me. But that was the very least: He was the only one who knew the Greek alphabet. He had learned it on his own, and since he wrote a great deal—regarding himself as a poet—the Greek letters became his secret code. He filled notebook after notebook, and when one was finished, he handed it to me; I leafed through it, unable to read a single word. He didn't let me hold it for long; scarcely had I expressed my admiration for his ability when he took the notebook back and with incredible speed he began a new one right before my eyes. As for Greek history, he was no less enthusiastic than I. Eugen Müller, who taught us that subject, was a wonderful teacher, but while I was concerned with the freedom of the Greeks, Ganzhorn cared only about their great writers. His ignorance of the language was something he didn't like to admit. Perhaps he had already begun studying it on his own, for we spoke about the fact that our ways would part as of the third year—he wanted to attend the literary *Gymnasium*—and when I said, respectfully and a bit enviously, "Then you'll have Greek!", he arrogantly declared: "I'll know it beforehand." I believed him, he was no braggart; he always carried out anything he announced, and he did a lot of things he hadn't announced. In his scorn for anything ordinary, he reminded me of the attitude that I was familar with at home. But he never put it into words; if the conversation touched upon anything that seemed unworthy of a great writer, he turned away and lapsed into silence. His head, long and narrow, as though squeezed together, held very high and at an angle, would then have something of an open penknife, which, however, stayed open, it wouldn't close; Ganzhorn was not capable of a mean or nasty word. In the midst of the class, he seemed sharply separated from it. No one who copied from him felt comfortable about it, he always pretended not to notice, never pushing his notebook over, or pulling it away; since he disapproved of cheating, he left every detail of the action to the other person.

When we found out about Socrates, the class had fun nicknaming me Socrates, thereby perhaps unburdening itself of the seriousness of his fate. This happened casually and with no deeper significance, but it stuck, and the joke got on Ganzhorn's nerves. For a whole while, I saw him busy writing, sometimes giving me a searching look and solemnly shaking his head. A week later, he had completed another notebook, but this time he said he wanted to read it to me. It was a dialogue between a poet and a philosopher. The poet was named Cornutotum, literally "whole horn," that was Ganzhorn himself, he liked translating his name into Latin; the philosopher was I. He had read my name backwards, hitting upon the two ugly words Saile Ittenacus. The latter was nothing like Socrates, just a run-of-the-mill sophist, one of those people whom Socrates had picked on. But that was only a side issue of the dialogue; the more important fact was that the poet harshly browbeat the poor philosopher on all sides, finally chopping him to bits, nothing was left of him. And that was what Ganzhorn, certain of victory, read to me; I wasn't the least bit offended. Because of the reversal of my name, I didn't apply it to myself; had he used my own name, I would have been touchier. I was glad that he was reading one of his notebooks to me. I felt elevated, as though he had initiated me into his Greek mysteries. Nothing changed between us, and after a while, when he asked me—timidly for him—whether I wasn't planning to write a counter-dialogue, I was sincerely amazed: He was right, after all; I was on his side—what was a philosopher next to a poet anyway? I wouldn't have had an inkling of what to write in a counter-dialogue.

Ludwig Ellenbogen impressed me in a totally different way. He came from Vienna with his mother, and he too had no father. Wilhelm Ellenbogen was a member of the Austrian parliament, a renowned orator; I had often heard his name in Vienna. When I asked the boy about him, I was struck with his calm way of saying: "That's my uncle." He sounded as if he didn't care one way or another. I soon realized he was like that about everything, he seemed more grown-up than I, not just taller, for pretty much all of them were taller. He was interested in things I knew nothing about; you found out by chance and casually, for he never boasted, he always kept aloof, without pride or false modesty, as though his ambition were not within the class. He was by no means reticent, he was open to any conversation; he merely didn't like coming out with *his* things, perhaps because none of us knew anything about them. He had special short talks with our Latin teacher, Billeter, who was different from the other teachers, not only because of his goiter; they read the same books, told each other the titles, which none of us had ever heard of, they discussed the books, expressed their opinions, and often felt the same way about them. Ellenbogen spoke quietly and matter-ox-factly, without boyish emotions; it was really Billeter who acted capriciously. If such a conversation began, the entire class listened uncomprehendingly, no one had the foggiest notion of what was being discussed. At the end, Ellenbogen was as imperturbable as at the start, but Billeter showed a certain satisfaction about such talks; and he respected Ellenbogen, who didn't care what they were learning in school at that point. I was sure that Ellenbogen knew everything anyhow, I actually didn't count him among the other boys. I liked him, but in a way that I would have liked him as an adult; and I was a bit embarrassed with him that I was so vehemently interested

in certain things, especially all the things we learned from Eugen
Müller in history class.

For the really new thing that first grabbed hold of me at this school
was Greek history. We had Öchsli's history books, one on general and
one on Swiss history, I went through both of them immediately, and
they followed each other in such rapid succession that they blended
together for me. The freedom of the Swiss fell together with that of
the Greeks. Starting all over again, I read now one and now the other
book. The sacrifice of the Thermopylae was made up for by the victory
at Morgarten. I experienced the freedom of the Swiss as present and
felt it in myself; because *they* had self-determination, because they were
not ruled by an emperor, they had managed not to get drawn into the
world war. I felt queasy about emperors as commanders-in-chief. Kaiser Franz Joseph wasn't much on my mind, he was very old and said
little when coming forward, usually a single sentence; next to my
grandfather, he seemed lifeless and dull. Every day, we had sung the
Austrian national anthem, asking God to preserve and protect our
Kaiser; he appeared to need this protection. While singing, I never
looked at his portrait, which hung on the wall behind the teacher's
desk, and I tried not to imagine him. Maybe I had absorbed some
dislike of him from Fanny, our Bohemian maid; she never batted an
eyelash when he was mentioned, as though he didn't exist for her, and
once, when I came home from school, she had scornfully asked: "Didja
sing for Kaiser again?"

But as for Wilhelm, the German kaiser, I saw pictures of him in
shining armor, and I also heard his blasts against England. When
England was at stake, I was always her partisan, and after everything
I had absorbed in Manchester, I was of the unshakable opinion that
the British did not want a war and that it was the German kaiser who
had started it by invading Belgium. Nor was I any less biased against
the Russian Tsar. At ten, while visiting Bulgaria, I had heard the name
Tolstoy, and I was told he was a wonderful man who regarded war as
murder and had never been afraid to say so to his emperors. Although
he'd been dead for several years, people spoke of him as though he
hadn't really died. Now, for the first time, I found myself in a republic,
far from any imperial doings, and I eagerly plunged into its history.
It was possible to get rid of an emperor, you had to *fight* for your
freedom. Long before the Swiss, much, much earlier, the Greeks had
successfully risen against a tremendous superior power, maintaining
the freedom that they had already won.

It sounds terribly vapid to me when I say that now, for back then I
was intoxicated with this new realization, I pounced on everyone with

it, and I devised barbaric tunes to the names of Marathon and Salamis, and kept vehemently chanting them at home, a thousand times over, just to the three syllables of those names, until Mother and my brothers said their heads were buzzing and they forced me to stop. Professor Eugen Müller's history lessons had the same effect each time. He spoke to us about the Greeks, his big wide-open eyes seemed like those of an intoxicated seer; he didn't even look at us, he looked at what he was talking about. His speech wasn't fast, but it never stopped, it had the rhythm of sluggish waves; whether the fighting was on land or at sea, you always felt you were out on the ocean. He ran his fingertips over his forehead, which was covered with a light sweat; less frequently, he stroked his curly hair as though a wind were puffing across it. The hour waned in his sips of enthusiasm; if he took a breath for new enthusiasm, it was as if he were drinking.

But occasionally, time was wasted, namely when he quizzed us. He had us write essays and discussed them with us. Then we were sorry for every moment that he might otherwise have taken us out on the ocean. Often, I raised my hand to answer his questions, if for no other reason than to get them over with fast, but also to show him my love for each one of his sentences. My words may have sounded like part of his own excitement, annoying my classmates, some of whom were slower. They didn't come from an empire, Greek freedom couldn't mean much to them. They took freedom for granted and didn't first have to be won over by way of the Greeks as proxies.

At this point, I was absorbing as much at school as normally through books. Whatever I learned through the living words of a teacher retained the shape of that teacher and was always linked to his shape in my memory. But while there were some teachers from whom I learned nothing, they nevertheless did make an impact through their own selves, their peculiar appearance, their movements, their way of speaking, and especially their like or dislike of you, the way you happened to feel it. There were all degrees of warmth and benevolence, and I do not recall a single teacher who did not strive to be fair. But not all of them succeeded in handling fairness effectively enough to hide dislike or benevolence. Then there were the differences in inner resources—patience, sensitivity, expectation. Eugen Müller, by his very subject, was obligated to a high measure of ardor and narrative talent, but he brought something along that went far beyond this obligation. So I was entranced by him from the very start and counted the days of the week by his lessons.

Fritz Hunziker, the German teacher, had a harder time; he was somewhat dry by nature, perhaps also hampered by his not very clear stature, whose effect was not improved by his slightly strident voice. He was tall, with a narrow chest, and stood as though on one long leg; he lapsed into patient silence when waiting for an answer. He never attacked anyone, but he also never probed into anyone either, his shield was a sarcastic smirk, to which he held fast; it was often still there even when it no longer seemed apt. His knowledge was balanced, perhaps overly categorized; we weren't swept off our feet by him, but he didn't lead us astray either. His sense of moderation and practical behavior was highly developed. He didn't care much for precociousness or over-enthusiasm. I saw him—and this wasn't so unjust—as Eugen Müller's antipode. Later, when Hunziker returned after a period of absence, I noticed how well-read he was, but his wide reading lacked arbitrariness and excitement.

Gustav Billeter, the Latin teacher, had a lot more individual peculiarity. His courage in facing the class day after day with his gigantic goiter fills me with admiration even today. He preferred staying in the left-hand corner of the classroom, turning the less apparent side of his goiter towards us, and keeping his left foot on a stool. He would then speak fluently, gently, and rather softly, with no excess excitement; if ever he grew angry, for which he sometimes had reasons, he never raised his voice, he only spoke somewhat faster. Elementary Latin, which he taught, must have bored him, and perhaps that was why he always acted so human. No one who knew little could feel pressured, much less destroyed, by him, and those who were good in Latin didn't feel particularly important. His reactions could never be predicted, but you didn't have to fear them either. A soft and brief ironical comment was really all he ever made to anyone, you didn't always understand it, it was like a private witty remark which he made to himself. He devoured books, but I never heard anything about those he was occupied with, so I didn't note a single title. Ellenbogen, whom he liked and enjoyed talking to, had—without his irony—the same superior unemotional way, and he did not overestimate the importance of the Latin that we learned from him. Billeter felt that my head start over the class was unfair, and he once told me as much very clearly: "You're quicker than the others, the Swiss develop more slowly. But then they catch up. You'll be amazed later on." Yet he was by no means xenophobic, as I could see by his friendship with Ellenbogen. I sensed that Billeter was very open to people, his attitude was cosmopolitan, and I believe that he probably also wrote—not just for himself.

The variety among the teachers was astonishing; it is the first variety one is conscious of in life. Their standing so long in front of you, exposed in all their emotions, incessantly observed, the actual focus of interest hour after hour, and—since you cannot leave—always for the same, precisely demarcated time; their superiority, which you refuse to acknowledge once and for all, and which makes you keen-sighted and critical and malicious; the necessity of getting at them without making it too hard for yourself, for you still haven't become a devoted, exclusive worker; even the mystery of their outside life, throughout the time that they don't stand there in front of you, acting themselves; and then the alternation of their appearances, each one in turn appearing before you, in the same place, in the same role, with the same goal, thus eminently comparable—all those things, working together, form a very different school from the declared one, a school for the variety of human beings; and, if you take it halfway seriously, the first conscious school for the knowledge of human nature.

It would not be difficult, and it might be interesting, to scrutinize one's later life in terms of which and how many of these teachers were encountered again under different names, which people were liked because of that, which people were dropped only because of an old grudge, which decisions were made because of such early knowledge, what would probably have been done differently without that knowledge. The early childhood typology, which is based on animals, and which always remains effective, is overlaid by a typology based on teachers. Every class has pupils who mimic the teachers particularly well and perform for their classmates; a class without such teacher-mimics would have something lifeless about it.

Now, as I let them pass before me, I am amazed at the variety, the peculiarity, the wealth of my Zurich teachers. I learned from many of them, as was their goal, and the gratitude I feel towards them after fifty years keeps growing from year to year, odd as it may sound. But even those from whom I learned little stand so clearly before me as people or as figures that I owe them something just for that. They were the first representatives of what I later took in as the intrinsic factor of the world, its population. They are non-interchangeable, one of the supreme qualities in the hierarchy; their having become figures as well takes nothing away from their personalities. The fluid boundary between individuals and types is a true concern of the real writer.

The Skull
Dispute with an Officer

I was twelve when I got passionately interested in the Greek wars of liberation, and that same year, 1917, was the year of the Russian Revolution. Even before his journey in the sealed freight car, people were speaking about Lenin living in Zurich. Mother, who was filled with an insatiable hatred of the war, followed every event that might terminate it. She had no political ties, but Zurich had become a center for war opponents of the most diverse countries and tendencies. Once, when we were passing a coffeehouse, she pointed at the enormous skull of a man sitting near the window, a huge pile of newspapers lay next to him; he had seized one paper and held it close to his eyes. Suddenly, he threw back his head, turned to a man sitting at his side and fiercely spoke away at him. Mother said: "Take a good look at him. That's Lenin. You'll be hearing about him." We had halted, she was slightly embarrassed about standing like that and staring (she would always reproach me for such impoliteness), but his sudden movement had struck into her, the energy of his jolting turn towards the other man had transmitted itself to her. I was amazed at the other man's rich, black, curly hair, which so glaringly contradicted Lenin's baldness right next to it; but I was even more astonished at Mother's immobility. She said: "Come on, we can't just stand here," and she pulled me along.

A few short months later, she told me about Lenin's arrival in Russia, and I began to understand that something important was happening. The Russians had had enough of the killing, she said, everyone had had enough of the killing, and soon it would be finished, whether with or against the governments. She never called the war anything but "the killing." Since our arrival in Zurich, she had talked about it very openly to me; in Vienna, she had held back to prevent my having any conflicts at school. "You will never kill a person who hasn't done anything to you," she said beseechingly; and proud as she was of having three sons, I could sense how worried she was that we too might become such "killers" some day. Her hatred of war had something elemental to it: Once, when telling me the story of *Faust*, which she didn't want me to read as yet, she disapproved of his pact with the devil. There was only *one* justification for such a pact: to put an end to war. You could even ally yourself with the devil for that, but not for anything else.

On some evenings, friends of Mother's gathered in our home, Bulgarian and Turkish Sephardim, whom the war had driven to Zurich. Most of them were married couples, who were middle-aged but seemed old to me; I didn't particularly like them, they were too Oriental for me and spoke only about uninteresting things.

One man came alone, a widower, Herr Adjubel; he was different from the others. He carried himself erect and had opinions that he advocated with conviction, and he calmly and chivalrously let Mother's vehemence, which afflicted him harshly, run off his back. He had fought in the Balkan War as a Bulgarian officer, had been seriously wounded, and left with an incurable ailment. People knew that he suffered awful pains, but he never so much as gave a hint. If the pains became unbearable, he would stand up, plead an urgent appointment, bow to Mother, and depart somewhat stiffly. Then the others would talk about him, discussing the nature of his sufferings in detail, praising and pitying him and doing the very thing that his pride wanted to avoid. I noticed that Mother made an effort to stop such conversations. She had been fighting with him until the very last moment, and since she could become very sharp and abusive in such debates, namely about war, she took everything upon herself and said: "Nonsense! He didn't have any pains. He was insulted by me. He thinks that a woman who hasn't gone through war has no right to talk about it. He's right. But if none of you tells him your opinion, then I have to do it. He was insulted. But he just happens to be proud and he took his leave in the most cordial way."

It could then happen that someone made an insolent joke and said: "You'll see, Mathilde. He's fallen in love with you and he's going to ask for your hand!"

"Just let him dare!" she promptly said with wrathful nostrils. "I wouldn't advise him to do so! I respect him because he's a *man*, but that's all." This was a nasty jab at the other men present, who were all here with their wives. But it ended the insufferable conversations about Herr Adjubel's sufferings.

I preferred him to stay till the last. From these arguments, I learned a lot of things that were new to me. Herr Adjubel was in a very difficult situation. He was devoted to the Bulgarian army, perhaps even more than to Bulgaria. He was filled with the traditional pro-Russian sentiments of the Bulgarians, who owed Russia their independence from the Turks. And he was now having a rough time of it because the Bulgarians were on the side of Russia's enemies. He would certainly have fought under these circumstances too, but with a tortured conscience, so perhaps it was good that he couldn't fight. Yet now the situation had gotten more complicated through the new turn of events in Russia. The fact that the Russians were leaving the war spelled, he thought, the destruction of the Central Powers. The infection, as he called it, would spread; first the Austrian and next the German soldiers would want to stop fighting. But then what would become of Bulgaria? Not only would they have to bear the mark of Cain—ingratitude—towards their liberators forever, but all the powers would pounce upon them as in the Second Balkan War and slice up the country among themselves. *Finis Bulgariae!*

One can imagine how Mother grabbed each point of his argument and tore it apart. Basically, she had everyone against her, for even though they welcomed a speedy end to the war, they regarded that end as a dangerous threat if brought by the activities of the Bolsheviks in Russia. They were all middle-class people, more or less well-to-do; those among them who came from Bulgaria feared that the revolution would spread there; those who came from Turkey saw the old Russian foe, albeit wearing a new garb, in Constantinople. Mother didn't care one way or another. All that mattered for her was who truly wanted to end the war. She, who came from one of the wealthiest families in Bulgaria, defended Lenin. She couldn't see a devil in him, as the others did, she saw a benefactor of mankind.

Herr Adjubel, with whom she actually fought, was the only one to understand her, for he had an opinion himself. He once asked her (it was the most dramatic moment of all these get-togethers): "And if I were a Russian officer, Madame, and I were determined to keep fighting with my men against the Germans—would you have me shot?" She didn't even hesitate: "I would have any man shot if he opposed the end of the war. He would be an enemy of mankind."

She was not discouraged by the horror of the others—compromising businessmen and their sentimental wives. Everyone spoke at once: "What? You would have the heart to do that? You would have the heart to shoot Herr Adjubel?"

"He's no coward. He knows how to die, he's not like the rest of you—isn't that so, Herr Adjubel?"

He was the one who agreed with her. "Yes, Madame, from your point of view, you would be right. You have the intransigence of a man. And you are a true Arditti!" These last words, which were a tribute (to her family, whom, in contrast to my father's, I didn't like at all), appealed less to me; but, I have to say, despite the vehemence of those exchanges, I was never jealous of Herr Adjubel, and when he succumbed to his illness a short time later, we both mourned him, and Mother said; "It's good that he didn't live to see the collapse of Bulgaria."

Reading Day and Night
The Life of Gifts

Perhaps it was because of the altered circumstances in the household that we didn't continue the old literary evenings. Until the three of us were in bed, Mother simply had no time. She went about her new duties with a grim determination. Everything she did was put into words; without a reflecting commentary, such chores would have overly bored her. She imagined that everything would have to run like clockwork, although that was not her nature; so she sought and found the clockwork in her words: "Let's get organized, children!" she would tell us. "Organized!" And she kept reiterating that word so often that we found it comical and repeated it in chorus. But she took that problem of organization very seriously and forbade our making fun of it. "You'll see, when you're on your own. If you don't get organized, you'll never get anywhere!" What she meant by this was doing everything in turn; and in the simple things that were concerned, nothing was simpler or easier. But the word egged her on, she had a word for everything, and perhaps the fact that everything was spoken about made up the brightness of our home life.

But in reality, she lived for the evening, when we were in bed and she finally had a chance to read. It was the time of her great Strindberg readings. I lay awake in bed, watching the shimmer of light under the door from the living room. She was kneeling on her chair, her elbows on the table, her head propped on her right fist, the tall stack of yellow Strindberg volumes in front of her. At every birthday and Christmas, a volume was added; that was what she wanted from us. It was particularly exciting for me that I wasn't allowed to read these volumes. I never made any attempt at peering into one; I loved the prohibition. The yellow volumes had a charisma that I can only ascribe to that prohibition, and there was nothing that made me happier than handing her a new volume, of which I only knew the title. When we had eaten supper, and the table was cleared, when the little brothers had been put to bed, I carried the stack of yellow volumes to the table for her and piled it up in the right spot. We then spoke a little, I sensed her impatience; since I had the stack before my eyes, I understood her impatience, and I went to bed quietly without tormenting her. I shut the living-room door behind me, and while undressing, I heard her walking to and fro a bit. I lay down and listened to the grating of the chair as she climbed upon it, then I felt her taking the volume into her hand, and when I was certain she had opened it, I turned my eyes to the shimmer of light under the door. Now I knew that she wouldn't stand up again for anything in the world; I switched on my tiny flashlight and read my own book under the blanket. That was my secret, which no one must know about, and it stood for the secret of her books.

She read until deep into the night. I had to economize with the battery of the flashlight, which I paid for out of my modest allowance, out of a fraction of the allowance, for most of it was tenaciously saved for presents for Mother. Thus, I could seldom read for more than a quarter hour. When I was finally found out, there was a big tumult; Mother could stand deception less than anything. I did succeed in replacing the confiscated flashlight; but, to make sure, she had appointed the little brothers as guards; they were terribly eager to suddenly snatch the blanket away from my body. If they awoke, they could easily tell from their beds whether my head was under the blanket. They would then sneak over without a sound, preferably together; and from under the blanket, I heard nothing and was defenseless. Suddenly, I lay there uncovered. I scarcely knew what had happened to me, and already the howl of triumph was booming in my ears. Mother, furious at the disturbance, stood up from her chair, found the line to destroy me with—"So I have no one in the world I can trust!"—and confiscated the book for a week.

The punishment was harsh, for it was Dickens. That was the author she gave me at that time, and I had never read any writer with greater passion. She started with *Oliver Twist* and *Nicholas Nickleby*, and especially the latter book, which told about contemporary conditions at English schools, so utterly entranced me that I just couldn't put it down. Once I finished, I began all over again, reading it through from start to finish. That happened three or four times, probably more often. "Why, you already know it," she said, "wouldn't you rather read something else?" But the better I got to know it, the more I wanted to reread it. She considered this a bad juvenile habit on my part and blamed it on the early books that I had gotten from Father and sometimes reread forty times, even though I already knew them by heart. She tried to break me of this habit by alluringly describing new books; fortunately, there were a lot by Dickens. *David Copperfield*, which was her favorite and which she regarded as his literary best, was to be the last one for me. She powerfully intensified my eagerness for it, hoping

that this bait would wean me off from eternally rereading the other
novels. I was torn between love for what I knew well and curiosity,
which she enflamed in every way. "Let's not talk about it anymore,"
she said in annoyance and gave me an unspeakably bored look, "we've
already talked about it. Do you want me to repeat the same thing to
you? I'm not like you. Let's talk about the next one now!" Since my
conversations with her were still the most important thing in my life,
since I couldn't stand not discussing every detail of a wonderful book
with her, since I noticed that she didn't want to say anything more and
that my stubborness was really beginning to bore her, I gradually gave
in and limited myself to reading each Dickens book only twice. I
bitterly regretted giving up a Dickens once and for all and perhaps
taking it back myself to the lending library where she had borrowed
it. (We had left everything in Vienna, the furniture and the library had
been put in storage, and so, for most books, she depended on the
Hottingen Reading Circle.) But the prospect of talking with her about
the new Dickens was stronger, and so it was she herself to whom I owe
all the wonders and who brought me away from my obstinacy, my best
quality in these things.

Sometimes she got scared of the passions she stoked in me, and she
then tried diverting me to other authors. Her biggest setback in this
area was Walter Scott. Perhaps she hadn't worked up enough ardor
when she first spoke about him, perhaps he really is as vapid as he
seemed at the time. Not only didn't I reread him, but after two or three
novels, I refused to take anything of his in my hand again, and I
rebelled so intensely that she was delighted at the resolute direction of
my taste and said the highest thing that I could hear from her: "You
are my son, after all. I never liked him either. I thought you were so
interested in history."

"History!" I cried indignantly. "Why, that's not history! That's just
dumb knights and their armor!" That, to our mutual satisfaction,
ended the brief Scott intermezzo.

In everything concerning my intellectual education, she paid little
heed to what others said; but at one point, someone must have impressed
her with something. Maybe she had heard something at school, where
she came from time to time like other parents; maybe she was unsettled
by one of the various lectures she attended. At any rate, she declared
one day, that I would have to know what other boys of my age were
reading, otherwise I soon wouldn't be able to understand my schoolmates. She got me a subscription to *Der Gute Kamerad* (a boys' weekly),
and incomprehensible as it now seems to me, I read it not without
enjoyment, at the same time as Dickens. There were exciting things in

it, like "The Gold of Sacramento," about the Swiss gold-hunter Sutter in California, and the most suspenseful thing of all was a story about Seianus, the minion of Emperor Tiberius. That was my first and authentic encounter with later Roman history, and this emperor, whom I despised as a figure of power, continued something in me that had begun five years earlier in England, with the story of Napoleon.

Mother did not read Strindberg alone, though he occupied her most at that time. A special group of books was made up of antiwar writings published by the Rascher publishing house. Latzko's *People in War*, Leonhard Frank's *Man is Good*, Barbusse's *Fire*—those were the three she talked to me about most frequently. She had wanted these too, like Strindberg, as presents from us. Our allowances alone, being very modest, would not have sufficed, although we saved nearly all of them for this purpose. But I also received a few rappens every day to buy a doughnut from the school janitor for my morning snack. I *was* hungry, but it was far more exciting to save that money until there was enough to get Mother a new book. First, I had gone to Rascher to learn the price, and it was already a pleasure just to enter that very lively book shop on *Limmatquai*, to see the people, who often asked for our future gifts, and naturally to take in with one glance all the books that I would eventually read. It was not so much that I felt bigger and more responsible among these adults, it was really the promise of future things to read, which would never run out. For if, in those days, I felt anything like concern about the future, it was really in regard to the world's supply of books. What would happen when I had read them all? Of course, best of all, I loved rereading the ones I liked, over and over, but this pleasure included the certainty that it would be followed by more and more.

Once I knew the price of the planned gift, the calculations began: How many ten-rappen morning snacks would I have to skip in order to have enough for the book? It always took several months: thus the book came together, bit by bit. The temptation to actually buy a doughnut just once, like some of my schoolmates, and eat it in front of them, was insignificant against this goal. On the contrary, I enjoyed standing close to someone consuming a doughnut and with something like a feeling of pleasure—I can't put it any other way—I pictured Mother's surprise when we handed her the book.

She was always surprised, although it was repeated. She never knew what book it would be. But if she sent me to get her a new book at the Hottingen Reading Circle and the book was already taken out because everyone was talking about it and wanted it—if she sent me again and became impatient, I knew that this would have to be the new present and I made it the next goal of my "politics." This enterprise also involved consistently misleading her. I asked for the book again at the Reading Circle and returned with a disappointed expression, saying: "The Latzko was out again!" The disappointment grew as the day of the surprise approached; and on the preceding day, it might happen that I stamped my foot angrily and suggested that Mother leave the Hottingen Reading Circle as a sign of protest. "That won't help," she said pensively, "then we shan't get any books at all."

The very next day, she had a brand-new copy of the Latzko in her hand, so how could she help but be surprised! Of course, I had to promise never to do it again and to eat the doughnuts at school from now on, but she never threatened to withdraw the tiny sum for them. That may have been part of her policy of character-building, and perhaps the book especially delighted her because I had saved up for it by small daily acts of renunciation. She herself was a person who ate with gusto, her taste for refined dishes was highly developed. During our puritanical meals, she had no qualms about speaking of things she missed, and she alone suffered from her decision to accustom us to modest and simple food.

It must have been this special kind of book that ultimately politicized her intellectual interests. Barbusse's *Fire* haunted her for a long time. She talked to me about it more than she considered right. I pestered her to allow me to read it; she remained firm, but she told me all about it in a somewhat milder form. Nevertheless, she was a loner and never joined any pacifist group. She heard Leonhard Ragaz speak and came home so agitated that the two of us stayed up most of the night. But her timidity about any public activities on her part remained invincible. She explained it away by saying that she only lived for us three, and what she couldn't get done herself, because no one would listen to a woman in this male world of war, we three, when grown up, would advocate in her sense, each in terms of his own abilities.

All sorts of things were happening in Zurich at that time, and she did her best to follow up on everything she heard about, not just the antiwar things. She had no one to advise her; intellectually, she was truly alone; among the friends who sometimes came to visit, she appeared to be by far the most open-minded and most intelligent person; and when I remember all the things she undertook on her own, I can only be amazed today. Even when it came to her strongest conviction, she formed her own opinion. I recall the scornful way she came down on Stefan Zweig's *Jeremiah*: "Paper! Empty straw! You can tell he hasn't experienced anything himself. He ought to read Barbusse instead of writing this nonsense!" Her respect for real *experience* was enormous.

She wouldn't have dared to open her mouth about actual warfare, for she had never personally been in a trench; and she went so far as to say it would be better if women were conscripted too, then they could fight against it seriously. Thus, when it came to those very things, it must have been her timidity that prevented her from finding a way to like-minded people. Claptrap, whether spoken or written, was something she hated fiercely, and if I ventured to say something imprecise, she would pull me up sharply.

During this period, when I was starting to think myself, I admired her unreservedly. I compared her with my teachers at the canton school, more than one of whom I accepted or even revered. Only Eugen Müller had her fire, bound with her earnestness; only he, when speaking, had her wide-open eyes and gazed ahead, unswervably, at the topic, which overwhelmed him. I told her about everything I heard in his classes, and it fascinated her because she knew the Greeks only from the classical dramas. She learned Greek history from me and wasn't ashamed to ask. For once, our roles were reversed, she didn't read history books on her own because they talked about wars so much. But it could happen that when we sat down for lunch, she promptly questioned me about Solon or Themistocles. She particularly liked Solon because he refused to set himself up as a dictator and withdrew from power. She was surprised that there was no play about him; she knew of none that dealt with him. But she found it unjust that the mothers of such men were barely mentioned by the Greeks. She undauntedly saw the mother of the Gracchi as her own ideal.

It is hard for me not to list everything she was involved in. For whatever it was, something of it passed on to me. I was the only one to whom she could recount everything in every detail. Only I took her stern judgments seriously, for I knew what enthusiasm they sprang from. She condemned many things, but never without first expatiating on what she had against them with vehement but convincing reasons. The time of our readings may have been over, the dramas and great performers were no longer the chief substance of the world; but a different and by no means smaller "wealth" had replaced them: the monstrous events happening now, their effects and their roots. She was distrustful by nature and in Strindberg, whom she considered the most intelligent of all men, she found a justification for her distrust, which she grew used to and could no longer do without. She caught herself going too far and telling me things that became the source of my own, still very young distrust. She would then feel scared and, by way of balance, tell me about some deed that she particularly admired. Mostly it was something tied to incomprehensible difficulties, but magnanimity always played a part too. During such attempts at balance, I felt closest to her. She thought I didn't perceive the reason for this change in tone. But I was already a bit like her and I practiced seeing through things. Acting naive, I took in the "noble" tale, I always liked it. But I knew why she was bringing it up now of all times, and I kept my knowledge to myself. Thus both of us held back slightly, and since it was actually the same, each of us had the identical secret from the other. It was no wonder that at such moments, feeling myself her *mute* equal, I loved her the most. She was certain that she had once again concealed her distrust from me; I perceived both things: her ruthless acumen and her magnanimity. At the time, I didn't know what *vastness* is, but I *felt* it: being able to comprise so many and such conflicting things, knowing that seeming incompatibles can all be valid at once, being able to feel that without perishing of fear, having to name that and think about it, the true glory of human nature—that was really what I learned from her.

Hypnosis and Jealousy
The Seriously Wounded

She went to concerts often; music remained important for her, though she seldom touched the piano after Father's death. Perhaps she had also become more demanding by having more opportunity to hear the masters of her instrument, some of whom were living in Zurich. She never missed a recital by Busoni, and it confused her a bit that he lived nearby. At first, she wouldn't believe me when I told her about running into him, and only when she learned from others that it really was Busoni did she accept it, and she upbraided me for calling him "Dschoddo-come-to-Papa," like the neighborhood children, instead of "Busoni." She promised she would take me to hear him some day, but only on condition that I never again call him by that false name. She said he was the greatest keyboard master she had ever heard, and it was nonsense referring to all the others as "pianists" just like him.

She also regularly attended the performances of the Schaichet Quartet, named after the first violinist, and she always came home in a state of inexplicable agitation, which I finally understood only when she once angrily said to me that Father would have loved to become such a violinist; it had been his dream to play so well that he could perform in a quartet. Why not do a solo concert, she had once asked him. But he had shaken his head and replied that he could never become that good, he knew the limits of his talent, he might possibly have been good enough for a quartet or for first violin in an orchestra if his father hadn't prevented him from playing so early on. "Grandfather was such a tyrant, such a despot, he tore the violin away from him and beat him when he heard him play. Once, he punished him by having his eldest brother tie him up in the cellar overnight." She was letting herself go, and to mellow the effect of her anger on me, she sadly added: "And Father was so modest." It ended with her noticing my confusion—how was he modest if Grandfather beat him?—and instead of explaining that his modesty consisted in his not believing himself capable of becoming more than perhaps a concertmaster, she said sarcastically: "In that way, you really take after *me!*" I didn't like hearing that, I couldn't stand it when she spoke about Father's lack of ambition, as though he had been a good person only because of that lack.

Hearing the *Saint Matthew Passion* put her in a state that I remember if for no other reason than because she was incapable of a real conversation with me for days afterwards. She couldn't read all week. She would open her book, but not see a single line; instead, she heard Ilona Durigo's alto. One night, she came into my bedroom with tears in her eyes and said: "It's all over with books, I'll never be able to read again." I tried to comfort her, I suggested sitting next to her while she read, then she wouldn't hear the voice anymore. That only happened, I said, because she was alone; if I sat next to her at the table, I could always say something, then the voices would fade. "But I *want* to hear them, don't you understand, I never want to hear anything else again!" It was such a passionate outburst that I was frightened. But I was full of admiration for her and said nothing more. During the next few days, I sometimes gave her an inquisitive look, she understood and said in a blend of happiness and despair: "I can still hear them."

I watched over her as she over me, and if you are close to someone, you gain an unerring sense for all emotions consistent with him. Overwhelmed as I may have been by her passions, I would not have let a false note pass. It wasn't presumption on my part but familiarity that gave me the right to be watchful, and I didn't hesitate to swoop down on her when I detected an alien, unwonted influence. For a while, she went to Rudolf Steiner's lectures. What she reported about them didn't sound like her at all, as though she were suddenly speaking in a foreign language. I didn't know who had gotten her to attend those lectures, she wouldn't let on, and when the remark escaped her that Rudolf Steiner had something *hypnotic* about him, I began storming her with questions. Since I knew nothing about him, I could gain an idea of him only from her own accounts, and I soon realized that he had won her over with frequent quotations from Goethe.

I asked her whether they were really new to her; after all, she must
be familiar with them since she claimed she'd read everything of
Goethe's. "Well, you know, nobody's read *all* of him," she admitted,
fairly embarrassed, "and I can't remember any of these things." She
seemed very unsure of herself, for I was accustomed to her knowing
every syllable of her writer; she always violently attacked other people
for their defective knowledge of an author, calling them "chatterboxes"
and "muddleheads," who confused everything because they were too
lazy to experience something thoroughly. I wasn't satisfied with her
answer and I then asked whether she would like me to believe these
things too. After all, we couldn't believe *different* things, and if she
joined Steiner after a few lectures because he was so hypnotic, then I
would force myself to likewise believe everything she said, so that
nothing would keep us apart. It must have sounded like a threat,
perhaps it was only a ruse: I wanted to find out how strongly this new
power had grabbed her, a power that was utterly alien to me, that I
had never heard or read about; it broke in upon us so suddenly, I had
the feeling that now everything would change between us. Most of all,
I feared it would make no difference to her whether or not I joined,
which would have meant that what happened to me would no longer
be so important to her. But things hadn't gone that far at all, for she
absolutely refused to let me "take part"; she vehemently said: "You're
too young. That's not for you. You shouldn't believe any of it. I'll
never tell you anything about it again." I had just saved up some money
to buy her a new Strindberg. Instead, on the spur of the moment, I
purchased a book by Rudolf Steiner. Solemnly, I presented it to her
with the hypocritical words: "You *are* interested in it and you can't
retain everything. You said it's not easy to understand, it has to be
properly studied. Now you can read it in peace and quiet and you'll be
better prepared for the lectures."

But she didn't care for that at all. Why had I bought it, she kept
asking. She said she didn't really know whether she wanted to keep it.
Perhaps she wouldn't like it. Why, she had read nothing of his. One
can only buy a book if one is positive one wants to keep it. She was
afraid I would read it myself and, she felt, be pushed into a specific
direction much too early. She was hesitant about anything that didn't
come from completely personal experience and she distrusted hurried
conversions, she made fun of people who let themselves be converted
too easily, and she often said of them: "Just another reed in the wind."
She was embarrassed about the word "hypnosis," which she had used,
and she explained that she hadn't been referring to herself, she had
noticed that the other spectators appeared hypnotized. Maybe it would

be better, she said, if we put all this off for some later time, when I was more mature and could understand it more readily. At bottom, she cared more about the things we could discuss between us, without distortions or contortions, without pretending anything that wasn't already a part of us. That wasn't the first time that I felt her coming halfway towards my jealousy. She also had no more time, she said, to go to those lectures; it was such an inconvenient hour for her, and they made her miss other things that she understood better. So she sacrificed Rudolf Steiner to me, never mentioning him again. I did not feel the unworthiness of victory over a man of whom I had not refuted a single sentence because I didn't know a single sentence. I had hindered his ideas from taking root in her mind, for I sensed that they didn't relate to anything we ever discussed; all I cared about was repelling those ideas from her.

But what should I think of that jealousy? I can neither approve nor condemn, I can only record it. It became part of my nature so early that it would be dishonest to conceal it. It always stirred whenever someone became important to me, and there were few such people who didn't have to suffer from it. My jealousy developed into something rich and versatile in my relationship to my mother. It enabled me to fight for something that was superior to me in every way, stronger, more experienced, more knowledgeable, and also more selfless. It never struck me how selfish I was in this struggle, and if someone had told me that I was making Mother unhappy, I would have been highly astonished. After all, it was she who gave me this right to her, she attached herself so close to me in her loneliness because she knew no one who was her equal. Had she socialized with a man like Busoni, then I would have been doomed. I was absorbed in her because she presented herself totally to me, she told me all the important thoughts that were on her mind, and her reticence in covering up certain things because of my youth was only feigned. She obstinately kept all eroticism from me, the taboo she had placed upon it on the balcony of our apartment in Vienna remained as powerful in me as though it had been proclaimed by God himself on Mount Sinai. I never asked about sex, it was never on my mind; and while she ardently and intelligently filled me with all the things in the world, that one thing, which had confused me, remained blank. Since I didn't know how greatly people need this kind of love, I couldn't guess what she was deprived of. She was thirty-two at the time and living alone, and that seemed as natural to me as my own life. At times, when she got angry at us for disappointing or irritating her, she did say she was sacrificing her life for us, and if we didn't deserve it, she would put us in the strong hands of a man, who would teach us what was what. But I didn't realize, I couldn't realize, that she was also thinking of her lonely life as a woman. I saw her sacrifice as devoting so much time to us, whereas she would much rather have *read* all the time.

This taboo, which often triggers the most dangerous counter-emotions in other people's lives, is something I am still grateful for even today. I cannot say that it has preserved any innocence in me, for in my jealousy I was nothing less than innocent. But it kept me fresh and naive for anything I wished to know. I learned in all possible ways, without ever feeling it as a restraint or burden, for there was nothing that irritated me or secretly occupied me more. Whatever happened to me took solid root in me, there was space for everything, I never had a feeling of anything being kept from me; on the contrary, it seemed as if everything were spread out before me, and I need only grab it. No sooner was it in me than it related to something else, got attached to that, kept growing, created an atmosphere, and called for something new. That was the freshness: everything taking shape and not merely adding up. The naiveté may have been that everything remained at hand, the lack of sleep.

A second good deed that Mother did for me during those years in Zurich together had even greater consequences: she exempted me from *calculation*. I was never told that one does something for practical reasons. Nothing was done that might be "useful." All the things I wanted to grasp were equally valid. I moved along a hundred roads at once without having to hear that any was more comfortable, more profitable, more productive. It was the things themselves that were important, and not their usefulness. One had to be precise and thorough and know how to advocate an opinion without trickery, but this thoroughness applied to the thing itself and not to some use it might have. There was scarcely any mention of what I might do some day. The thought of a profession receded so far into the background that all professions remained open. Success didn't mean that one advanced for oneself, success benefited everybody, or it wasn't true success. It is a mystery to me how a woman of her background, well aware of the commercial prestige of her family, with great pride in it, never denying it, managed to achieve such freedom, breadth, and unselfishness of vista. It can only have been the shock of the war, the sympathy for all who had lost their most precious people to the war, that made her suddenly leave her limits behind and turned her into sheer magnanimity towards everyone who thought and felt and suffered, with admiration for the radiant process of thinking, which was given to everyone, at the top of the list.

I once saw her aghast; it is my mutest recollection of her and the only time that I saw her crying on the street. She was normally too self-controlled to let herself go in public. We were strolling along *Limmatquai,* I wanted to show her something in the window display at Rascher. All at once, a group of French officers came towards us in their conspicuous uniforms. Some of them had trouble walking, the others adjusted their pace to them, we stopped to let them slowly trudge by. "They're badly wounded," said Mother, "they're in Switzerland to convalesce. They're being exchanged for Germans." And at that moment, a group of Germans came from the other side, several of them with crutches too, and the rest trudging slowly for their sake. I still remember how I shuddered from head to foot: What would happen now, would they charge one another? We were so disconcerted that we didn't step aside in time and suddenly found ourselves between the two groups who were trying to pass each other, we were enclosed, right in the middle. It was under the arcades, there was certainly enough room, but now we were peering very closely into their faces as they thronged past one another. No face was twisted with hate or anger, as I had expected. They gazed calmly and amiably at one another as though there were nothing odd about the situation, a few saluted. They moved a lot slower than other people, and it took a while, it seemed like an eternity until they had gotten by each other. One of the Frenchmen turned back, raised his crutch aloft, waved it about a little, and then cried to the Germans, who were already past: "Salut!" A German who had heard it did the same, he too had a crutch, which he waved, and he returned the greeting in French: "Salut!" One might think, upon hearing this, that the crutches were brandished *threateningly,* but that wasn't the case at all, they were simply showing each other, by way of farewell, what had remained for them jointly: crutches. Mother had stepped over to the curb and was standing in front of the window display with her back to me. I saw that she was trembling; I went up next to her, cautiously eyed her askance. She was weeping. We pretended to be gazing at the display, I didn't say a word; when she pulled herself together, we went home in a hush, nor did we ever speak about that incident afterwards.

The Gottfried Keller Celebration

I formed a literary friendship with Walter Wreschner from a parallel class. He was the son of a psychology professor from Breslau. He always spoke in an "educated" way and never used the dialect with me. Our friendship emerged very naturally, we spoke about books. But there was an enormous difference between us, he was interested in the most modern stuff, which people were talking about, and at the time that was Wedekind.

Wedekind sometimes came to Zurich and performed at the *Schauspielhaus* in *Earth Spirit*. He was a subject of violent controversy, parties formed for or against him, the one against him was more powerful, the one for him was more interesting. I knew nothing about him from personal experience, and Mother, who had seen him at the *Schauspielhaus* gave a colorful account of him (she described in detail his appearance with the whip), but her verdict was quite shaky. She had hoped for something like Strindberg, and without totally denying the kinship between them, she felt that Wedekind had something of a preacher and also of a yellow journalist, always wanting to make a splash and be noticed, not caring how he drew attention, so long as he got it. Strindberg, however, she said, was always rigorous and superior, although he saw through everything. *He* had something of a doctor— but not one for healing and also not one for the body. She said I would only understand what she meant when I read him myself, later on. As for Wedekind, I got a very inadequate notion of him too, and since I didn't wish to jump ahead and was exceedingly patient when warned by the right person, he couldn't attract me as yet

Wreschner, on the other hand, spoke about him constantly; he had even written a play in his manner and let me read it. Everyone on stage just shot up the place, suddenly, groundlessly, I couldn't see why. The whole thing was more alien to me than if it had taken place on the moon. At this time, I was combing all bookshops for *David Copperfield*, which was to be the crown of one and one half years of Dickens enthusiasm and a present for me. Wreschner came along when I went to the bookshops; *David Copperfield* was nowhere to be found. Totally uninterested in such an old-fashioned book, Wreschner made fun of me, saying it was a bad sign that *David Copperfield*, as he belittled it, wasn't anywhere, it meant that nobody wanted to read it. "You're the only one," he added ironically.

At last, I found the novel, but in German, and I told Wreschner how silly I found his Wedekind (whom I only knew from his imitation).

However, this tension between us was pleasant; he listened carefully when I told him about my books, he even got to hear the plot of *Copperfield*, while I heard about all the utterly weird things that took place in the Wedekind dramas. It didn't bother him that I kept saying: "That can't be, that's impossible!" On the contrary, he enjoyed surprising me. Today, however, I find it peculiar that I can't remember anything he amazed me with. It slid off me as though it didn't exist anywhere; since there was nothing in me to which it could connect, I regarded it all as stuff and nonsense.

A moment came when our mutual arrogance united in one, and we stood as a party of two against an entire crowd. In July 1919, the Gottfried Keller centennial was celebrated. Our entire school was to gather in the Preacher Church on that occasion. Wreschner and I walked down together from *Rämistrasse* to *Predigerplatz*. We had never heard anything about Gottfried Keller; we only knew that he was a Zurich writer, born one hundred years ago. We were surprised that the celebration was to take place in the Preacher Church; it was the first time that such a thing happened. At home, I had asked, to no avail, just who he was: Mother didn't even know the title of a single one of his works. Wreschner hadn't picked up anything about him either, and he only said: "He's simply Swiss." We were in a cheery mood because we felt excluded, for we were interested only in the literature of the great world, I in English and he in contemporary German. During the war, we had been enemies of sorts; I swore by Wilson's Fourteen Points, he wanted the Germans to win. But after the collapse of the Central Powers, I turned away from the victors, I already felt an antipathy against victors, and when I saw that the Germans weren't being treated as Wilson had promised, I switched over to their side. So we were really only separated by Wedekind, but though I understood nothing of him, I never doubted his fame for an instant.

The Preacher Church was jammed to the hilt, the mood was lugubrious. There was music, and then came a big speech. I no longer remember who gave it, it must have been a professor at our school, but no one that we had. I only know that he got more and more worked up about Gottfried Keller's importance. Wreschner and I kept sneaking ironic glances at each other. We believed we knew what a great writer is, and if we didn't know anything about a writer, then he just wasn't great. But when the speaker kept making loftier and loftier claims for Keller, talking about him as I was used to hearing about Shakespeare,

Goethe, Victor Hugo, about Dickens, Tolstoy, and Strindberg, I was seized with a horror such as I can scarcely describe, as though somebody had profaned the most sublime thing in the world, the glory of the great writers. I became so furious that I really wanted to heckle. I thought I could feel the devotion of the mass around me, perhaps also because the whole thing was taking place in a church, for I was well aware at the same time of how indifferent many of the students were to Keller, if for no other reason than because writers, especially those that some of them had in school, were actually a bother. The devotion consisted in the way they all took it mutely, nobody made a peep, I myself was too self-conscious or too well bred to cause any disturbance in a church, our anger went inward, turning into an oath that was no less solemn than the occasion it sprang from. No sooner were we out of the church than, deadly earnest, I said to Wreschner, who would rather have made his sarcastic remarks: "We have to swear, both of us have to swear, never to become local celebrities!" He saw I was in no mood for fun, and he swore the oath to me as I to him, but I doubt if his heart was really in it, for he regarded Dickens, whom he had no more read than I Keller, as *my* local celebrity.

That speech may really have been full of claptrap; I had a good sense of such things at an early age, but what struck me to the core of my naive attitude was the lofty claim for a writer whom not even Mother had read. My account stunned her, and she said: "I don't know, I finally have to read something by him now." The next time that I went to the Hottingen Reading Circle, I, reserved until the end, asked for a copy of Keller's *The Field People of Seldwyla*. The girl at the counter smiled, a gentleman who had come for something himself corrected me like an illiterate: *The* People *of Seldwyla*. It wouldn't have taken much for him to ask me: "Can you read already?" I was very embarrassed and, in the future, I acted even more reticent about Keller. But at the time, I couldn't guess with what delight I would some day read *Green Henry*; and when I, as a student, in Vienna, again became utterly enthralled by Gogol, I felt that German literature, to the extent that I knew it then, had only one story like his stories: "The Three Just Kammachers." Had I the luck to be alive in the year 2019 and the honor to be standing at the Keller bicentennial in the Preacher Church and to celebrate him with a speech, I would find quite different praises for him, which would compel even the ignorant arrogance of a fourteen-year-old.

Vienna in Trouble
The Slave from Milan

Mother endured that life with us for two years; we had her all to ourselves. I thought she was happy because I was. I didn't guess that it was hard for her and that she was missing something. But what had happened in Vienna, now recurred; after two years of concentrating on us, her energy began to wane. Something inside her crumbled without my noticing. The calamity returned in the form of an illness. Since it was one striking all the world, the big influenza epidemic in the winter of 1918-19, and since the three of us caught it, like everyone we knew, schoolmates, teachers, friends, we saw nothing special about her falling ill too. Perhaps she lacked proper care, perhaps she got back up too early; suddenly, complications set in, and she had a thrombosis. She had to go to the hospital, where she remained for several weeks, and when she came home she was no longer the same person. She had to lie down a lot, she had to take care of herself, the housework was too much for her, she felt confined and oppressed in the small apartment.

She no longer knelt in her chair at night, leaning her head on her fist; the high stack of books, which I prepared as before, stayed untouched. Strindberg was in disgrace. "I'm too restless," she said, "he depresses me, I can't read him now." At night, when I was lying in bed in the adjacent room, she would abruptly sit down at the piano and play sad songs. She played softly to avoid waking me, as she thought; she hummed along even more softly, and then I heard her weep and talk to my father, who had been dead for six years.

The months that followed were a period of gradual dissolution. Recurrent states of feebleness convinced her and me that it couldn't go on like that. She would have to give up the household. We conferred this way and that way what to do with the children and myself. The little brothers were both already attending school in Oberstrass, but it was still a primary school, and so they wouldn't lose anything by transfering back to the boarding school in Lausanne, where they had already spent a few months in 1916. They would be able to improve their French, which wasn't particularly good yet. But I was already at the *Realgymnasium* of the canton school, where I felt fine and liked most of my teachers. I loved one of them so much that I told Mother I would never go to any school where he wasn't teaching. She knew the intensity of my passions, both negative and positive, and she realized this was no joking matter. And so, throughout the long period of deliberations, it was regarded as settled that I would have to stay in Zurich and board somewhere here.

She herself would do everything to restore her health, which was deeply shaken. We would spend the summer together in the Bern highlands. Then, after the three of us were settled in our various places, she would go to Vienna for a thorough examination by good specialists, who could still be found there. They would advise the proper treatments, and she would follow all their advice to the letter. Perhaps it would take a year before we could live together again, perhaps longer. The war was over, she felt drawn back to Vienna. Our furniture and books were stored in Vienna; who could tell what state they were in after three years? There were so many reasons for going to Vienna; the chief reason was Vienna itself. We kept hearing how bad things were in Vienna. Along with all the private reasons, she felt something like an obligation to see how things stood. Austria had crumbled; the land she had thought of with a kind of bitterness so long as it had waged war, now mainly consisted of Vienna for her. She had wanted defeat for the Central Powers because she was convinced that they had started the war. Now she felt responsible for, nay, almost guilty about Vienna, as though her attitude had plunged the city into disaster. One night, she told me in earnest that she had to see for herself what it was like there; she couldn't bear the thought of Vienna going under totally. I started to realize, albeit still unclearly, that the crumbling of her health, of her clarity and solidity, of her feelings about us, were linked to the end of the war, which end she had so passionately wished for, and to the collapse of Austria.

We had resigned ourselves to the idea of the imminent separation when we traveled to Kandersteg once again, for the summer. I was accustomed to being in grand hotels with her; she had never gone to any other kind since her youth. She liked the subdued atmosphere, the cordial service, the changing guests, whom one could observe from one's own table during the *table d'hôte* without seeming overly curious. She liked talking about all those people to us, speculating about them, trying to figure out their background, quietly deprecating them or pointing them out. She felt I would thereby experience something of the great world without getting too close to it, for which she thought it was too early.

The previous summer, we had been in Seelisberg, on a terrace high over Lake Urner. We often walked down through the forest with her to Rütli Meadow, at first in honor of William Tell, but very soon in order to pick the strongly fragrant cyclamens, whose scent she loved. She never noticed flowers that didn't have a perfume, it was as if they didn't exist, but she was all the more passionate about lilies of the valley, hyacinths, cyclamens, and roses. She loved talking about them, explaining that it was due to the roses of her childhood in her father's garden. When I brought home natural-science booklets from school, copying the pictures assiduously—a real strain on a bad draughtsman— she pushed them away; I could never get her interested in them. "Dead!" she would say. "It's all dead! It doesn't smell, it only makes me sad!" But she was entranced with Rütli Meadow. "No wonder Switzerland was born here! I would have sworn any oath amid this fragrance of cyclamens. They *knew* what they were defending. I would be ready to give my life for this fragrance." All at once, she confessed that something had always been missing for her in Schiller's *William Tell*. Now she knew what it was: the smell. I argued that maybe there hadn't been any forest cyclamens at that time.

"Of *course* there were. Otherwise Switzerland wouldn't exist today. Do you think they would have sworn their oath? It was here, right here, and this fragrance gave them the strength for the oath. Do you believe there were no other peasants who were ever oppressed by their masters? Why Switzerland of all places? Why these inner cantons? Switzerland was born on Rütli Meadow, and now I know where they got their courage." For the first time, she exposed her doubts about Schiller; she had always spared me so that I wouldn't get confused. The fragrance made her throw her qualms overboard, and she confided something that had long been troubling her: Schiller's rotten apples. "I think he was different when he wrote *The Brigands*, he didn't need any rotten apples then."

"What about *Don Carlos*? And *Wallenstein*?"

"Yes, yes," she said, "it's good that you know it. You'll find out soon enough that there are writers who *borrow* their life. Others *have* it, like Shakespeare."

I was so indignant at her betrayal of our Vienna evenings, when we had read both of them, Shakespeare *and* Schiller, that I rather disrespectfully said: "I think you're drunk from the cyclamens. That's why you're saying things that you usually don't believe."

She let it go at that, she may have felt that I was partly right, she liked me to draw my own conclusions and not let myself be caught unawares. I also kept a clear head in regard to the hotel life and was never taken in at all by the fine guests, even those who really *were* fine.

We stayed in the Grand Hotel; one ought to live in a suitable style now and again, at least during holidays, she said. Nor was it all that bad, she went on, getting used to changing circumstances early enough. After all, at school, I had highly diverse classmates. That's why I liked being there, she said. She hoped I didn't like it because I learned more easily than the others.

"But that's what you *want*! You'd despise me if I were bad at school!"

"That's not what I mean. I'm not even thinking of that. But you like talking to me and you wouldn't like to bore me, and so you have to know a lot. I can't talk to a numbskull after all. I have to take you seriously."

I realized that. But I still didn't really grasp the connection with life in a posh hotel. I fully understood that it was linked to her background, to what she called "a good family." There were bad people in her family, more than one, she often spoke about them quite openly to me. In my presence, her cousin and brother-in-law had yelled at her, calling her a "thief" and accusing her in the lowest way. Wasn't he from the same family? And what was good about that? He wanted more money than he already had, that was how she had finally explained it. Whenever she talked about her "good family," I came up against a wall. On this topic, she was absolutely narrow-minded, unshakable, and inaccessible to any argument. At times, I felt such despair about it that I grabbed her violently and shouted: "You are you! You're a lot more than any family!"

"And you're impudent. You're hurting me. Let go!" I let go, but first I added: "You're more than anybody else in the world! I know you are! I know you are!"

"Some day, you'll talk differently. I won't remind you of this."

But I can't say that I felt unhappy in the Grand Hotel, so much was going on. We got into conversations, though gradually, with people who were well traveled. When we were in Seelisberg, an old gentleman told us about Siberia; and a few days later, we met a married couple who had navigated the Amazon. The following summer, in Kandersteg, where naturally we stayed in a grand hotel again, a very taciturn Englishman named Mr. Newton sat at the next table and kept reading the same India-paper book. Mother didn't rest until she found out it was a volume of Dickens, *David Copperfield* of all things. My heart went out to Mr. Newton, but that made no impact on him. He held his peace for another few weeks, then he took me and two other children of my age on an excursion. We hiked for six hours, but he never emitted more than a syllable—now and then. Upon returning us to our respective parents in the hotel, he observed that this landscape of the Bern highlands couldn't be compared to Tibet. I gaped at him as though he were Sven Hedin in person, but that was all I ever got out of him.

Here in Kandersteg, Mother had an outburst, which, more than her states of feebleness, more than all our deliberations in Zurich, proved what sinister things were going on inside her. A family from Milan arrived in the hotel: the wife a lovely and opulent lady of Italian society, the husband a Swiss industrialist, who had been living in Milan for a long time. They had their very own painter in tow, Micheletti—"a famous painter," who could paint only for the family and was always watched by them: a small man who acted as though he wore physical shackles, in bondage to the industrialist for his money, to the woman for her beauty. He admired Mother and, one evening, as they left the dining room, he paid her a compliment. He didn't dare, of course, tell her that he wanted to paint her portrait, but she was certain he wanted to and she said, as we rode the elevator up to our floor: "He's going to paint me! I'm going to be immortal!" Then she paced up and down her hotel room and kept repeating: "He's going to paint me! I'm going to be immortal!" She couldn't calm down; for a long time (the "children" were already in bed) I remained up with her, she was incapable of sitting, she kept walking back and forth as on a stage, declaiming and singing and not really saying anything, but merely repeating in every possible key: "I'm going to be immortal!"

I tried to calm her down; her excitement surprised and frightened me. "But he didn't say he wanted to paint you!"

"His eyes told me, his eyes, his eyes! He couldn't actually articulate it, the woman was standing right next to us, how could he have said so! They watch him, he's their slave, he's sold himself to them, he's sold himself to them for an annuity, everything he paints belongs to them, they force him to paint what *they* want. Such a great artist and so weak! But he wants to paint *me*! He'll find the courage and tell them! He'll threaten never to paint again! He'll force the issue. He'll paint me and I'm going to be immortal!" Then it resumed, the last sentence as a litany. I was ashamed for her and found it wretched, and when my initial terror was past, I grew angry and attacked her in every way, merely to sober her. She never used to speak about painting, it was the one art that barely interested her and that she didn't understand. So it was all the more shameful to see how important it had suddenly become for her. "But you've never seen a single painting by him! Maybe you wouldn't like what he does. Why, you've never even heard his name before. How do you know he's so famous?"

"They said so themselves, his slavekeepers, they didn't shrink from saying so: a famous portraitist from Milan, and they've got him imprisoned! He always keeps looking at me. He looks over at me from their table. He's a painter, it's a higher power, I've inspired him and he has to paint me!"

She was looked at by so many people, and never in a cheap or insolent way. It couldn't mean anything to her for she never spoke about it, I assumed she didn't notice; she was always absorbed in some thoughts or other. I did notice the stares, I never missed a single one, and perhaps it was jealousy and not just respect that kept me from ever saying a word about it to her. But now she made up for the past in a dreadful way; I was ashamed for her, not because she wanted to be immortal—I understood that, although I had never guessed how intense, nay, how powerful that desire was in her—but the fact that she wanted to place the fulfillment of that desire in the hands of another person, and one who had sold himself to boot, a man whom she herself regarded as an ignoble slave. The fact that it hinged on the cowardice of this creature and on the whim of his masters, the rich family from Milan, who kept him like a dog on a leash and whistled for him in front of everyone when he got into a conversation with anyone else: I found that horrifying, I saw it as a humiliation of my mother, a humiliation that I couldn't stand; and in my anger, which she kept stoking, I smashed her hope by ruthlessly demonstrating that he paid compliments to every woman he happened to be near when leaving the dining room, and they were always brief compliments, until his masters grabbed his arm and pulled him away.

But she didn't give in right away; she fought like a lioness for her compliment from Micheletti, refuting what I had just demonstrated, throwing up at me every stare he had ever granted her, she had missed none and forgotten none; in the few days since the arrival of the Milanese, she had, as it turned out, registered nothing else. She had lain in wait for his compliments, making sure that she reached the exit from the dining room at the same time as he, and, though loathing his owner, the lovely society woman, like poison, she admitted that she understood the woman's motives, she herself would love to be painted by him as often as possible, and he, a somewhat frivolous man, who knew his own character, had entered this slavery willingly, she said, so as not to degenerate, and for the sake of his art, which was more important to him than anything else in the world, and he had done right in doing so. It had been absolutely wise of him, what did people like us know anyway about the temptations of a genius, and all we could do in such a case was to step aside and wait quietly to see whether we appealed to him and might contribute anything to his development. In any case, she was quite positive, she said, that he wanted to paint her and make her immortal.

Since Vienna, since Herr Professor's visits to tea, I had never felt such hatred for her. Yet it had come so suddenly; it had taken only a remark by the Swiss industrialist from Milan to a group of hotel guests about little Micheletti on the evening of their arrival. The Swiss had pointed to his white spats, shaken his head, and said: "I don't know why people are making such a fuss over him. Everybody in Milan wants him to paint them, he doesn't have more than two hands, eh?"

Mother may have felt something of my hatred; she had experienced my loathing in Vienna for several bad weeks, and in spite of her delusion at this point, she felt my antagonism first as disturbing and then as dangerous. She obstinately insisted on the portrait, which she had to believe in; even when I sensed that her strength was waning, she kept repeating the same words. But all at once, pacing through the room, she ominously halted before me and said sarcastically: "You're not envious of me, are you? Should I tell him he can only paint the two of us together? Are you in such a big hurry? Wouldn't you rather earn it on your own?"

This accusation was so low and so wrong that I couldn't retort. It lamed my tongue but not my brain. Since she had finally looked at me amidst her sentences, she could read their effect in my face, she collapsed and broke into vehement laments: "You think I'm crazy. You have your whole life ahead of you. My life is over. Are you an old man that you don't understand me? Has your Grandfather gotten into you? He's always hated me. But not your father, not your father. If he were alive, he would protect me from you now."

She was so exhausted that she burst into tears. I hugged and caressed her, and felt so sorry for her that I granted her the portrait she yearned for. "It will be very beautiful. You have to be alone on it. You all alone. Everyone will admire it. I'll tell him he has to make you a present of it. But it would be better if it got into a museum." This suggestion pleased her, and she gradually calmed down. But she felt very weak; I helped her into bed. Her head lay weary and drained on the pillow. She said: "Today I'm the child and you're the mother," and she fell asleep.

The next day, she nervously avoided Micheletti's eyes. Worried, I observed her. Her enthusiasm had vanished, she expected nothing. The painter paid compliments to other women and was dragged off by his keepers. She didn't notice. After a few days, the Milanese group left the hotel; the woman was dissatisfied with something. When they were gone, Herr Loosli, the hotelier, came to our table and told Mother that he didn't like such guests. The painter wasn't all that famous, Herr Loosli had made inquiries. The couple had obviously been looking for commissions for him. The hotelier said he kept a decent house and this wasn't the right place for adventurers. Mr. Newton, at the next table, glanced up from his India-paper book, nodded, and swallowed a sentence. That was a lot from him and was taken by Herr Loosli and ourselves as disapproval. Mother said to Herr Loosli: "He did not act properly." The hotelier continued his round, apologizing to the other guests. Everyone seemed relieved that the Milanese were gone.

Part Five

Zurich— *Tiefenbrunnen* *1919–1921*

The Nice Old Maids of the Yalta Villa
Dr. Wedekind

I didn't know the origin of the name Yalta, but it sounded familiar because there was something Turkish about it. The house was out in Tiefenbrunnen, very near the lake, separated from it only by a road and a railway line; the house stood, slightly elevated, in a garden filled with trees. You reached the left side of the villa after a brief ride up; a high poplar stood at each of its four corners, so close that the trees looked as if they were carrying the house. They mellowed the heaviness of the burly structure, they were visible from rather far away, on the lake, and they marked the location of the house.

The front garden was shielded from the road by ivy and evergreen trees; there were enough places to hide in. A mighty yew tree stood closer to the house, with broad branches, as though meant to be climbed; you were up the tree in no time.

Behind the house, a few stone steps led up to an old tennis court; it was no longer maintained, the ground was uneven and rough, it was suitable for anything but tennis playing and served for all public activities. An apple tree next to the stone steps was a miracle of fruitfulness; when I moved in, it was so overladen with apples that it had to be multiply supported. If you ran up the steps, apples plopped on the ground. To the left, a small adjacent house with a trellis-covered wall was rented to a cellist and his wife; you could hear him practicing from the tennis court.

The real orchard only began in back of the court. It was plentiful and bounteous, but next to the one apple tree, which always stuck in your eye because of its location, the orchard didn't actually stand out.

From the driveway you entered the house through a huge hall, sober as a cleared-out schoolroom. At a long table, there were usually a few young girls sitting over homework and letters. The Yalta Villa had been a girls' boarding school for years. A short time ago, it had been turned into a boarding house; the inhabitants were still young girls from every country on earth, but they were no longer taught in the house. They attended outside institutions, but ate together and were watched over by the ladies.

The long dining room on the lower floor, which always smelled fusty, was no less bare than the hall. I slept in a tiny garret on the third floor; it was narrow and meagerly furnished. Through the trees of the garden I could glimpse the lake.

Tiefenbrunnen's railroad depot was nearby; from Seefeldstrasse, where the house was located, a footbridge led over the tracks to the depot. At certain times of the year, the sun was just rising when I stood on the footbridge; even though I was late and in a hurry, I never failed to halt and pay tribute to the sun. Then I raced down the wooden steps to the depot, leapt into the train, and rode one station through the tunnel, to Stadelhofen. On *Rämistrasse*, I ran up to the canton school, but kept stopping wherever there was something to see, and I always came late to school.

I went home on foot, along *Zollikerstrasse*, which lay higher; I usually walked with a schoolmate who also lived in Tiefenbrunnen. We were absorbed in weighty conversations; I was sorry when we arrived and had to part company. I never spoke to him about the women and young girls I lived with, I was afraid he might despise me for so much femininity.

Trudi Gladosch, the Brazilian girl, had been living at the Yalta for six years; she was a pianist and attended the conservatory and she was a fixture in the house. It was hard to enter without hearing her practice. Her room was upstairs and she practiced at least six hours a day, often longer. You got so used to it that you missed the sound when it stopped. In wintertime, she was always wrapped in several sweaters, for she was terribly cold. She suffered from the climate, never growing accustomed to it. There was no vacation for her ever; Rio de Janiero, where her parents lived, was too far away, she hadn't been home in six years. She missed it, but only because of the sun. She never spoke about her parents, mentioning them at most when a letter came from home, and that was seldom the case, once or twice a year. The name Gladosch was Czech, her father had migrated from Bohemia to Brazil not all that long ago; she herself had been born in Brazil. Her voice was high, somewhat croaking; we liked to talk, there was nothing we didn't talk about. She had a way of getting excited that charmed me. We shared many noble opinions, we were of one and the same mind in scorning all venality; but I insisted I knew more than Trudi though she was five years my senior, and when she, coming from a savage land, as it were, championed the cause of the feelings against knowledge and I defended the necessity of knowledge too, which she regarded as harmful and corruptive, we were invariably at daggers drawn. This led to out-and-out fisticuffs; I tried to force her down with my hands, whereby I stretched out my arms to keep her from getting too close, for, especially during our arguments, she emitted a powerful smell, which I couldn't bear. She may not even have known how horribly she smelled, and the unphysical manner of our fighting was something she may have explained with my timidity about her being older. In the summer, she wore what she called her merida dress, a white, shirtlike creation with a round neckline; when she bent over, you could see her breasts, which I noticed, but which meant nothing to me, and it was only when I spotted a gigantic furuncle on her breast one day that I suddenly felt something like an ardent pity for her, as though she were a leper and an outcast. She *was* an outcast, for her family hadn't paid her board for years and kept putting Fräulein Mina off till the following year. Trudi felt she was living on a sort of charity, and for this reason she had an especially intimate relation with Caesar, the old St. Bernard, who usually just slept and smelled bad. I soon realized, with some embarrassment, that Trudi and Caesar smelled alike.

But we were friends and I liked her, for we could talk about anything together. Actually, we were pace-setters, she with her eternal practicing and her six years' experience in the house, I as the newest member and the only male. She was the eldest of the boarders, I the youngest. She knew the ladies of the house from all sides, I only from the best. She despised hypocrisy and always shot straight from the shoulder when anything bothered her in any of the ladies. But she was neither cunning nor nasty nor hateful, she was a good-natured, though somewhat obtrusive person, as though born to be set back or ignored, evidently accustomed to this fate very early on by her parents, and, of course—what offended me very deeply when I found out—unhappily in love. Peter Speiser—whom she knew from the conservatorium—a far better pianist than she, in his outward behavior the accomplished and self-assured concert virtuoso, also attended the canton school; he was in a parallel class and he was the first person whom Trudi and I talked about together. I was too naive to notice why she enjoyed bringing him up, and it was only six months later, when I chanced upon a draft of a letter from her to him, that the scales fell from my eyes. I confronted her, and she confessed that she was unhappily in love with him.

Throughout this period, I had taken Trudi for granted as a kind of property that I didn't have to make much of an effort for, that was always there and simply belonged to me, whereby "belong" still had a fully harmless meaning. It was only after her confession that I realized she didn't belong to me. Now, I felt as if I had lost her, and she became important to me as something lost. I told myself that I despised her. For her account of trying to get Peter interested in her sounded woeful. She thought only of submissiveness, her instincts were those of a slave girl. She wanted to be stepped on by him, she threw herself—in her letter—at his feet. But it was easy for him, who was proud and haughty, to ignore her. He didn't see her at his feet, and if he stepped on her, it was an accident that he didn't even notice. She herself was not without her own kind of pride; she guarded her feelings, just as she generally took feelings seriously and respected them. She championed the independence of feelings, that was her patriotism; she did not share my patriotism for Switzerland, for the school, for the house we both lived in. She regarded that patriotism as immature; Peter was more important to her than the whole of Switzerland. Of all their musical colleagues (they had the same teacher), he was the best, his career was deemed certain, his parents provided for him in every way, he was spoiled and always beautifully dressed, he had an artistic mane of hair and a big mouth which he used loudly without seeming unnatural; but he was also friendly to everyone, already affable for his age, never overlooked anyone, for anyone is capable of offering applause, yet he could not endure Trudi's passion-colored applause. When he perceived how she felt about him (after many love letters to him, which she never sent but, in her negligent way, forgot to destroy, she sent him one that she had made a clean copy of), he stopped talking to her and greeted her only coolly from a distance. It was around this time (Trudi lamented her woe to me, it was summer, and she had her eternal merida dress on) that she bent forward to proclaim the measure of her submissiveness to Peter's will and I spotted the gigantic furuncle on her breast, and my pity for her was kindled.

Fräulein Mina wrote her name with one "n," she had nothing to do, as she said, with Minna von Barnhelm, her full name was Hermine Herder. She was the head of the four-leaf clover that ran the boarding house, and she was the only one of the four who had a primary profession, on which she plumed herself to no small degree: she was a painter. Her somewhat overly round head was wedged deep within her shoulders on a short body; it sat right upon it, as though there had never been such a thing as a neck, what a superfluous contraption. The head was very big, too big for the body, the face was filled with countless tiny red arteries, which accumulated on the cheeks. She was sixty-five, but looked unworn; if complimented on her freshness of mind, she replied that painting had kept her young. She spoke slowly and clearly, just as she walked; she always wore dark colors, her skirt reached down to the ground, and you noticed her steps underneath only when she climbed the stairs to the third floor, the "sparrow's nest," her studio, where she retreated to paint. There, she painted nothing but flowers and called them her children. She had started by illustrating botanical books; she knew about the peculiarities of flowers and enjoyed the confidence of botanists, who would ask her to illustrate their books. She spoke of them as of good friends; two names that she often mentioned were Professor Schröter and Professor Schellenberg. Schröter's *Alpine Flora* was the best-known of her works. Professor Schellenberg still visited the house in my day, bringing along an interesting lichen or a special moss, which he explained to Fräulein Herder in great detail, as though lecturing, and in standard (rather than Swiss) German.

Her leisurely manner must have been linked to her painting. As soon as she got to like me a bit, she invited me to the "sparrow's nest," permitting me to watch as she painted. I was greatly astonished at how slow, how solemn and dignified her work was. The very smell of the studio made it into a special place, unlike any other, I sniffed to catch the smell the instant I entered, but like everything else that occurred here, the sniffing also proceeded deliberately. As soon as she picked up her brush, she started reporting on what she was doing. "And now I'm taking a little white, just a wee bit of white. Yes, I'm taking white, because nothing else will do here, I simply have to take white." She would repeat the name of the color as often as she could, and that was really all she said. In between, she kept mentioning the names of the flowers she was painting, and it was always their botanical names. Since she painted each species by itself very meticulously, not caring to mix it with others (for that was what she had always done with the botanical illustrations), one learned those Latin names from her, together with the colors. She said nothing else, whether about the habitat, or about the structure and functions of the plant; everything that we learned from our science teacher, everything that was new and fascinating and that had to be drawn in our notebooks, she left out, and so the visits to the sparrow's nest had something ritualistic about them, made up of the turpentine smell, the pure colors on the palette, and the Latin names of the flowers. Fräulein Mina saw something venerable and sacred in this institution, and once, in a solemn moment, she confided to me that she was a vestal virgin and that was why she had never married; a person who has devoted his life to art, she said, must forgo the happiness of normal mortals.

Fräulein Mina had a peaceful nature and never hurt anybody; this was due to the flowers. She had no bad opinion of herself; for her gravestone she wanted one sentence: "She was good."

We lived close to the lake and went rowing; Kilchberg lay right on the other side. We once rowed over to visit the grave of Conrad Ferdinand Meyer, who became my poet at this time. I was struck by the simplicity of the inscription on the headstone. It said nothing about a "poet," no one mourned, he was unforgettable to nobody; all it said was: "Here lies Conrad Ferdinand Meyer. 1825-1898." I understood that any word would merely have diminished the name, and I realized here for the first time that the name alone mattered, that the name alone held, and everything else paled next to it. On the way back, it wasn't my turn to row; I couldn't speak a word, the hush of the inscription had carried over to me, but it suddenly turned out that I was not the only one thinking about the grave, for Fräulein Mina said: "I would like only one line on my grave: 'She was good.'" At that moment, I didn't like Fräulein Mina at all, for I sensed that the poet whose grave we had just visited meant nothing to her.

She often spoke of Italy, a country she knew well. In earlier years, she had been a governess for Count Rasponi's family, and the younger countess, her ex-pupil, invited her to her home once every two years, in Rocca di Sant'Arcangelo, near Rimini. The Rasponis were cultured people, frequented by interesting guests, whom Fräulein Mina had met over the years. But Fräulein Mina always had something to carp about in truly famous people. She preferred quiet artists who blossomed in secrecy, perhaps she was thinking about herself. It was striking that not only she, but also Fräulein Rosy and the other women in the house accepted any poet who had published at all. If there was a series of readings by the middle or younger generation of Swiss poets, then at least Fräulein Rosy went regularly, being more responsible for literature than painting, and the next day, in the hall, she would give us a detailed report on the peculiarities of the man. The women were deadly serious, and even if they didn't understand his poems, they liked this or that in the poet's manner, his shyness when bowing, or his confusion when making a mistake. They had the opposite attitude towards people who were the talk of the town. They viewed them with very different, with critical eyes, and particularly resented every characteristic that was unlike their own.

When the house had been a girls' boarding school, not that many

years ago, the ladies would occasionally invite a poet to read some of
his works to the girls. Carl Spitteler came all the way from Lucerne
and felt comfortable among the girls. He liked chess and sought out
the best player, Lalka, a Bulgarian, as his partner. Thus he sat in the
hall, a man of over seventy, propping his head on his hand, gazing at
the girl, and saying slowly, not after each of her moves, but still more
often than proper: "She is beautiful and she is intelligent." They never
forgave him for that, it was repeated often with an indignation that
grew every time.

Among the four ladies, there was one who *was* good, but who never
said it about herself. She didn't paint and never went to lectures, and
most of all she liked working in the garden. That's where one normally
found her, the season permitting; she always had a friendly word, but
only one word and not whole lessons, I don't recall ever hearing the
Latin name of a flower from her, although she was busy with plants
all day long. Frau Sigrist was Fräulein Mina's elder sister, and at
sixty-eight she really looked old. She had a very weathered, a totally
wrinkled face; she was a widow and had a daughter, the daughter was
Fräulein Rosy, who had always been a teacher and, in contrast to her
mother, never stopped talking.

You never thought about one being the daughter and one the mother;
you knew it, but it didn't enter your daily conception of them. The four
ladies formed a unity that you didn't associate with any man. It never
occurred to you that they had had fathers, it was as if they had come
into the world without fathers. Frau Sigrist was the most maternal of
the four, also the most tolerant, I never heard any prejudice or any
condemnation from her, but she never uttered a mother's claim. I never
heard her say "my daughter"; if I hadn't found it out from Trudi, I
would never have noticed anything. Thus, the maternal quality had
been highly restricted among the four ladies, almost as if it were rather
a bit indecent. Frau Sigrist was the calmest of the four; she never put
herself in the limelight, she never gave instructions, she never issued
an order; perhaps one heard a sound of agreement from her, but only
when one met her alone in the garden. In the living room, where the
four of them sat together every evening, she was usually wordless. She
sat a bit on the edge; her round head, which wasn't quite as large as
Fräulein Mina's, leaning slightly, always at the same angle; with her
deep wrinkles, she looked like a grandmother, but no one said that,
nor did anyone ever mention that she and Fräulein Mina were sisters.

The third was Fräulein Lotti, a cousin, perhaps a poor cousin, for
she had the least authority. She was the thinnest and plainest, as small
as the two sisters, almost as old, with sharp features, both her conduct

and expression fearlessly those of an old maid. She was a bit neglected, for she had no intellectual demands. She never spoke about paintings or books, she left that to the others. One always saw her sewing, that was something she was good at; whenever I stood next to her, waiting for a button she was sewing on for me, she emitted a few resolute sentences; in her small chores, she displayed more energy than others in the greatest. She was the least-traveled and had connections in the closer surroundings of the town. A younger cousin of hers lived in a farmhouse in Itschnach; we sometimes visited her when taking a long walk. Fräulein Lotti, who had plenty to do in the house (she also helped in the kitchen), would not come along, she had no time, which she said sternly and without complaining, for her most pronounced feature was her sense of duty. It was her pride to go without things that she particularly cared for. If another excursion to Itschnach was being discussed, rumor had it that she might, just might, come along this time, we just shouldn't nag her, when the time came and she saw us gathered in the garden, she would suddenly join us. It is true that she always did come over then, but only to send very detailed greetings to the cousin. Wasn't she coming too, she was asked. Goodness, what had gotten into us! There was enough work in the house for three days, and it had to be done by tomorrow! But she did take the visit, to which she never let herself be enticed, very seriously. She highly valued the greetings we brought back from the cousin and a detailed account of the events, each of us taking a turn. If anything didn't suit her, she asked questions or shook her head. Those were important moments in the life of Fräulein Lotti, they were actually the only demands she made; if she was left too long without reports from her cousin, her caustic remarks increased, and she became unendurable. But that seldom happened; it was part of the house routine to think about it without ever openly discussing it.

There remains the youngest and tallest of the four, whom I have already mentioned, Fräulein Rosy. She was in her prime, not yet forty, hale, hearty, and strong, a gymnast; she oversaw our games in the tennis court. She was a teacher to the core and liked talking. She talked a lot, at too regular a tempo, and her explanations always became too detailed. She had plenty of interests, especially the young Swiss poets, for she had also taught German. But it didn't matter what she talked about, it always sounded the same. She viewed it as her bounden duty to examine everything, and there was hardly anything she wouldn't respond to. But one seldom managed to ask her anything, for she was always in the middle of holding forth on her own, her initiatives were inexhaustible. You found out from her what had happened in the Yalta since the beginning of time, you got to know all the boarders from all the countries in the world and, if possible, their parents too, who had sometimes, alas not always, come along on the first visit; you found out about their merits and deficiencies, and what eventually happened to them, their ingratitude, their loyalty. It could happen that you weren't even listening after an hour, but Fräulein Rosy didn't realize it, for if she had to break off for any reason, she noted precisely where, steadfastly resuming at the right place later on. Once a month, she withdrew for two days. She remained in her room and didn't come down for meals, she had a "buzzing skull," that was her somewhat jaunty label for a headache. One might have thought that those would be days of relief; but far from it, we all missed her, and we also felt sorry for her, for if *we* missed the monotony of her talking, how greatly must she miss it herself, spending two whole days alone and mute in her room!

She did not regard herself as an artist like Fräulein Mina, who was owed supreme deference, and it was taken for granted that Fräulein Mina should withdraw into the sparrow's nest for the major part of the day, while the other three were continually occupied with some practical work. Fräulein Mina also wrote out the bills for the boarders, sending them to the parents at regular intervals. She would always add a long letter, stressing how reluctantly she wrote bills, for her area was the flowers that she painted and not money. The letters also dealt with the behavior and progress of the pupils, clearly showing her deeper interest in them. It was all very emotional, selfless, and noble.

As a unit, the four ladies were called the Fräuleins Herder, although two of them now had other names. But it was correct according to the distaff side. They appeared together as a unit for black coffee in the parlor, when the weather was nice, then on the veranda in front of it, and for a glass of beer in the evening. At such times, they were alone with each other, away from work, and you were not allowed to disturb them for any reason whatsoever. It was considered a special privilege that I was permitted to enter the parlor. It smelled of cushions and of old clothes, the ones that the ladies had on, it smelled of half-dried apples and, according to the season, of flowers too. These changed, like the young girls who boarded in the house; the basic smell, that of the four ladies, remained the same and always dominated. I didn't find it unpleasant, for I was treated benevolently. I did tell myself that there was something ridiculous about this household, nothing but women, and, with the pure exception of Frau Sigrist, nothing but old maids; but that was sheer hypocrisy. I, as the sole male among them all, old and young, couldn't have been better off, I was something special for them, merely because I, as it was put in Swiss German, was a "lad," and I didn't consider that any other "lad" would have been just as special in my place. I basically did what I wanted to, I read and learned what I desired. That was why I entered the parlor of the ladies in the evening: it contained a bookcase in which I could browse to my heart's content. I looked at illustrated books on the spot, others I took to read in the hall. There was Mörike, whose poems and tales I read with delight, there were the dark-green volumes of Storm and the red volumes of Conrad Ferdinand Meyer. For a while, Meyer became my favorite writer; the lake tied me to him, at all times of the day and evening, the frequent tolling of bells, the rich harvests of fruit, but also the historical subjects, especially Italy, whose art I finally learned about, and which I also heard a great deal about orally. In this bookcase, I first stumbled upon Jacob Burckhardt and I plunged into his *Civilization of the Renaissance*, without being able to get much out of it at that time. For a fourteen-year-old, the book had too many facets, it presumed experience and reflection in areas of which some were still fully closed to me. But even then this book was a kind of spur for me, a stimulus for breadth and variety, and a strengthening of my distrust of power. I was amazed to see how modest, indeed how meager my thirst for knowledge was, compared with that of a man like Burckhardt, and that there were degrees and intensities unheard of which I would never have dared to dream. He himself, as a figure, did not appear to me behind this book; he melted and dissolved in it, and I recall my impatience when replacing it on the bookshelf, as though he had eluded me into a different, almost unfamiliar language.

The opus that I eyed with true envy, a "luxury edition," was entitled *The Miracles of Nature*, in three volumes, and looked so costly that I couldn't hope ever to own it myself. Nor did I dare ask if I could take it to the hall; the girls weren't interested in it, and it would have been a sacrilege. So I only perused it in the parlor of the ladies. I would sometimes sit there for an hour, silently gazing at pictures of radiolarians, chameleons, and sea anemones. Since the ladies were on their own time, I didn't trouble them with questions, I showed them nothing; when I discovered something particularly exciting, I kept it to myself and was amazed by myself, which wasn't so easy, I would at least have liked to emit an exclamation, and it would have been fun determining that they didn't know about something they had had in their bookcase for many years.

I was not supposed to sit there for too long, however, for it might have led the girls out in the hall to believe I was enjoying special privileges. Well, actually I *was*, but they didn't resent it so long as it was limited to affection and attention. There was only one point in which there would have been bad blood, and that was the food. For the meals weren't especially good or copious. The ladies ate a piece of bread with their beer in the evening, and nobody was to think that I got anything extra from them, which indeed was never the case, for I would have been ashamed of such favors.

There would be a lot to tell about the girls, but I do not now intend to describe all of them. Trudi Gladosch, the Brazilian, has already been introduced. She was the most important, for she was always there, and had been there long before I or others came. Thus, she was not really typical or characteristic of the others, and no one else came from as far away as she. There were girls from Holland, Sweden, England, France, Italy, Germany, and from the French, Italian, and German parts of Switzerland. There was a student from Vienna, she was here to be "fattened" (it was the period of starvation after World War I), and there were always individual children from Vienna. These boarders weren't all there at the same time, however, the tenants changed throughout the two years, only Trudi never changed, and since her father, as I have already said, owed for her room and board, the situation was quite embarrassing for her.

Everyone worked together at the large table in the hall, here they did their homework and wrote their letters. If I had to be undisturbed, I was permitted to use a small schoolroom in the back of the house.

Shortly after moving into the Yalta, I heard the name "Wedekind" from the ladies; but here, the name was preceded by a "Doctor," which confused me slightly. They seemed to know him well, he often came by; after everything I had heard about him, from Wreschner, from Mother, and what not—his name was in the air—I couldn't quite understand what he was doing here. He had died recently, but he was spoken of as though alive. The name was borne by confidence; it sounded like the name of a man whom one relied on, they said with great respect that he had uttered this or that at his last visit, and the next time he came, they would have to consult him about something important. I was struck blind, dazzled by the name, which, in my eyes, belonged to only *one* man; I didn't dare ask for any details, though I normally had a ready tongue, and I explained it for myself by assuming that this must be a case of a double life. The ladies obviously didn't know what he had written, I myself knew it only from hearsay; so he wasn't really dead, he was still practicing, known only to his patients, in that section of our street, *Seefeldstrasse,* that lay closer to town.

Then one of the girls fell ill and Dr. Wedekind was summoned. Curious, I waited for him in the hall. He came, he looked stern and ordinary, like one of the few teachers whom I didn't like. He went upstairs to the patient, soon came back down, and resolutely informed Fräulein Rosy, waiting below, about the girl's sickness. He sat down at the long table in the hall, wrote out a prescription, got to his feet, and, while standing, became involved in a conversation with Fräulein Rosy. He spoke Swiss German like a Swiss, the deception of the double role was perfect; even though I didn't care for him at all, I began to admire him slightly for this theatrical achievement. I then heard him say very decisively (I don't know how the subject came up) that his brother had always been the black sheep of the family, people simply couldn't imagine how that brother had hurt him professionally. Some patients had been so frightened because of his brother that they had never returned to his office. Others, he said, had asked him: It just wasn't possible that such a man could be his brother? He had always, he said, given one and the same answer: Hadn't anyone ever heard that someone in a family can go the wrong way? There were impostors, check forgers, confidence men, crooks, and similar riffraff, and such people, as he could confirm from his medical practice, often came from the most decent families. Why, that was what prisons were for, he said, and he was in favor of those criminals being punished with utmost severity and with no consideration of their background. Now the brother was dead, he went on, he could say a few things about that brother which would not make his image any better in the eyes of decent people. But he preferred to hold his peace and think to himself: It's good that he's gone. It would have been better had he never lived. He stood there, solid and positive, and spoke with such wrath that I strode over to him, forgetting myself in my anger, planted myself in front of him, and said: "But he was a *writer!*"

"That's just it!" he snapped at me. "People like him give wrong ideals. Mark my words, my boy, there are good writers and there are bad writers. My brother was one of the worst. It is better not to become a writer in the first place and to learn something useful!—What's wrong with our boy here?" he turned to Fräulein Rosy: "Is he already coming out with such stuff too?"

She defended me; he turned away, he did not shake my hand when leaving. Thus, long before I read Wedekind, the doctor succeeded in filling me with affection and respect for him, and during my two years in the Yalta, I never got sick once, so as not be treated by that narrow-minded brother.

Phylogeny of Spinach
Junius Brutus

Mother spent a good part of those two years in Arosa, at the *Waldsanatorium*. I saw her—as I wrote to her—hovering at a great altitude above Zurich, and whenever I thought of her, I automatically gazed aloft. My brothers were at Lake Geneva, in Lausanne; so after the small, crowded apartment on *Scheuchzerstrasse,* the family had moved quite far apart, forming a triangle: Arosa-Zurich-Lausanne. Letters did pass back and forth every week, discussing everything (at least mine did). But most of the time I was independent of the family, and thus they gave way to new things. For the daily rule of life, my mother was replaced by the committee—one may phrase it thus—of the four ladies. I would never have dreamt of putting them in her stead, but in point of fact it was they I turned to when I wanted permission to go out or whatever. I was a lot freer than before; they knew what sort of wishes I had and denied me nothing. It was only when it got to be too much, when I attended lectures three days in a row, that Fräulein Mina grew skeptical and almost timidly said no. But that seldom came up, there weren't all that many lectures accessible to me, and mostly I myself preferred to have free time at home, for after every lecture, no matter what the topic, there was plenty to be read. Whatever was touched sent off waves of new things, spreading out on all sides.

I felt every new experience physically, as a sense of bodily expansion. Part of it was already knowing something else to which the new thing had no connection whatsoever. Something separate from everything else came to roost where previously there was nothing. A door suddenly flew open where one had not suspected anything to be, and one found oneself in a landscape with its own light, where everything bore a new name, stretching further and further, to infinity. One moved about, astonished, here, there, wherever one felt like, and it was as if one had never been anywhere else. "Scientific" became a magic word for me at that time. It did not signify, as later on, restricting oneself, gaining a right to something by forgoing everything else; on the contrary, it meant expansion, liberation from limits and boundaries, truly new landscapes that were populated differently, and they weren't imaginary as in stories or fairy tales, if you spoke their names they were not to be refuted. I had my difficulties with the much older stories, which I clutched as though life hinged on them. They were smiled at; I couldn't, for instance, come out with them in front of my schoolmates. Some of them had already lost all stories; being grown-up meant making scornful comments about them. I kept all the stories by spinning them further and using them as starting points to invent new ones for myself; but I was no less enticed by the areas of knowledge. I imagined new subjects at school in addition to the old ones, I devised names for some, names so odd that I never dared say them aloud, guarding them as a secret later too. But something about them remained unsatisfying, they were valid only for myself, they signified nothing to anyone, and I certainly also felt, as I spun them out, that I couldn't put anything into them that I didn't already know. The yearning for the new was not really stilled by them, the new had to be gotten where it existed independently of me, and that was the function, then, of the "sciences."

Furthermore, my altered circumstances had released forces that had long been bound. I no longer *watched over* Mother as in Vienna and in *Scheuchzerstrasse*. Perhaps that had been a cause of her periodic illnesses. Whether or not we cared to admit it, so long as we lived together we were accountable to each other. Each of us not only knew what the other did, but also sensed the other's thoughts, and what made up the happiness and denseness of this rapport was also its tyranny. Now, this watchfulness was reduced to letters, in which one could easily hide with some cleverness. She, in any case, by no means wrote me everything about herself: there were only reports on her illness, which I believed and went into. As for some of the people she met, she told me about them on her visits, her letters themselves contained quite little about them. She did the right thing, for if I found out anything about a figure in her sanatorium, I pounced on him with concentrated strength and tore him to bits. She lived among many new people, several of whom meant something to her intellectually; they were mature and diseased people, mostly older than she, but articulate and fascinating precisely because of their special kind of leisure. By socializing with them she thought of herself as really ill, and allowed herself the special sort of precise self-observation that she had once renounced for our sake. Thus, she too was free of us as I of her and my brothers, and our energy individually developed in an independent way.

However, I didn't want to keep any of my newly gained wonders from her. Any lecture that I went to and was inspired by I would tell her about, in factual detail. She got to hear things that had never interested her: e.g., about the Bushmen in the Kalahari, about the fauna of East Africa, about the island of Jamaica; but also about the architectural history of Zurich or the problem of free will. The art of the Renaissance in Italy—that was still acceptable, she was planning a trip to Florence that spring and received my precise instructions on what she absolutely had to see. She was embarrassed about her inexperience in the area of fine art and was not unwilling to be instructed occasionally. But she scoffed at my reports on primitive peoples, not to mention natural history. Since she herself prudently concealed so much from me, she assumed I was doing the same. She was firmly convinced that these many pages of reports on topics that bored her to tears were meant to camouflage personal things I was dealing with. She kept asking for real news of my life instead of the "Phylogeny of Spinach," as she scornfully called anything smacking of science. My regarding myself as a writer was something she accepted not unwillingly, and she never balked at ideas for plays and poems that I laid before her, or even at a completed drama that I dedicated to her and sent her. Her doubts as to the value of this concoction were never stated; perhaps too, her judgment was uncertain since I was the author. But she ruthlessly rejected anything smacking of "science," she refused to hear anything about it in letters, saying it had absolutely nothing to do with me and was an attempt at misleading her.

That period produced the first seeds of the later estrangement between us. When my curiosity, which she had fostered in every way, struck off in a direction alien to her, she began doubting my truthfulness and my character and was frightened of my possibly taking after Grandfather, whom she regarded as a wily actor: her most irreconcilable enemy.

Nevertheless, it was a slow process, it had to take time; I had to attend enough lectures to let my accounts of them and their effect on her accumulate. At Christmas 1919, three months after my entrance into Yalta, she was still under the impact of the drama I had dedicated to her: *Junius Brutus*. Since early October, I had been working on it evening after evening; in the schoolroom in back, which had been given over to me for studying, I remained every evening after supper until nine o'clock or later. I had long since finished my homework, and if I was deceiving anyone, it was the "Fräuleins Herder." They had no idea that I was working on a drama for Mother two hours daily. It was a secret, no one must find out about it.

Junius Brutus, who had overthrown the Tarquinii, was the first consul of the Roman Republic. He took its laws so seriously that he condemned his own sons to death and had them executed for participating in a conspiracy against the Roman Republic. I got the story from Livy, and it made an indelible impact on me, because I was certain that my father would have pardoned his sons had he been in Brutus' place. And yet *his* own father had been capable of cursing him for disobedience. In the ensuing years, I had seen how Grandfather had been unable to get over that curse, which Mother bitterly threw up to him. Livy didn't have much on this topic, a brief section. I invented a wife for Brutus, who fights with him over the lives of their sons. She gets nowhere with him, their sons are executed, in her despair she hurls herself from a cliff into the Tiber. The drama ends in an apotheosis of the mother. The last words (they are put in Brutus' mouth, he has just learned of her death) are: "The father's curs'd who murders his own sons!"

It was a double tribute to Mother; I was aware of one tribute, which had such great control of me during the months of writing, that I thought she would be so overjoyed as to recover. For her illness was mysterious, the doctors couldn't quite tell what was wrong; no wonder that I tried to aid her with such devices. As for the hidden second tribute, I was unaware of its existence: The final line of my play was a condemnation of Grandfather, who, as some of the family and particularly my mother were convinced, had killed his son with his curse. Thus, in the struggle between Grandfather and Mother, which I had witnessed in Vienna, I resolutely sided with her. Perhaps she also received this hidden message; we never discussed it, and I therefore cannot say for sure.

There may have been young writers revealing talent at the age of fourteen. I was definitely not one of them. The play was wretched, it was written in iambs that mock all description, awkward, bumpy, and bloated, not so much influenced by Schiller as determined in every detail, but in such a way that everything was ludicrous, dripping with ethics and nobility, garrulous and shallow, as though having passed through six pairs of hands, each less gifted than the earlier pair and thus making the origin unrecognizable. It is not advisable for a child to solemnly march about in the garments of an adult, and I would never had mentioned this wretched concoction if it hadn't revealed something with a genuine core: the early horror at the death penalty and at the order to carry it out. The connection between an order and a death penalty, albeit of a different nature than I could know at that time, occupied me later for many decades and has not released me even today.

Among Great Men

I finished the drama on time and wrote out the clean copy during the weeks before Christmas. Carrying through such a long work, which I began on October 8 and finished on December 23, filled me with a new kind of rapture. In the past, I had spun yarns for weeks on end, telling them to my brothers in installments; but as I never wrote them down, I didn't see them before me. *Junius Brutus,* a tragedy in five acts, filling a lovely, light-gray notebook, stretched out for over one hundred twenty-one pages and ran to 2,298 blank verses. This labor was my most important activity for ten weeks, and its significance was heightened by my keeping it a secret from the ladies and girls in the Yalta, even Trudi, who was my confidante. While so many other new things moved in on me, things I was passionately caught up in, the true meaning of my life seemed to be contained in the two daily hours of glorifying my mother. My weekly letters to her, reporting on all sorts of things, climaxed in the proudly ornate signature, with the following words underneath: *"In spe poeta clarus."* She had never learned Latin at any school, but her knowledge of Romance languages helped her guess pretty much of it. Still, being worried that she might misunderstand *"clarus"* as "clear," I put the German translation below the Latin.

It must have been pleasant to see the thing before me, which I did not then doubt: twice, in Latin and German, in my own hand and in a letter to Mother, whose highest veneration was for great writers. But it was not just my love for her that nourished my ambition at that time. The real fault, if it can be called a fault, lay with the *Pestalozzi School Calendar.* It had been accompanying me for three years now, and while I read the whole thing (there were so many interesting facts to learn from it), something in it had become a kind of tablet of the laws for me: the pictures of the great men in the actual calendar. There were one hundred eighty-two, one for every two days: an impressively drawn portrait and, underneath, the man's vital statistics and a few terse lines about his achievements and works. The calendar had already delighted me in 1917, when it first came into my hands: there were the globe-trotters whom I admired, Columbus, Cook, Humboldt, Livingstone, Stanley, Amundsen. There were also the great writers: the first on whom I set eyes when opening the calendar happened to be Dickens; it was also the first picture I ever saw of him, at the top left of the page for February 6, and, as a quotation next to the picture, under the date: "Cast a glance at the lowest in the human tumult!"—a sentence that became so much a part of me that now it is hard to imagine that it was ever new for me. But Shakespeare was there too, and Defoe, whose *Robinson Crusoe* had been one of the earliest English books my father gave me; likewise Dante and Cervantes; Schiller, of course, Molière and Victor Hugo, whom Mother often spoke about; Homer, whom I knew from the *Myths of Classical Antiquity,* and Goethe, whose *Faust,* despite so many stories about it, was still kept from me at home; Hebel, whose "Treasure Chest" we used in school as a reader in stenography; and many others whom I knew from poems in the German reader. I wanted to remove Walter Scott, whom I couldn't stand, and I started to smear him up with ink. But I didn't feel right about it, and so, having just begun, I grimly revealed my plan. "That's a childish prank," said Mother. "He can't defend himself. That won't get him out of the world. He is one of the most famous writers, and he'll still be in everything. And if anybody sees your calendar, you'll be ashamed." I *was* ashamed even beforehand, and I halted my destructive work immediately.

It was a wonderful life that I led with these great men. All nations were represented, and all fields. I knew a little about the musicians already; I was taking piano lessons and going to concerts. There was Bach, Beethoven, Haydn, Mozart, and Schubert. I had witnessed the impact of the *Saint Matthew Passion* on Mother. As for the others, I could already play pieces of theirs and heard them as well. The names of the painters and sculptors became meaningful only in the Yalta period; for two or three years I had looked at their portraits timidly and felt guilty. Socrates was there, Plato, Aristotle, and Kant. There were mathematicians, physicists, and chemists, and naturalists that I had never heard of. *Scheuchzerstrasse,* the street we lived on, was named after one of them; and the calendar fairly teemed with inventors. I can scarcely describe how rich this Olympus was. I presented each individual physician to Mother, letting her feel how high they stood over Herr Professor. The nicest thing was that conquerors and generals played an exceedingly woeful part. It was the deliberate policy of the calendar maker to gather the *benefactors* of mankind and not the destroyers. Alexander the Great, Caesar, and Napoleon did have their portraits, but I can't recall anyone else of that crew, and I remember them only because they were dumped out of the calendar in 1920. "That's only possible in Switzerland," said Mother. "I'm glad we live here."

Perhaps one quarter of the great men in the calendar were Swiss. Most of them I had never heard of. Nor did I go to any trouble to find out more about them; I accepted them with an odd kind of neutrality. The man whom the calendar was named after, Pestalozzi, made up for many. The same could hold for the rest. But it was also possible that they were included because it was a Swiss calendar. I respected the history of the Swiss; being republicans, they were as dear to me as the ancient Greeks. So I did my best not to question any of them, and I hoped that each one's merit would also crystalize for me.

It is no exaggeration to say that I lived with these names. Not a day passed without my leafing through these pictures, and I knew the sentences beneath them by heart. The more definite they sounded, the better I liked them. The calendar bristled with superlatives; countless examples of "the greatest this" and "the greatest that" have lodged in my memory. There was an intensification of that too: the greatest this or that "of all times." Böcklin was one of the greatest painters of all time, Holbein the greatest portraitist of all time; I knew a thing or two about explorers, and I didn't find it right that Stanley figured as the greatest explorer of Africa, I liked Livingstone a lot more because he was also a physician and had waxed indignant at slavery. In all other areas, I swallowed whatever I read. For two men, I noticed, "great" had been supplanted by "tremendous"; Michelangelo and Beethoven had their special place.

It is hard to decide whether this stimulus was a good thing; there can be no doubt that it filled me with blustering hopes. I never asked myself whether I had any right to tarry among these gentlemen. I riffled through the calendar to wherever I found them, they belonged to me, they were my saintly icons. In any event, this intercourse heightened not only the ambition, of which I had gotten a major part anyhow from my mother; it was pure veneration imbuing me. It was not taken lightly, the distance to the venerated figures seemed immeasurable. One admired their hard lives no less than their achievements. And although one enigmatically dared to emulate one or the other, there still remained the huge number of the rest, active in fields one knew nothing about, and at whose work-processes one could only be astonished, knowing one could never imitate them, and that was the very reason why they were the actual miracles. The wealth of minds, the variety of their accomplishments, the sort of equal rights obtaining for them, the diversity of their backgrounds, their languages, their eras, but also the difference in their life spans (some of them had died very young)—I wouldn't know what else could ever have given me a stronger sense of the vastness, richness, and hope of mankind than this gathering of one hundred eighty-two of its best minds.

Shackling the Ogre

On December 23, *Junius Brutus* went off to Arosa, with a long letter containing instructions on how Mother was to read it: First at one sitting, to gain an overall impression, but then a second time, piece by piece, with a pencil in hand to take a critical position on the details and report to me about them. It was a grand moment, my demands and expectations at a high pitch, and when I remember how miserable this "work" was, and that it didn't entitle me to the slightest hopes and, moreover, that I realized it myself so quickly, I must date from that time the distrust that I later felt against everything I wrote down in haughtiness and self-assurance.

The crash came the next day, before Mother had the play in her hands. I was supposed to see Grandmother and Aunt Ernestine, who still lived in Zurich and whom I visited once a week. After that stormy nocturnal scene in Fräulein Vogler's house, when I had virtually fought for my mother's hand and won it, my relationship to my grandmother and my aunt had changed. They knew it made no sense trying to talk Mother into remarrying, she wouldn't hear of doing something that would have destroyed me. Something like a rapport even developed between Mother's middle sister and myself; she began to understand that I was not taking after the Ardittis and that I was determined not to concentrate on earning money but to go into an "ideal" profession.

I found Grandmother alone, she received me with some important news: Uncle Solomon of Manchester had come, my aunt would be back with him any moment. So he had arrived in Zurich, the ogre of my English childhood, whom I hadn't seen in six and a half years, since we had left Manchester. In between lay Vienna and the world war, which had ended with the hope placed in Wilson and his Fourteen Points, and now, just recently, the great disillusion: Versailles. My uncle had often been talked about, Mother's admiration for him had not abated. But it was founded exclusively on his commercial success, and so many more important things had happened since then between her and me, such great figures had emerged in our evening readings and then in the real world of events, which I eagerly followed, that my uncle and his power had shrunk in my eyes. I still, as always, considered him a monster, the embodiment of all infamy, and his image had formed for me into something brutal and horrible, which fitted in completely—but I no longer saw him as dangerous. Not to worry, I would get the better of him. When my aunt came and said he was waiting for us downstairs to take us out, I felt something like elation; I, a dramatist at fourteen (the drama was in the mail already) wanted to confront him and measure myself against him.

I didn't recognize him at all; he looked finer than I had expected, his face was not unattractive at first glance and in any event not that of an ogre. I was amazed that he still spoke German fluently after all the years in England, it was a new language between us. I perceived it almost as noble on his part that he didn't force me to speak English with him; for some time now, my English had been rusty; in the serious conversation that was expected, I felt more secure with German.

"Which is the finest pastry shop in Zurich?" he promptly asked. "That's where I want to take you." Aunt Ernestine mentioned Sprüngli; she was thrifty by nature and had qualms about mentioning Huguenin, which was supposed to be even more posh. We went to Sprüngli on foot, along *Bahnhofstrasse*; my aunt, who had to take care of something, stayed behind a while; and, as is proper among men, we instantly plunged into politics. I vehemently attacked the Allies and especially England, since he came from there; I said that Versailles was unjust and contradicted everything that Wilson had promised. He pointed various things out to me, quite calmly; I sense that my vehemence amused him, he simply wanted to hear what sort of a person I was, and he let me talk. But even though he said very little, I noticed that he didn't really want to express any opinion on Wilson. In regard to Versailles, he said: "Economic factors play a role here. You don't understand that yet. . . . No country wages a four-year war free of charge." But what truly struck me was the question: "What do you think of Brest-Litowsk? Do you believe the Germans would have behaved any differently if they had won? The victor is the victor." He now fixed his eyes fully upon me for the first time: they were icy and blue, I recognized him.

Aunt Ernestine joined us in Sprüngli. In his arrogant way, the uncle ordered hot chocolate and pastry for us, but touched none of it himself, it all lay before him as though it weren't there; he said he was on an important trip and had little time, but he did want to visit Mother at Arosa during the next few days. "What is this disease?" he then asked and promptly answered himself: "I'm never sick, I don't have the time." But he added that he hadn't seen us all for such a long while and wanted to catch up. "You don't have a man in the family, that won't do." It didn't sound malevolent, though somewhat hurried. "And what are you *doing?*" he suddenly asked me, as if we hadn't spoken with one another at all. The stress lay on *doing*, *doing* was what mattered, everything else was chitchat for him. I sensed that things were getting serious, and I hesitated slightly. My aunt helped me, she had eyes like velvet, and if she had to, she could speak that way too.

"You know," she said, "he wants to go to the university."

"That's out of the question. He's going to be a businessman!" He pronounced his words with a Viennese accent, that pronunciation put him more decisively into his element. There now came a long sermon on the family's vocation for business. All had been businessmen, and he himself was living proof of how far one could get in business. The only one who had tried anything else, his cousin, Dr. Arditti, had soon regretted it. A doctor earned nothing and was a messenger boy for rich people. He had to come running for the least little thing, and the people didn't even have anything wrong with them. "Like your father," he said, "and now your mother." That was why Dr. Arditti had soon given up the profession and was now a businessman again like all of them. The moron had lost fifteen years with his studies and the illnesses of people who didn't concern him. But now he had made it after all. Perhaps he would still get rich despite the fifteen years. "Ask him! He'll tell you the same thing!" This Dr. Arditti, the black sheep of the family, was always getting in my way. I despised him beyond words, that traitor to his real profession, and I would never have dreamt of asking him anything, even though he was living in Zurich.

My aunt sensed what was happening to me, perhaps she was also frightened because he had mentioned my father in such a heartless way. "You know," she said, "he has such a thirst for knowledge."

"Fine, fine! A general education, a commercial school, then an apprenticeship in the business, then he can enter into it!" He stared straight ahead at what he wanted, he never so much as deigned to glance at me, but then he turned to his sister and even smiled when saying to her, as though it were really meant just for her: "You know, I want to gather all my nephews in my business. Nissim will be a businessman, George too; by the time my Frank is grown up, they'll be able to do business with him in charge!"

Frank in charge! I a businessman! I felt like pouncing upon him and hitting him. I controlled myself and took leave of them, although I still had time. I walked out into the street, my head on fire, and ran all the way back to Tiefenbrunnen in that angry delirium, ran as if the wretched business were at my heels. The first emotion that took a more solid shape was my pride. "Frank in charge, I a clerk, I, I," and then came my name. At that moment, I retreated to my name, as whenever I was in danger. I used it seldom and didn't like to be called by it. It was the reservoir of my strength, perhaps any name could have been that by belonging to me alone, but this name was more of a reservoir.

I repeated the sentence of indignation over and over to myself. But ultimately, only the name was left. When I arrived at the Yalta, I had reiterated it hundreds of times to myself and drawn so much strength from it that no one noticed anything odd about me.

It was the evening of the twenty-fourth, and they were about to celebrate Christmas at the Yalta. For weeks now, they had been talking of nothing else. The preparations were made in secret; it was, as Trudi told me, the biggest event of the year. She, who fought hypocrisy with a vengeance, promised me it would be beautiful. At home, we had always exchanged presents, but that was all. Mother wasn't religious, and didn't distinguish between the various religions. A performance of Lessing's *Nathan the Wise* at the *Burgtheater* had determined her attitude in these matters once and for all. But her memory of the customs at home, perhaps also her natural dignity, prevented her from taking over the Christmas feast in its entirety. So she had stuck to the somewhat meager compromise of gifts.

At the Yalta, everything was decked out; the hall where we spent most of our time was normally bare and sober, but tonight it radiated in warm colors and smelled of fir sprigs. In a much smaller area, the "reception room" right behind it, the celebration began. There stood the piano, which served at house concerts. On the wall above it hung a picture, that always seemed gigantic to me because of the small proportions of the space: Böcklin's *Sacred Grove*. Initially, I had thought it an original and gazed at it abashedly as the first "real" painting I had ever become aware of in a private house. But then one day, Fräulein Mina divulged to me that *she* was the painter, it was a copy from her own hands. She had done it at an early period, before devoting herself exclusively to her "flower-children"; and the picture was so faithful that any visitor in the house who wasn't enlightened about it mistook it for an original. There sat Fräulein Mina now, in front of her work, accompanying us as we sang the carols. She was certainly not the best pianist in the house, but the feeling she worked up for the songs was contagious. We all stood crowded together in the room; there wasn't much space, and we sang for all we were worth. After "Silent Night, Holy Night" and "Oh, You Happy, Oh, You Blissful," everyone was allowed to suggest a carol that he regarded as suitable and that he liked. It took fairly long until all requests were filled, and I especially enjoyed the fact that it went on and on, and no one hurried. You could not tell that anybody was waiting for presents, his own or the surprises he had planned for the others. But then, the procession formed and we filed off into the backmost room of the house, somewhat more hurried now; the youngest, a Viennese boy on holiday, took the lead; I, in those weeks the second youngest, right after him, and everyone according to age until the last. Then we finally stood at the big table, every present was attractively wrapped, and as a bonus, everyone got a few satirical verses from me; I never missed any chance for rhyming. Here I found the statuette of a Tuareg, high on a camel, in bold movement, and underneath, the words *The Africa Traveler*, together with the name. Even the books complied with my notion of a better future: Nansen's *Eskimo Life*, *Old Zurich* with views from earlier times, *Sisto e Sesto*, travel sketches from Umbria. There was thus a combination of many things that enticed me and occupied me at that time, and my uncle, who had no idea of all this, and whose icy, ugly words I could still hear during the caroling, was finally banished and silent.

After the holiday dinner, there was music till late at night. A former boarder, a singer, was visiting; Herr Gamper, a cellist at the municipal orchestra, who lived with his wife in a small adjacent building, played; and our pianists, Trudi and a Dutch girl, excelled as his accompanists. It was so beautiful that I dreamt of revenge. I shackled my uncle to a chair and forced him to sit and listen. Back in Manchester, he had never been able to endure music. He didn't sit still for long, he tried to jump up. But I had shackled him so fast to the chair that he couldn't get away. Finally, he forgot that he was a gentleman and hopped out of the house with the chair on his back, a ridiculous spectacle—in front of all the girls, Herr Gamper, and the ladies. I wished that my mother could see him like that, and I planned to write her everything tomorrow.

Making Oneself Hated

That first winter of my separation from Mother and my brothers brought a crisis in the school. During the past few months, I had sensed an unusual restraint among some of my schoolmates, but this restraint was articulated in ironical comments by only one or two of them. I had no idea what it was about. It didn't strike me that my own behavior could irritate anyone, nothing about it had changed, my schoolmates were the same except for a very few, and I had known them for over two years now. The class had already gotten a lot smaller in spring 1919; the few who wanted to learn Greek had switched to the *Literargymnasium*. The rest, who had opted for Latin and other languages, were divided into four parallel classes at the *Realgymnasium*.

With this redistribution, several newcomers had joined us; one of them, Hans Wehrli, lived in Tiefenbrunnen. We had the same road home and grew closer. His face looked as if the skin were stretched tight over the bones, it had something haggard and furrowed about it, which made it look older than the other faces. But that wasn't the only reason he seemed more grown-up to me: he was reflective and critical and never made remarks about girls, which some of the others had already started doing. On the way home, we always talked about "real" things, by which I meant everything connected to knowledge and the arts and the greater world. He could listen quietly and then suddenly and vividly react with his own opinions, which he grounded intelligently. This alternation of quietness and vividness attracted me, for quietness was not my thing; I was always lively with other people. I felt his quickness as his most intrinsic quality, he instantly knew what you meant without your having to say a lot, and he was always ready with an answer, agreeing or rejecting; the unpredictable nature of his reactions enlivened our talks. But no less than with the external course of these conversations, I was occupied with his self-assurance, whose roots I didn't know. All I knew about his family was that they operated the large mill in Tiefenbrunnen, which ground the flour for Zurich's bread. That seemed very useful to me, it was a very different kind of work than what I feared and hated in my uncle and the menace of the "business." As soon as I got to know someone a bit better, I made no bones about my distaste for everything linked to business and mere personal advantage. Hans Wehrli appeared to understand this, for he accepted it calmly and never criticized me for it; at the same time, it struck me that he never said anything against his own family. A year later, he gave a talk in school about Switzerland at the Congress of Vienna. I now learned that one of his forebears had represented Switzerland at the Congress, and I started to realize that Hans Wehrli was a "historical" person. At the time, I couldn't have put it in clear terms, but I sensed that he lived in peace with his family background.

For me, the matter was more complicated. Father stood as a good spirit at the outset of my life, and my feeling for Mother, to whom I owed just about everything, still seemed unshakable. But then right away, there came the circle of those, especially on Mother's side, whom I profoundly distrusted. It began with her successful brother in Manchester, but it did not stop with him. In summer 1915, during the visit to Ruschuk, there was also Mother's awful and crazy cousin, who was convinced that every single member of the family was robbing him, and who could breathe only in litigation until the end of his life. Then there was Dr. Arditti, the only one in the clan who had chosen what I felt was a "beautiful" profession, the kind, namely, in which one lives for other people; but he had betrayed this profession as a physician and was now in business like the others. On my father's side, it was less bleak, and even Grandfather, who had abundantly proved his proficiency and, in certain situations, his hardness, had so many other qualities that his overall picture was more complex and more fascinating. Nor did I have the impression that he wanted to rape me into business. The misfortune he had caused was already done, my father's death was in his bones, and all the evil he had caused there benefited me now. But deeply as he impressed me, I could not admire him, and thus, starting with him and going backwards, there stretched, for me, a history of ancestors who had led an Oriental life in the Balkans, different from *their* ancestors in Spain, four or five hundred years earlier. They were people to be proud of, physicians, poets, and philosophers, but there was only general information about them, having little to do with the family specifically.

In this period of a sensitive, precarious, and uncertain relationship to my background, an event occurred, which, seen from the outside, must certainly appear insignificant, but which had far-reaching consequences for my further development. I cannot skip it, much as I dislike talking about it, for it was the only painful event in the five Zurich years, to which I otherwise think back with a feeling of effusive gratitude; and its failure to submerge utterly into the wealth of joy has to do merely with later events in the world.

In the years of my childhood, I had never personally been made to feel any animosity towards me as a Jew. In both Bulgaria and England such things, I believe, were unknown then. What I noticed of them in Vienna never went against me, and whenever I told my mother about hearing or seeing anything of that sort, she would interpret it, with the arrogance of her caste pride, as being meant for others but never Sephardim. That was all the more bizarre since, after all, our entire history was based on the expulsion from Spain; but by shifting the persecutions so emphatically into a far past, she thought she might keep them away more effectively from the present.

In Zurich, Billeter, the Latin professor, had once criticized me for sticking my hand up too quickly when he asked us a question; when I blurted out the answer ahead of Erni, a rather slow boy from Lucerne, Billeter insisted that Erni work out the answer himself; he encouraged him, saying, "Just think, Erni, you'll come upon it. We won't let a Viennese Jew take everything away from us." That was somewhat sharp; and at the time, it had to offend me. But I knew that Billeter was a good man, that he wanted to protect a ponderous boy against a quick-minded one, and although it had been against me, I basically liked him for it and tried to tone down my eagerness.

But what should one think of this eagerness of excelling? Part of it, certainly, was a greater liveliness, the swiftness of Ladino, which I had spoken as a child and which had remained, as a peculiar tempo, in the slower languages like German and even English. But that can't be all: the most important thing must have been my desire to hold my own against my mother. She expected instant answers; anything one didn't have at hand wasn't valid for her. The speed with which she had taught me German in just a few weeks in Lausanne seemed justified, in her eyes, by the success of that method. So later on, everything took place in the same tempo. Basically, it all proceeded between us as in stage plays; one person spoke, the other replied; long pauses were an exception and had to mean something very special. But such exceptions weren't given to us; during our scenes, everything went like clockwork, one person had barely finished his last sentence and the other was already replying. With this dexterity, I held my own with Mother.

Thus, having a natural liveliness, I also felt the need to increase it in order to hold my own with her. In the altered situation of the classroom, I acted as I did at home. I behaved toward the teacher as though he were my mother. The only difference was that I had to stretch my hand up before bursting out with the answer. But then it came right away, and the others were left out in the cold. I never dreamt that this conduct could get on their nerves, much less offend them. The behavior of the teachers toward such swiftness varied. Some took it as an easing of their job when a few pupils reacted all the time. It helped their own work, the atmosphere didn't get stodgy, something was happening, they could feel that their teaching was good if it promptly triggered the right reactions. Others saw it as unjust and feared that certain slow minds might lose all hope of getting anywhere, precisely because of the opposite responses that steadily confronted them. These teachers, who were not all that wrong, acted coolly toward me and viewed me as some kind of evil. But then again, there were several who were glad that respect was paid to *knowledge*, and it was they who were most closely on the track of the motives for my flagrant alertness.

For I believe that part of knowledge is its desire to show itself and its refusal to put up with a merely hidden existence. I find mute knowledge dangerous, for it grows ever more mute and ultimately secret, and must then avenge itself for being secret. Knowledge that comes forth by imparting itself to others is good knowledge; it does seek attention, but it does not turn against anyone. The contagion coming from teachers and books tries to spread out. In that innocent phase, it does not doubt itself, it both gains a foothold and spreads, it radiates and wishes to expand everything along with itself. One ascribes the qualities of light to it, the speed at which it would like to spread is the highest, and one honors it by describing it as enlightenment. That was the form in which the Greeks knew it, before it was squeezed into boxes by Aristotle. One doesn't care to believe that it was dangerous before being split up and stowed away. Herodotus strikes me as the purest expression of a knowledge that was innocent because it had to radiate. His divisions are those of the nations who speak and live differently. He does not strengthen the divisions when speaking about them; instead, he makes room for the most diverse things in himself and makes room in other people who are informed by him. There is a small Herodotus in every young man who hears about hundreds of things, and it is important that no one should attempt to raise him beyond that by expecting restriction towards a profession.

Now the essential part of a life that is starting to know takes place in school, it is a young person's first public experience. He may want to distinguish himself, but even more, he wishes to radiate knowledge as soon as it takes hold of him, so that it won't become mere property for him. Other pupils, slower than he, have to believe that he is trying to suck up to the teacher and they look upon him as an eager beaver. But he has no goal in sight that he is aiming at, he precisely wants to get beyond such goals and draw the teachers into his drive for freedom. He measures himself against the teachers and not his schoolmates. He dreams of driving the practical notions out of his teachers, he wants to overcome them. And only those teachers who have not given in to the practical aims, who emanate their knowledge for its own sake—only those teachers are the ones he loves rapturously; and he pays tribute to them by reacting swiftly to them, he thanks them incessantly for their incessant emanation.

But these tributes set him apart from the others, in front of whom he pays the tributes. He pays no heed to them while putting himself forward. He is not filled with any bad wishes towards them, but he does leave them out of the game; they do not join in and they exist only as spectators. Not being seized by the teacher's substance as he is, they are unable to admit to themselves that *he* is seized, and they must think he is acting on base motives. They resent him as a spectacle in which no part is allotted to them; perhaps they are slightly envious that he can hold out. But mainly, they regard him as a troublemaker, who confounds their natural opposition to the teacher, which he, however, transforms into a homage right before their eyes.

The Petition

In fall 1919, when I moved to Tiefenbrunnen, the class was divided again. There were sixteen of us; Färber and I were the only Jews in the class. We had geometrical drawing in a special room; everyone had a locker assigned to him there, it was locked and had a name plate. One day in October, right in the middle of my dramatic efforts, which were accompanied by all kinds of elated feelings, I found my name plate in that room smeared up with insults: "Abrahamli, Isaakli, jewboys, get out of school, we don't need you." There were similar things on Färber's name plate; they weren't identical, and it may be that my memory is mixing some of his insults in among mine. I was so amazed that at first I couldn't believe it. Until now, no one had ever insulted me or fought against me, and I had been with most of my schoolmates for over two and a half years already. My amazement soon turned into anger; I was deeply affected by the insult, my ears had been filled with "honor" since early childhood. My mother especially went out of her way to dwell on this point, whether in regard to the Sephardim, the family, or each single one of us.

Naturally, no one admitted to it; other classes also were taught geometrical drawing in this room, but I sensed something like malicious satisfaction in one or two classmates when they saw how hard the blow had been.

From that instant, everything was changed. There may have been earlier taunts, which I barely heeded; but from now on, I experienced them with a sharp awareness; not the slightest remark against Jews could escape me. The taunts increased, and whereas they had once come only from a single pupil, they now seemed to come from several. The boys with the most developed minds, who had been with us at first, were no longer here; : Ganzhorn, who had competed with me and was my superior in many ways, had chosen the *Literargymnasium*, where I really belonged with my interests. Ellenbogen, intellectually the most adult, had gone to another division. I had been together with Hans Wehrli for six months, but he was now in the parallel class; we still had the same walk home, but he didn't take part in the inner life of the class at this time. Richard Bleuler, a dreamy, imaginative boy whom I had always wanted to be friends with, kept aloof from me. The action, so I felt, came from another boy, a kind of anti-intelligence, in the class. Perhaps he felt a particularly strong dislike of my "lively bustle," as the later formula put it. He had his own smartness, which didn't coincide with school smartness; he was also more mature and starting to get interested in things I had no notion of, matters of life so to speak, which, as he must have thought, were more important in the long run. Of the group of boys who were more or less like-minded, for whom matters of knowledge were important or who at least acted as if they were, I seemed to be the only one left, and it never struck me how irritating this "monopoly" must have appeared to the others.

Thus now the attacks threw me together with Färber, with whom I really had nothing in common. He knew Jews in other classes and told me what was happening there. Similar information came from all classes; the dislike of Jews seemed to be growing in all of them and being expressed more and more openly. Perhaps Färber was exaggerating what he transmitted; he was an unreflecting, emotional person. He also felt threatened in more than one way: he was lazy and a bad pupil. He was tall and rather heavy, and was the only one with red hair in class. He couldn't be overlooked; when he stood in front on a group photograph of the class, he covered the boys in back. His face had been crossed out in such a photo by others in the class. It looked as if they didn't care to have him so far in front; yet it was a sign that they wanted him out of the class altogether. But he was Swiss, his father was Swiss, his native language was the dialect, the idea of living anywhere else would never have occurred to him. He was afraid of not being promoted to the next grade and, since he usually did badly in front of the teachers, he perceived their dissatisfaction with him as part of the same hostility shown him by his classmates. It was not surprising that the information he brought me from the Jews in the parallel classes was increased by his own disquiet. I didn't know the other Jewish pupils, nor did I try to talk to them individually. This was his function from the very start, and he did his job zealously and with growing panic. It was only when he told me about one boy—"Dreyfus said he's so desperate he doesn't want to go on living"—that I too became panicky. I asked him, horrified: "Do you think he wants to kill himself?"

"He can't stand it, he's going to kill himself."

I didn't really believe it, it wasn't all that bad, as I knew from personal experience, there were just taunts, which, however, increased from week to week. But the thought that Dreyfus could kill himself, the very words "kill himself," gave the finishing stroke to my peace of mind. "Kill" was a horrible word, the war had made it profoundly loathsome, but now the war had been over for a year, and I lived in hope of an Eternal Peace. The stories I had kept inventing for myself and my little brothers, about abolishing war, had always ended in the same way, with the resurrection of the dead soldiers; but now they seemed like something more than stories. In Wilson, the American president, Eternal Peace had found a spokesman in whom most people believed. Today, no one can adequately visualize the power of this hope, which seized the world at that time. I live as a witness that it also took hold of children; I was by no means the only one, my conversations with Hans Wehrli on our way home were filled with it, we shared this attitude, and the dignity and seriousness of our conversations were determined by it to a large extent.

But there was something even more horrifying to me than "killing," and that was doing it to oneself. I had never really been able to grasp that Socrates took the cup of hemlock *calmly.* I don't know what made me think that every suicide can be prevented, but I know I was already convinced of this back then. You only had to find out about the intention in time and do something about it on the spot. I figured out what to tell a potential suicide: He would be sorry if he could find out about it after a while, but then it would be too late. He'd be better off waiting, and then he could still find out. I held this argument to be irresistible, I rehearsed it in monologues until presented with an opportunity to use it; but as yet, no opportunity had presented itself. The Dreyfus business was different, perhaps others were toying with the same idea. I knew about mass suicides from Greek and Jewish history, and although they were usually involved with freedom, the accounts had left me with mixed feelings. I hit upon the plan of a "public action," the first and only one during those early years. In all five parallel classes of our year, there were seventeen Jews in total. I proposed that we all convene—most of us didn't know each other—in order to discuss what was to be done, whereby I thought of setting up a petition to the administration, who might not realize what sort of pressure we were under.

We met in the Rigiblick restaurant on Mount Zurich, in the place where I had gotten my first glimpse of Zurich six years ago. All seventeen came, the petition was voted on and drafted immediately. In a few business-like sentences, we, the collected Jewish pupils of the third year, called the attention of the administration to the increasing anti-Semitism prevailing in these classes and we asked that measures be taken against it. All the Jews signed their names; there was great relief. We put our trust in the headmaster, who was slightly feared as being stern, but was also considered very just. I was to present the petition to the administration. We expected miracles from it, and Dreyfus declared that he wanted to stay alive.

Now came weeks of waiting. I assumed we would all be summoned together to the administration, and I thought about what I ought to say. It would have to be dignified words, we must not compromise ourselves, everything had to be terse and clear and we mustn't whine, for goodness' sake. But we had to bring up honor, for that was the crux. Nothing happened, and I feared that the petition had landed in the wastebasket. Any response, even a scolding for our independent action, would have been preferable to me. The taunts did stop for the moment, and that surprised me even more, for if the other pupils had been reprimanded behind our backs, I would have had to find out from someone or other whom I was closer to.

After five or six weeks, perhaps it was more, I was summoned to the headmaster's office alone. I was not received by stern Headmaster Amberg. His assistant, Usteri, stood there, with the petition in his hand, as though he had only just gotten it and was reading it for the first time. He was a short man, and his high-slung eyebrows made him look as if he were always merrily smiling. But he wasn't merry now, he merely asked: "Did you write this?" I said yes; it was my handwriting, and I had actually composed and not just penned it. "You raise your hand too much," he then said, as though the affair concerned only me; he tore up the paper with the signatures before my eyes and threw the pieces into the wastebasket. With that, I was dismissed. The whole thing had happened so fast that I couldn't say anything. "Yes," in answer to his question, had been my only word. I found myself outside the headmaster's door, as though I hadn't even knocked in the first place, and if the pieces of the petition, which had landed in the wastebasket, hadn't made such an impact on me, I would have thought I'd been dreaming.

The closed season in the class was over now, the taunts resumed as before, except that now they were more resolute and hardly ever stopped. Each day brought a well-aimed remark, and it confused me that they were against Jews in general or against Färber in particular, but left me out, as though I didn't belong. I regarded that as a deliberate tactic to pull us apart, and I cudgeled my brain a great deal to figure out what the assistant headmaster had meant with my raising my hand too much. Until this moment, when he had uttered his six words, it had never crossed my mind that I ever did anything wrong by sticking my arm aloft incessantly. I really did have the answer ready before the teacher had quite finished asking his question. Hunziker resisted this haste by ignoring me until I lowered my hand again. Perhaps that was the wisest tactic, but this too altered little in my lively reactions. Whether an answer was permitted or not, my arm incessantly shot into the air. Never *once* in all those years had it occurred to me that it might bother the other pupils. Instead of telling me so, they had nicknamed me Socrates, much earlier, in the second year, encouraging me even more with that honor, for that was how I took it. It was only Usteri's lean sentence, "You raise your hand too much," that lamed my arm; it was high time, and it did stay down, to the extent that I could keep it down. Besides, I had lost interest, I didn't enjoy school anymore. Instead of waiting for the questions in class, I waited for the next taunt at recess. Every put-down of Jews triggered counter-thoughts in me. I would have liked to refute everything, but things didn't reach that point; it was not a political debate, but, as I would phrase it today, the formation of a mob. In my mind, I formed the elements of a new ideology; Wilson had taken over the goal of saving humanity from war. I left that goal to him without losing my own interest in it; all my open conversations were still on that theme. But my secret thoughts, which I kept to myself—for whom could I have talked to about it?—concerned the fate of the Jews.

Färber had a harder time than I, for he did poorly with the teachers. He was indolent by nature, but now he gave up trying altogether. He dully waited for the next humiliation and then suddenly flared up. He flew into a temper and struck back, perhaps not noticing that his angry reactions warmed the cockles of his enemies' hearts. But that was an internal feud, for he retorted to insults with good Swiss curses, in which he was inferior to no one. After a few weeks, he resolved upon a serious measure. During recess, he went to Hunziker and complained about the hostile behavior of the class. He told him that his father was asking Hunziker in due form to convey this complaint to the headmaster's office. If nothing changed, he said, his father then planned to go to the headmaster himself.

Now we again waited for an answer, and again nothing came. We discussed what Färber would say if he were called into the headmaster's office for questioning. I urged him not to lose patience. He had to stay calm, I told him, and simply report on what was happening. He asked me to rehearse it with him, and we did it more than once. His face turned red even with me when he started talking, he got muddled and cursed our adversaries. I sometimes went to his place to help him with his homework. At the end of each tutoring session, we practiced the speech for the headmaster's office. So much time passed that he actually managed to learn it, and when I finally could tell him that it was okay, I remembered Demosthenes, and I comforted Färber by telling him about the Greek's difficulties. Now we were armed and we kept on waiting. No reaction ever came, the headmaster's office remained silent, as did Hunziker, whom we observed during his classes to catch even the slightest sign of a change. Hunziker got drier and drier, he outdid himself in his sobriety and assigned an essay topic for which I never forgave him: a letter to a friend, asking him to order a room, a bicycle, or a camera for us.

However, the atmosphere in the class did change. In February, four months after the start of the campaign, the taunts stopped at one swoop. I didn't trust the situation, I was sure they would start again, but this time I was wrong. The other pupils behaved as in earlier days. They no longer attacked, they no longer mocked, indeed, it even seemed to me as if they were deliberately avoiding the word that concentrated all the humiliation. Most of all, I was surprised at the true enemies, who had launched the action in the first place. Their voices had a warm ring when they talked to me, and I was delirious with joy when they asked me something they didn't know. I reduced my hand-raising to a minimum, and I succeeded in what was a peak of self-renunciation—I sometimes kept to myself things that I knew and I sat there dully, though I itched all over.

At Easter, the old school year ended; this brought some drastic changes, the most important being that the teachers now used the polite form *Sie* with us. The class had been in the square, merloned main building of the *Gymnasium*, which was thrust, oblique and fairly sober, into a bend in *Rämistrasse*, an ascending street. From this building, which dominated the nearby urban landscape, the class was moved into the *Schanzenberg* (the entrenchment mountain), very close by on its own hill; and, not having been meant as a schoolhouse originally, it had an almost private character. The classroom had a veranda and faced a garden; during lessons, we kept the windows open, and the room was fragrant with trees and flowers; the Latin sentences were accompanied by bird sounds. It was almost like the garden of the Yalta in Tiefenbrunnen. Färber had been left back, which was certainly not unjust, considering his performance, and he was not the only one. The class had gotten more compact, and there was a new mood about it. Everyone took part in the lessons in his own way, I made sure not to keep raising my hand immeasurably, and the others' resentment against me seemed gone. To the extent that one can imagine a community in a school class, we really had one. Each pupil had his qualities and each one counted. No longer feeling threatened, I noticed that my classmates were not uninteresting, even those who did not excel in any special school knowledge. I listened to their conversations, I recognized my ignorance in many areas outside of school, and I lost something of the arrogance that had contributed to the misfortune of the past winter. It was obvious that some, who had developed slowly, were now catching up. In a sort of chess club that formed, I was often thoroughly beaten. I entered the role that others had once had towards me, I admired the better players and began thinking about them. I was entranced with an essay of Richard Bleuler's, which was so good that it was read aloud in class, it was free of all schoolishness, inventive, light, and full of imaginative ideas; it made it seem as if there were no such thing as books. I was proud of Bleuler, and during recess I went to him and said: "You're a real writer." I wanted—as he couldn't realize—to tell him that I was no writer, for my eyes had meanwhile opened in regard to the "drama." He must have gotten a wonderful upbringing at home, for he waved me off modestly and said: "It's nothing special." He meant it too, his modesty was genuine. For I had had to read my essay aloud before him, it was full of the inexplicable self-confidence I was stamped with, and when I returned to my seat and he then passed me while going up front, he quickly whispered to me: "Mine is better." Thus he knew it, and now I saw how right he was, and now, when I sincerely bowed to him, he just as sincerely said to me: "It's nothing special." I realized that he lived among writers at home—his mother and her friend Ricarda Huch; I pictured him being present when they read their new works aloud, and I wondered if they also said: "It's nothing special." It was a lesson: One could do something special and not preen oneself on it. Something of this newly experienced modesty left its mark in my letters to Mother; it didn't last long, but now my conceitedness had a worm, which prevented me from carrying out further drama plans of the same sort. This was the same Bleuler whose rejection had hurt me so deeply the previous winter, for I had always liked him, and now it became clear to me that he had good reason not to like a lot of things about me.

All told, the winter had been a drastic one: getting used to the Yalta, without a single other male, doing what I felt like, borne by a blind affection, nay, a kind of worship, by females of all ages; the sharp attack by my uncle, who wanted to suffocate me in his business dealings; the daily campaign of the class. When the campaign was finished, in March, I wrote my mother that for a while I had hated people, I had lost all *joie de vivre*. But now it was different, I said, now I felt forgiving and no longer vengeful. In the subsequent happy period at the *Schanzenberg*, a time of forgiveness and newly aroused love of humanity, some things did remain in doubt, but the doubts—this was something new—were aimed at myself.

The attacks, incidentally—as I later found out—had been stopped from above, in an intelligent way, without noise or ado. True, the petition, which I was so proud of, had landed in the wastebasket, but individual pupils had been questioned in the headmaster's office. The comment that Usteri had made so casually, "You raise your hand too much!" had been one of the results. Because of its enigmatic isolation, it had struck me deeply and it got me to change my behavior. And there must have been useful comments to our adversaries too, otherwise they wouldn't have suddenly stopped their campaign. Since everything had happened so quietly, I must have gotten the impression, during the period of humiliation, that no one was doing anything about it; but in reality, the opposite was the case.

Getting Prepared for Prohibitions

The earliest prohibition that I recall from my childhood had to do with space; it referred to our garden, where I played and which I was not allowed to leave. I was not permitted to set foot in the street outside our gate. I cannot, however, determine who uttered the prohibition, perhaps it was my cane-wielding grandfather, whose house stood by the gate. That prohibition was seen to by the little Bulgarian girls and the servant; Gypsies in the street outside, as I often heard, simply thrust stray children into a sack and took them along, and that fear may have contributed to my observing the prohibition. There must have been other prohibitions of a similar nature, but they have drifted away, for they vanished behind one that broke in upon me with utter passion, when I, at five, in a dreadful moment, nearly became a murderer. At that time, when I, with a war whoop on my lips—"Now I'm going to kill Laurica!"—dashed towards my playmate with a raised ax because she had always, and in the most tormenting manner, refused to let me see her school writing; at that time, when I would certainly have struck her down if I had managed to get close enough to her, Grandfather, as wrathful as God himself, strode towards me, waving his cane, and grabbed the ax away from me. The horror with which I was then viewed by all, the seriousness of the family conferences on the homicidal child, the absence of my father, who was thus unable to tone anything down, so that Mother—an unusual event—secretly stepped in for him and tried to comfort me for my terror, despite severe punishment—all those things, but especially my grandfather's conduct (he subsequently caned me amid the most horrifying threats) had such a lasting effect on me, that I have to describe it as the actual, the primal prohibition in my life: the prohibition to kill.

Not only was I forbidden ever to touch the ax again, I was also ordered never again to enter the kitchen yard, where I had gotten it.

The Armenian servant, my friend, no longer sang for me, for I was even shooed away from the window of the big living room, from which I had always watched him. To keep me from ever seeing the ax, they forbade me to so much as glance into the kitchen yard; and once, when I yearned so strongly for the Armenian that I managed to sneak unnoticed to the window, the ax had vanished, the wood lay there unchopped; the Armenian, standing there idly, gave me a look of reproach and motioned at me with his hand to disappear as fast as possible.

It was a recurrent relief for me that I hadn't struck; for weeks afterwards, Grandfather kept scolding me, telling me—if my plan had worked—how dead Laurica would have been, how she would have looked in her blood, how her brain would have foamed out of the split skull, how I, punished by being chained up in a small kennel, would have had to spend the rest of my life alone, a pariah, never going to school, never learning how tho read or write, futilely begging and weeping for Laurica to come back to life and forgive me; Grandfather said there was no forgiveness for murder, for the dead person was never again in a situation to grant that forgiveness.

Thus, that was my Sinai, that was my shalt-not; and my true religion thus originated in a very definite, personal, unatonable event, which, despite its failure, adhered to me as long as I encountered Grandfather in the garden. Whenever I saw him in the following months, he threateningly brandished his cane, reminding me of the evil I might have committed, had he not interfered in the nick of time. Furthermore, I am convinced, though unable to prove it, that the curse he hurled at my father not many months later, before our removal to England, was connected with the grandson's wild behavior, as though I had prompted the threats and punishments with which his control over us finally crumbled.

I grew up under the domination of the commandment not to kill, and while no later prohibition ever attained its weight and meaning, they all did draw their strength from it. It was enough to designate something clearly as a prohibition, new threats were not pronounced, the old threat was still in force, the most effective threats were the horrible images that had been painted as the consequences of a successful homicide: the split head, the brain foaming out; and if later on, after my father's death, Grandfather turned into the mildest of all tyrants towards me, it altered nothing in the terror he had evoked. It is only now, when reflecting on these things, that I understand why I have never been able to touch the brain and other innards of animals; these are food prohibitions that came upon me of their own accord.

Another food prohibition, springing from my earliest religious lessons in Manchester, was nipped in the bud by a cruel action of my mother's. A few sons of our closer friends gathered for religious instruction in the Florentin mansion on Barlowmore Road. The teacher was Mr. Duke, a young man sporting a Vandyke and coming from Holland. There were not more than six or seven of us boys. Arthur, the son of the house and my best friend, also took part. There were only males present, and when Mirry, Arthur's eldest sister, entered the room where we were gathered—she may have done it out of curiosity or to look for something—Mr. Duke stopped talking and waited in silence until she had left again. What he was telling us must have been very much of a secret. The story of Noah and the Ark, which he told us, wasn't new to me. I was, however, surprised by Sodom and Gomorrha, perhaps that was the secret; for just as Lot's wife was about to turn into a pillar of salt, the English chambermaid came into the room and got something out of the buffet drawer. This time, Mr. Duke broke off in the middle of the sentence. Lot's wife had frivolously looked back, and we were in great suspense to hear about her punishment. Mr. Duke scowled, wrinkled his forehead, and eyed the maid's movements with unconcealed disapproval. Lot's wife got a deferred sentence; when the maid was outside, Mr. Duke shifted closer to us and said, almost whispering: "They don't like us. It's better if they don't hear what I tell you boys." Then he waited a bit and announced in a solemn voice: "We Jews do not eat pork. They don't like that, they enjoy their bacon at breakfast. You are not permitted to eat pork." It was like a conspiracy, and although Lot's wife still wasn't turned into a pillar of salt, the taboo sank into me, and I resolved never again to eat pork for anything in the world. It was only now that Mr. Duke cleared his throat, returned to Lot's wife, and announced her salty punishment to us, as we listened breathlessly.

Filled with the new prohibition, I went back home to Burton Road; I couldn't ask Father anymore. But I did report to Mother what had happened; I associated the destruction of Sodom with the pork; she smiled when I declared that the bacon the governess ate at breakfast was prohibited to us; she merely nodded without contradicting me, and so I assumed that she, albeit a woman, did belong "to us," as Mr. Duke would have put it.

Shortly thereafter, the three of us, Mother, the governess, and I, were having lunch in the dining room. There was a reddish meat that I didn't recognize; it was very salty and tasted very good. I was encouraged to have another piece and I enjoyed eating it. Then, Mother said in an innocent tone of voice: "It tastes good, doesn't it?"

"Oh, yes, very good. Will we have some more soon?"

"That was pork," she said. I thought she was making fun of me, but she was quite serious. I started feeling nauseated, I went out and vomited. Mother paid no attention. She didn't care for what Mr. Duke had done, she was determined to break the taboo; it worked, I didn't dare let him set eyes on me after what happened, and this form of religious instruction was done with.

Perhaps Mother wanted to be the sole authority, proclaiming shalts and shalt-nots. Having made up her mind to devote her life entirely to us and take full responsibility for us, she tolerated no other deep influence. From the writers whom she read, as others read the Bible, she drew the assurance that the individual development of the various religions didn't matter. She felt one had to find what was common to all of them and go by that. She distrusted anything leading to the acute and bloody fight of religions against one another, and she believed that it diverted attention from the more important things that people had to master. She was convinced that people were capable of the worst things, and the fact that they still fought wars was an irrefutable proof of how greatly all religions had failed. A short while later, when clergymen of all faiths were parties to blessing the weapons with which people who had never before seen each other were battling one another, her repugnance grew so powerful that she couldn't altogether hide it from me—even in the Vienna period.

She wanted to safeguard me against the influences of such authorities at any cost and she failed to realize that she thereby made herself the ultimate source of all proclamations. The force of supreme prohibitions was now with her. Never prey to the insanity of viewing herself as something godlike, she would have been very astonished had someone told her how outrageous her undertaking was. She had dealt swiftly with Mr. Duke's wretched affectations of secrecy. But it was far more difficult holding her own against Grandfather. His authority was shaken by his curse, and the fact that it had worked, as he was forced to believe, robbed him of his assurance towards us. He truly felt guilty when he kissed me and he pitied me for being an orphan. The word struck me as awkward whenever he used it, for it sounded as if Mother weren't still alive; however, he said it—which I didn't realize—against himself, it was his way of throwing up his guilt at himself. His fight with Mother over us was only half-hearted, and if she herself hadn't suffered from her own guilt she would have won the fight very easily. Both of them were weakened, but since his guilt was disproportionately greater, he got the worst of it.

All authority concentrated in her. I believed her blindly, it made me feel happy to believe her, and as soon as anything consequential and crucial was at stake, I awaited a pronouncement from her as others one from a god or his prophet. I was ten when she placed the second great taboo upon me, after that much earlier one against killing, which was imposed by Grandfather. Her taboo was against everything connected to sexual love: she wanted to keep it hidden from me as long as possible and convinced me that I wasn't interested in it. I really wasn't at the time, but her taboo kept its force during the entire Zurich period; I was almost sixteen and still refused to listen when other pupils spoke about the things that most preoccupied them. I wasn't so much repelled—at most, occasionally and only in particularly drastic circumstances—I was "bored." I, who had never known boredom, decided it was boring to talk about things that didn't really exist; and at seventeen, in Frankfurt, I still could astonish a friend by claiming that love was an invention of poets, it didn't exist, in reality everything was totally different. By that point, I had grown distrustful of the blank-verse poets, who had dominated my thoughts for so long, and I was, so to speak, extending Mother's taboo by letting it include "high" love.

While this taboo soon crumbled in a natural way, the prohibition against killing remained unshaken. It was so greatly nourished by the experiences of an entire and conscious life, that I would be incapable of doubting its justification, even if I hadn't already acquired it through my murder attempt at the age of five.

The Mouse Cure

At the sight of a mouse, Mother grew weak and lost all control. No sooner had she perceived some whooshing thing than she screamed, interrupted what she was doing (perhaps even dropping an object she was holding), and ran off with a shriek, whereby, probably in order to avoid the mouse, she moved in the strangest zigzags. I was used to this; I had experienced her carryings-on as far back as I could remember; but so long as Father was around, it didn't affect me very deeply, he liked being her protector and knew how to calm her down. In the twinkling of an eye, he had driven out the mouse, he took Mother in his arms, picked her up, and carried her about the room like a child, and he found the right words to soothe her. While doing so, he made— I might almost say—two different faces: a serious one, to acknowledge and share her terror, and a merry one, promising to clear up the terror and perhaps also meant for us children. A new mousetrap was then positioned cautiously and ceremoniously, he first held it up before her eyes, praising its efficiency, lauding the irresistible piece of cheese in it, and giving several demonstrations of how securely it closed. Then, as swiftly as it had come, everything was over. Mother, standing on her own feet again, laughed and said: "What would I do without you, Jacques!" Another sigh came: "Ough! How stupid of me!" And once the "Ough!" had been emitted, we recognized her, and she was her normal self.

In Vienna, when no father was with us anymore, I tried to assume his role, but that was too difficult. I couldn't take her in my arms, I was too small, I didn't have his words, I didn't have the same effect on the mouse as he, the mouse shot back and forth in the room for a fairly long time until I got rid of it. So first of all, I tried to shoo Mother into another room; my success hinged on her panic, which wasn't always equally intense. Sometimes she was so panicky that she actually remained in the same room as the mouse, then I had an extremely difficult time of it, for her own zigzagging crossed that of the mouse, both scurried back and forth for a while, head on, as though they couldn't stop frightening each other, in opposite directions, and then head on again, a senseless confusion. Fanny, already familiar with the screaming, came from the kitchen with a new mousetrap, that was *her* job, and it was actually Fanny who hit upon the effective words, which were always addressed to the mouse: "Here's some bacon for you, you stupid animal! Now get caught!"

Instead of explanations, which I asked Mother for afterwards, I only got stories about her girlhood: how she used to jump on the table, refusing to come down; how she infected her two elder sisters with her fright, and how they used to run around the room and all three of them once even fled up on the same table, standing there together, while a brother said: "Should I join you up there too?" There was no explanation; she didn't try to find one, she wanted to change back into the girl she used to be, and her only chance to do so was the appearance of a mouse.

Later, in Switzerland, whenever we moved into a hotel room, her first question to the chambermaid, whom she buzzed up for that very purpose, was whether there were any mice here. She was never satisfied with simple answers, and asked a few catch-questions to ferret out contradictions. She particularly had to know when the last mouse had been seen in the hotel, on what floor, in what room, how far away from our room, for it seemed inadmissible that any mouse had ever shown itself in this one. It was odd how this cross-examination put her mind at ease: no sooner was it done than she settled in and unpacked. She walked up and down the room a couple of times with an expert air, made her remarks about the furniture, then stepped out on the balcony and admired the view. She was once again sovereign and self-confident, just as I liked her.

The older I grew, the more ashamed I was about her transformation when the fear of mice came over her. In the Yalta period, I made a carefully thought-out effort to cure her. She came to visit me twice a year and spent a few days in the Yalta. She was given a nice, large room on the second floor, and she never failed to put her questions to the Herder ladies, who didn't have a totally clear conscience on this head; nor were they fit for cross-examination, they were evasive, humorous, and so unserious about the matter that Mother, in order to sleep peacefully, started in on me and interrogated me for something like an hour. This was a bad beginning, since I had so greatly looked forward to seeing her and there were so many things I wanted to talk about. Nor did I care for my mendacious replies, which served to calm her. As an early admirer of Odysseus, I did like completely invented stories in which someone turned into someone else and concealed himself, but I didn't like short-winged lies, which demanded no creativity. So once, right after her arrival, I tackled the matter à la Odysseus and, making my mind up on the spot, I said I had seen something wonderful and just had to tell her about it: A gathering of mice had taken place up in my small garret. They had arrived in the light of the full moon, lots of them, at least a dozen, and they had moved about in a circle and danced. I had been able to observe them from my bed, I could see every detail, it was so bright, it had really been a dance, in a circle, and always in the same direction, not as fast as they usually moved, more of a slogging than a scurrying, and there had been a mouse mother, who had held her young in her mouth and joined in the dancing. It was hard to describe how dainty the little mouse had looked, sticking halfway out of her mouth, but I had had the impression, I said, that the mother's circular motion with the others had not been pleasant for him, he had started squealing woefully, and since the mother was spellbound by the dancing and didn't want to interrupt it, the young had kept squealing louder and louder, until the mother, hesitantly, perhaps even reluctantly, had stepped out of the circle and begun nursing the child, a bit away from the dancers, though still in the moonlight. It was too bad, I told my mother, that she hadn't seen it herself, it was just like with human beings, the mother offers the baby her breast, I had forgotten that these were mice, they were so human, and it was only when my eyes fell on the dancers that I realized they were mice; but not even the dancing had had anything mouselike about it, it was too regular, too controlled.

Mother broke in and hastily asked whether I had spoken to anyone about it. No, of course not, you can't tell people a thing like that, why, nobody would believe it, the tenants of the Yalta would think I had gone crazy, I would most certainly take care not to tell them. "Well, then you know how bizarre your tale sounds. You dreamt it." But, despite the doubts she voiced, I noticed she would have preferred the story to be true. She was deeply affected by the suckling mouse-mother, she asked about details, over and over again; the more precisely I answered, the more I got the feeling that the thing was really true, even though I was quite aware that I had made the story up. She felt the same way, she warned me not to tell anyone else in the house about it; the harder I insisted that I hadn't dreamt it, and the more evidence I cited, the more important it seemed to her that I shouldn't say anything about it; she told me to wait until the next full moon and see what would happen. I had also described the dance as lasting until the moon had floated so far away that it no longer shone into my room. But the mouse-mother hadn't rejoined the circle of dancers, she had been busy with her offspring for a long time, cleaning it, not with her little paws, but with her tongue. The instant the full moon had stopped pouring into the garret, all the mice had vanished. I had promptly switched on the light, I said, and carefully inspected the area on the floor, where I then found mouse droppings. That had disappointed me, I said, for the dance had been so solemn; human beings would certainly not simply let themselves go on such an occasion.

"You're being unfair," she said, "that's just like you. You expect too much. Mice aren't people, after all, even if they do have a kind of dancing."

"But the way she nursed her young, that was human."

"That's true," Mother said, "that's true. I'm sure it wasn't the nursing mother who let herself go."

"No, it wasn't her, the droppings were in other spots." With these and similar details, I cemented her belief. We agreed to keep the matter to ourselves. She told me to be sure and report to her in Arosa at the next full moon.

That did away with my mother's fear of mice. Even in later years, I was careful not to admit I had invented the whole thing. She tried to shake my story in many different ways, such as by mocking my imagination, which had fooled me, or by worrying about my mendacious character. But I stuck to my guns, insisting that I had seen exactly what I described, albeit only that one time. No full moon ever brought the mice back; perhaps they had felt spied upon in my garret and had moved their dance to a less vulnerable area.

The Marked Man

After supper, which we ate together at a long table on the lower floor of the house, I sneaked into the orchard. It lay off to the side, separated by a fence from the actual grounds of the Yalta; we only entered it as a group during the fruit harvest, otherwise it was forgotten. A rise in the ground concealed it from the eyes of the house tenants; no one suspected you were there, you weren't looked for, even calls from the house sounded so muffled that you could ignore them. As soon as you had slipped unnoticed through the small opening in the fence, you found yourself alone in the evening twilight and you were open to any mute event. It was so nice sitting next to the cherry tree on a small rise in the grass. From here, you had a free view of the lake and you could follow the inexorable changes in its color.

One summer evening, an illuminated ship appeared; it moved so slowly that I thought it was standing still. I looked at it as though I had never seen a ship, it was the only one, there was nothing outside it. Near it, there was twilight and gradual darkness. It was radiant, its lights formed their own constellation, you could tell it was on water by the painless calm of its gliding. Its soundlessness spread out as expectation. It shone for a long time, without flickering, and took possession of me, as though I had come to the orchard for the sake of that ship. I had never seen it before, but I recognized it. It vanished in the full strength of its lights. I went into the house and talked to nobody; what could I have talked about?

I went to the orchard evening after evening and waited for the boat to come. I didn't dare entrust it to time; I was hesitant to place it in the hands of the clock. I was certain it would reappear. But it changed its time and did not reappear, it did not repeat itself, remaining an innocent wonder.

A sinister figure among the teachers was Jules Vodoz, whom we had in French for a while. I noticed him even before he came to us: he wore a hat wherever he was, even in the hallways of the school, and he had a somber, frozen smile. I wondered who he was, but I was afraid to ask others about him. His face had no color, it looked prematurely aged, I never saw him talking to another teacher. He always seemed to be alone, not out of arrogance, not out of scorn, but in some dreadful remoteness, as though hearing and seeing nothing around him, as though somewhere far away. I called him "the mask," but kept the nickname to myself, until he showed up in class one day, the hat on his head, our French teacher. He spoke—always smiling—softly, quickly, with a French accent, looked none of us in the face, and he now appeared to be listening hard into the distance. He paced nervously up and down, his hat made him look as if he were about to leave any minute. He stepped behind his desk, took off the hat, reemerged, and stood in front of the class. In the upper part of his forehead, he had a deep hole, which the hat normally covered. Now we knew why he always wore it and didn't like removing it.

The interest of the class was aroused by that hole, and we soon ferreted out who Vodoz was and what the hole was all about. He knew nothing about our investigations, but he was marked, and since he no longer concealed the hole in his forehead, he must have assumed that we knew about his background. Many years ago, he and another teacher had taken a class on an outing in the mountains. An avalanche had plunged down and buried them. Nine pupils and the other teacher perished, the rest were dug out alive, Vodoz with a serious injury on his head; it was doubtful whether he would survive. The numbers may have changed in my memory, but there can be no question that it was the worst disaster ever to strike the school.

Vodoz lived on with that mark of Cain, teaching at the same school. How could he ever have dealt with the issue of responsibility? The hat, shielding him from curious gazes, did not shield him against himself. He never took it off for long, he would soon get it from his desk and put it on again and then go along his path of a driven man. The sentences he used for instruction were distinct from him, as though someone else were speaking them, his smile was his horror, that was he. I would think about him, he entered my dreams, I listened like him to the approach of the avalanche. We didn't have him as a teacher for long, I was relieved when he left us. I think he often changed classes. Perhaps he couldn't stand being with the same pupils too long, perhaps they all soon turned into victims for him. I sometimes met him in the hallways and I greeted him cautiously, he didn't notice, he noticed nobody. None of my classmates ever spoke about him, he was the only teacher whom no one tried to mimic. I forgot him and never thought about him again; his image resurfaced before me only with the illuminated ship.

The Arrival of Animals

The kind of teacher you wish for, bright and energetic, was Karl Beck. He came into the classroom as swiftly as the wind, he was already standing in front, he lost no time, he was already in the middle of things. He was erect and slender, he held himself very straight, with no trace of rigidity. Was it because of the subject that his teaching never got involved in private complications? His mathematics was lucid and addressed everybody. He made no distinctions between us, everyone existed in his own right for Karl Beck. But he was candidly delighted if pupils responded well, he had a way of showing his delight, which you didn't take as preference, nor could anyone take his disappointment as discrimination. He didn't have very much hair for his age, but the hair he did have was silken and yellow; when I saw him, I had a joyous feeling of rays. But it wasn't that he subdued you with warmth, it was actually a kind of fearlessness. He courted us as little as he bullied us. A very slight mockery lay on his face, but no trace of irony; feigning superiority was not his thing, it was more as if he had retained his mockery from his own schooldays and had to make a little effort now not to show it as a teacher. He must have had a critical mind, I realize that in my memory of him; the detachment he maintained was an intellectual one. His effect was due not to importance, which teachers tend to show, but to his evenness of vitality and to his lucidity. The class was so unafraid of him that they initially tried to give him a hard time: one day, they greeted him with yells, he was already in the open doorway, the class kept on yelling. He took a very quick look, angrily said, "I'm not teaching!", slammed the door behind him, and was gone. No punishment, no court, no investigation, he was simply not there. The class remained alone with its yelling, and what was at first regarded as a victory ended with a feeling of ridiculousness and fizzled out.

Our geography book was written by Emil Letsch, and we also had him as our teacher. I knew his book before he came to us, I had half memorized it, for it contained very many numbers. The heights of mountains, the lengths of rivers, the populations of countries, cantons, and cities—I memorized whatever could be expressed in numbers, and I am still suffering from these mostly obsolete figures. I set great hopes on the author of such riches, anyone who had written a book was a king of god for me. But it turned out that the only thing this author had of God was the wrath. Letsch commanded more than he taught, and with any object he mentioned, he would add the price. He was so stern that he never once smiled or laughed. He soon bored me because he never said anything that wasn't in his book. He was maddeningly terse and expected the same terseness from us. Bad marks drummed down like beatings over the class, he was hated, and so intensely that this hatred became the only memory of him for many of his pupils. I had never seen such a concentratedly wrathful man, for other men, likewise wrathful, express themselves in greater detail. Maybe he was used to giving orders, maybe it was more taciturnity than wrathfulness. But the sobriety he emanated had a paralyzing effect. He wore a Vandyke; he was a short man, that may have contributed to this resoluteness.

I never gave up hope of eventually finding out something from him that would have justified his occupation with geography—he had even gone on expeditions. But the metamorphosis I experienced in him was of a different sort. He was present at a lecture on the Carolina and Mariana Islands, to which Fräulein Herder had taken me at a guild hall. The lecturer was General Haushofer from Munich, a scholarly geopolitician, superior to our Letsch not just in rank. It was a rich lecture, precise and lucid, which stimulated my subsequent occupation with the South Sea islands. His bias was unpleasant; I thought it was the military deportment that bothered me, and didn't hear any details about him until later. But I did learn a great deal in that short hour and I was in the expansive, cheerful mood one gets into on such occasions, when Professor Letsch suddenly greeted Fräulein Herder. They were old acquaintances who had met on a trip to Crete; and since he lived in Zollikon, we all walked home together. I couldn't believe my ears when I heard him conversing with Fräulein Mina. He spoke three, four, five sentences in a row, he smiled, he laughed. He expressed his amazement that I was living in the Yalta Villa, which he still remembered as a girls' boarding school. He said: "That's where our boy's geography comes from. He has it from you, Fräulein Herder!" But that was the least: he inquired about the other ladies, whom he called by name. He asked Fräulein Herder if she often got to Italy. He said he had run into Countess Rasponi on the island of Djerba a year ago. Thus it went, back and forth, all the way home; he was an affable, an almost courteous man, who finally took leave of us, emphatically, indeed heartily, albeit somewhat hoarsely.

On the journey, said Fräulein Mina, he had known all the prices and never stood for any cheating. The prices that that man had in his head—she still couldn't grasp it today.

Letsch's teaching meant nothing to me, and his book could just as

easily have been written by someone else. But I do owe him the experience of a sudden metamorphosis, certainly the last thing that I would
have expected from him.

There would be better things to report about Karl Fenner, the teacher
for natural history. Here, the man disappears in the immense landscape
that he opened up for me. He did not continue something for which
the groundwork had been laid at home, he began with something
completely new. Mother's ideas of nature were a conventional sort. She
not very convincingly enthused about sunsets and chose our apartments
in such a way that the rooms we used the most always faced west. She
loved the orchards of her childhood because she loved fruits and the
scent of roses. For her, Bulgaria was the land of melons, of peaches
and grapes, that was a matter of her strongly developed sense of taste
and smell. But we had no pets in the house, and she had never earnestly
talked to me about animals except as delicacies. She described how
geese had been crammed in her childhood, and while I practically died
of indignation and pity, she remarked how good such fat geese tasted.
She was quite aware of the cruelty of the fattening process, and the
implacable thumb of a maid stuffing more and more corn mush into
the beak of a bird, which I only knew from her description, became a
terrifying image in my dreams, in which I myself had turned into a
goose and was getting stuffed and stuffed, until I woke up screaming.
My mother was capable of smiling when I talked of such things, and
I knew she was now thinking of the taste of goose. She did make me
familiar with one kind of animal, the wolves on the frozen Danube;
she respected them because she had so greatly feared them. In Manchester, Father took me to the zoo. It didn't happen often, he was not
given enough time; she never came along, she never joined us, perhaps
because it bored her, she was utterly devoted to human beings. It was
thus my father who began my animal experiences, without which no
childhood is worth living. He mimicked the animals to my delight, he
was even able to change into the tiny turtle that we, like all children
in England, kept in the garden. Then, everything had broken off suddenly. For six or seven years now, I had been living in my mother's
world, which had no animals. Our life teemed with great men, but
none wore an animal's face. She was familiar with the heroes and gods
of the Greeks, although she preferred human beings to them too; it was
only as an adult that I learned about the dual-shaped deities of Egypt.

From the kitchen balcony of the apartment on *Scheuchzerstrasse*, we
looked down at a vacant lot. Here, the tenants of the surrounding
houses had started little vegetable gardens. One belonged to a policeman, who also kept a pig; he battened it devotedly and with all sorts

of cunning. In summertime, school began at seven; I got up by six and caught the policeman jumping over the fences of the neighboring gardens and hastily tearing up fodder for his pig. He first cautiously peered up at the windows of the houses to see if anybody was watching, all the people were still asleep, he didn't notice me, perhaps I was too small, then he hastily pulled out whatever he could and jumped back over to Sugie (that was what he called his pig). He wore police trousers, the long vertical stripe on each leg didn't seem to bother him in his undertaking, he leaped from one small vegetable bed to the other, a good jumper, helped himself, and thus spared his own truck. Sugie was insatiable, we liked hearing her grunt, and when George, my little brother, who had a terrible sweet tooth, had stolen chocolate again, we made fun of him by calling him Sugie and grunting tirelessly. He then cried and promised never to do it again, but the policeman had an irresistible effect on him, and the very next day, more chocolate disappeared.

In the morning, I awakened my little brothers; all three of us hid on the balcony and breathlessly waited for the policeman to emerge; then, not making a peep, we watched him jumping, and it was only when he was gone that we started grunting for all we were worth, Sugie had become our pet. Unfortunately, she didn't live very long, and, when she vanished, we were alone again, starving for animals, but without realizing it. Throughout that period, Mother was uninterested in Sugie, and the only thing on her mind was the dishonest policeman, whom we were profusely lectured on. She dilated zestfully on hypocrisy, got all the way to Tartuffe, and swore to us that the hypocrite would not escape his just deserts.

Our relationship to animals was still so miserable back then. This changed only with Fenner and his natural-history class at school; it changed thoroughly. With infinite patience, he explained the structure of plants and animals. He got us to do colored drawings, which we did at home, meticulously. He was not easily satisfied with these pictures, he went into every mistake, gently but doggedly urging us to improve them, and he often advised me to throw away the picture and start all over again. I spent nearly all my homework time on these natural-history notebooks. Because of the efforts they cost me, I was lovingly devoted to them. I admired my schoolmates' labors, which seemed marvelous to me; what effortless and beautiful drawings they did. I felt no envy, I felt astonishment at viewing such a notebook, there is nothing healthier for a child who learns easily than utter failure in some field or other. I was always the worst in drawing, so bad that I felt sympathy from Fenner, who was a warm and affectionate person.

He was short and somewhat pudgy, his voice was soft and quiet, but his teaching was down-to-earth and carefully planned, with a thoroughness that was sheer pleasure; we advanced only slowly, but the things we took up with him were never forgotten, they were inscribed in us forever.

He took us on excursions, which we all liked. They were merry and relaxed, nothing was overlooked; at Lake Rumen, we got all sorts of small water creatures, which we brought back to school. Under the microscope, he showed us this fantastic life in the smallest space, and everything we saw was then drawn. I have to hold myself back from going into detail and launching into a science course, which I can hardly force upon readers who know all this anyhow. But I must point out that he did not share my emerging sensitivity on all questions of eating and getting eaten. He took these things for granted; whatever happened in nature was not subject to our moral judgements. He was too plain, perhaps also too modest to let his opinion interfere with these inexhaustibly cruel processes. If there was any time to talk during an excursion and I let out some emotional remark in that direction, he kept silent and didn't answer, which was not really like him. He wanted to accustom us to a virile, stoic attitude in these things, but without dreary, sanctimonious claptrap, merely through his attitude. So I had to perceive his silence as disapproval and I restrained myself a bit.

He was preparing us for a planned visit to the slaughter house. During several lessons beforehand, he often talked about it, always explaining over and over again that they didn't let the animals suffer, they made sure—in contrast to earlier days—that the animals died a quick, painless death. He went so far as to use the world "humane" in this context, impressing upon us how to act towards animals, each of us in his milieu. I so greatly respected him, I liked him so much, that I also accepted these somewhat overly prudent preparations for the abattoir without feeling any aversion towards him. I sensed that he wanted to get us used to something inevitable, and I liked the fact that he was going to so much trouble and starting long before the visit. I pictured how Letsch, had he been in his place, would have ordered us off to the slaughter house and tried to solve the ticklish problem in the gruffest way, with no considerations for anyone. But I greatly feared the day of the visit, which came closer and closer. Fenner, who was a good observer and whom nothing easily escaped, even in people, noticed my fear, although I stubbornly locked it up inside myself and never said anything to my classmates, whose jokes I was scared of.

When the day came, and we were passing through the abattoir, he never left my side. He explained each device as though it had been thought up for the sake of the animals. His words imposed themselves as a protective layer between me and everything I viewed, so that I couldn't clearly describe it myself. When I think back upon it today, I felt that he acted like a priest trying to talk a person out of believing in death. It was the only time that his words seemed unctious to me, though serving to shield me against my horror. His plan worked, I took everything calmly, with no emotional outburst, he could be satisfied with himself, until his science ran away with him and he showed us something that destroyed everything. We came to a ewe, who had just been slaughtered and lay there open before us. In its water bag, a lamb was floating, tiny, scarely an inch long, its head and feet were perfectly recognizable, but everything about it looked transparent. Perhaps we wouldn't have noticed it, but he stopped us and explained, in his soft but unmoved voice, what we were seeing. We were all gathered around him, he had taken his eyes off me. But now I stared at him and quietly said: "Murder." The word came easily over my lips because of the war, which had just ended, but I think I was in a sort of trance when I said it. He must have heard, for he broke off and said: "Now we've seen everything," and he took us out of the slaughterhouse without stopping again. Perhaps we really had seen everything he wanted to show us, but he walked faster, he very much wanted to get us out.

My trust in him was shattered. The notebooks of drawings lay unopened. I did no more drawings. He knew it, he never asked me for any in class. When he walked up the aisles to criticize and correct the drawings, my notebook stayed shut. He never so much as glanced at me; I remained wordless in his lessons, I pretended to be sick at future excursions and had myself excused. No one but us perceived what had happened, I believe he understood me.

Today I fully realize that he was trying to help me through something that I wasn't meant to get over. He had confronted the slaughterhouse in his way. Had it been meaningless to him, as to most people, he wouldn't have taken us out again so quickly. In case he is still in the world today, at ninety or one hundred, I would like him to know I bow to him.

Kannitverstan; The Canary

Very early, in the second year of *Gymnasium*, we had stenography as an elective subject. I wanted to master it, but it was hard, I could tell how hard it was for me by the progress that Ganzhorn, in the next seat, was making. It went against my grain to use new signs for letters that

I knew well and had been using for a long time. Also, the shortenings deprived me of something. I did want to write faster, but I would have preferred a method of doing it without altering anything in the letters, and that was impossible. I memorized the signs with great difficulty; no sooner did I have one in my head than it vanished again, as though I had swiftly dumped it out. Ganzhorn was amazed, he found the signs as easy as Latin or German or as the Greek letters, in which he wrote his creative works. He felt no resistance against using *different* signs for the same words. I perceived each word as if it were made for eternity, and the visible form it appeared in was something inviolate for me.

I was used to the existence of different languages since my childhood, but not to the existence of different scripts. It was annoying that there were Gothic letters along with the Latin ones, but they were both alphabets with the same realm and the same application, fairly similar to each other. The shorthand syllables introduced a new principle, and the fact that they diminished writing so greatly made them suspicious in my eyes. I couldn't get through dictations, I made hair-raising mistakes. Ganzhorn saw the kettle of fish and corrected my mistakes with lifted eyebrows. Perhaps it would have gone on like that and I would eventually have given up stenography as something unnatural for me. But then Schoch, who also taught us calligraphy, brought us a reader in shorthand: Hebel's *The Treasure Chest*. I read a few of the stories in it, and without knowing what a special and famous book it was, I kept reading. I finished it in the briefest time, it was only a selection. I felt so sad when it was done that I promptly started all over again. I reread it several times, and the shorthand, which I didn't even think about— I would have read those stories in any script—had entered into me of its own accord. I reread the booklet many times, until it fell to pieces, and even when I later owned the book, in normal print, complete and in every available edition, I returned most of all to those crumbling pages, until they dissolved under my fingers.

The first story, "Memorabilia from the Orient," commenced with the words: "In Turkey, where queer things are said to happen occasionally. . . ." I always felt as if I came from Turkey, Grandfather had grown up there, Father had been born there. In my native city, there were many Turks, everyone at home understood and spoke their language. Though I hadn't really learned it as a child, I *had* heard it frequently; I knew a few Turkish words that had passed into our Ladino and I was generally aware of their origin. To all this were joined the tales of earliest days: how the Turkish sultan had invited us to live in Turkey when we had to leave Spain, how well the Turks had treated us ever since. With the very first words that I read in *The Treasure*

Chest, I had a warm feeling; what may have touched other readers as something exotic was familiar to me, as though it came from some kind of homeland of mine. Perhaps that was why I was also doubly receptive to the moral of the story: "One should not carry a rock in one's pocket for a foe or any revenge in the heart." At that time I was certainly not capable of putting the moral to any good use. I still cultivated an irreconcilable hatred for the two men whom I had named the chief foes of my early life: the bearded professor in Vienna and the ogre-uncle in Manchester. But a "moral" has to contrast with the way you feel and behave in order to strike you, and it has to remain in you for a long time before it finds its opportunity, suddenly braces itself, and strikes.

Hebel was full of such teachings, which are hard to forget, and each was tied to an unforgettable story. My life had begun with Kannitverstan's experience, when my parents spoke privately in a language I didn't know, and the things that had been heightened in his lack of understanding on individual occasions—the beautiful house with the windows full of tulips, asters, and gillyflowers; the riches that the sea washed ashore from the boat; the great funeral procession with the horses muffled in black—all those things had turned into a heightening of an entire language for me. I don't believe there is any book in the world that engraved itself in my mind as perfectly and as minutely as this one; I would like to follow all the trails it has left in me and express my gratitude to it in a tribute meant solely for this book. When the pompous iambic morality that dominated my surface in those years collapsed and fell into dust, every line that I had from that book survived intact. I have not written any book that I did not secretly measure by the language of that book, and I wrote each one first in the shorthand whose knowledge I owe to that book alone.

Karl Schoch, who brought us *The Treasure Chest*, had a hard time with himself and the pupils. He had a small, oval head with a ruddy face and canary-yellow hair, which stood out especially in his moustache— was it really that yellow or did it only seem that way to us? His movements, which had something jerky or hopping about them, may have contributed to his nickname: soon after we made his acquaintance, he became known as the "Canary," and he kept that sobriquet until the end. He was still a young man, he didn't have an easy time talking; it was as though he had problems moving his tongue. Before his tongue produced what he wanted to say, he had to prime himself well. Then the sentences came, but always very few. They sounded dry and monotonous, his voice was hollow, but very soon he lapsed into silence again. First, we had calligraphy with him; this subject, which I never got anything out of, may have made him seem pedantic. He took beautiful script as seriously as a pupil who had only just mastered it. Since he said so little, each word of his gained an exaggerated importance. He repeated himself, even when it wasn't necessary; anything he wanted to impress upon us had first to be wrested out of himself. No matter whom he addressed, his tone of voice was the same. You suspected that he had to practice in advance what he wanted to tell us. But then he frequently and inexplicably bogged down, and all his rehearsing was for nothing. He didn't seem feeble, so much as out of place. He wasn't put together right, he knew it and probably had to think about it all the time.

As long as it was calligraphy, he just barely passed the cruel examination of the pupils. There were some who made an effort and learned a good hand from him. All they had to do was cleanly copy the signs he chalked on the blackboard. It was the subject making the fewest mental demands, and it gave those who were still undeveloped the chance to prove themselves. But, while writing on the blackboard, he gained time for his silence. He then related to letters, not living pupils, he wrote them big and precise, for all together instead of for individuals, and it must have been a relief for him to momentarily turn his back on those gazes, which he feared.

It was disastrous that he subsequently replaced Letsch for geography. He was shaky in it, and the class delightedly grabbed the chance of getting back at Schoch for Letsch's tyranny. After the colonel, Schoch seemed like a minor recruit, and now he also had to speak all the time. He was welcomed with a soft twittering, which referred to the canary. After class, he was dismissed with a loud twittering. He hadn't even closed the door behind him when the twittering began. He never took any notice, he never wasted a single word on it, and there is no telling whether he knew what it meant.

We had come to South America; the big map hung behind him, he had us come forward one by one to indicate and name the rivers. Once, when it was my turn, the rivers I had to name included a Rio Desaguadero. I pronounced it correctly, which was no big thing; one of the most frequent words I had heard and used all my life was *agua* (water). He corrected me and said it was pronounced Rio Desag*a*dero, and the *u* was silent. I insisted that it was pronounced *agua*; he asked me how I knew. I stuck to my guns, saying I ought to know, because Spanish was my mother tongue. We faced each other in front of the entire class, neither gave in, I was annoyed that he wouldn't acknowledge my right to Spanish. He repeated, expressionless and rigid, but more resolute than I had ever seen him: "It is pronounced Rio Desag*a*dero." We hurled the two pronunciations at each other several times, his face got more and more rigid; had he been holding the pointer, which I was clutching, he would have lunged out at me. Then he got a saving flash, and dismissed me with the words: "In South America, it's pronounced differently."

I don't believe I would have gotten that opinionated with any other teacher. I didn't feel sorry for him, although he would certainly have deserved it in this embarrassing situation. We had a few more lessons with him; then once, as we were waiting for him—the twittering had already begun—another teacher appeared and said: "Herr Schoch will not come anymore." We thought he was sick, but we soon learned the truth. He was dead. He had cut open his wrists and bled to death.

The Enthusiast

The school year in the *Schanchzenberg*, the year of reconciliation, brought us a few new teachers. They used the polite form with us, *Sie*, it was the general rule, following it was easier for the "new" ones than for the teachers who had known us for a long while. Among those we had for the first time, there was a very old and a very young one. Emil Walder, the old one, had written the grammar book from which we studied Latin; aside from Letsch, he was the only textbook author I had as a teacher at the canton school. I awaited him with the curiosity and respect that I felt towards any "author." He had an enormous wart, which I see before me when I think of him, but I am unable to localize it. It was either right *or* left, near one eye, I believe the left one, but it has the obnoxious quality of wandering about in my memory, depending on from where I conversed with him. His German was very guttural, the Swiss stuck out more powerfully than in other teachers. That gave his diction, notwithstanding his age, something emphatic. He was uncommonly tolerant and allowed me to read during lessons. Since I had an easy time with Latin, I got used to a kind of double existence with him. My ears followed his instruction, so that, if called on, I could always reply. My eyes read a small volume that I kept open under my desk. He was curious, however and, upon passing my desk, he pulled out the book, held it up close to his eyes until he knew what it was, and then gave it back to me, still open. If he didn't say anything, then I took it as approval of what I was reading. He must have been a wide reader; once we had a brief talk about a writer whom he couldn't get anywhere with. I was absorbed in Robert Walser's *The*

Walk, it was a strange work which I couldn't put down, it was totally different from everything else I knew. It seemed to have no content and to be made up of polite formulas; I was caught up in it against my will and didn't want to stop reading. Walder approached from the left; I sensed the presence of the wart, but didn't look up, I was swept along too powerfully by the formulas, which I thought I despised. His hand came down upon the book, interrupting my reading—to my annoyance, right in the middle of one of the lengthiest sentences. Then he lifted the book up to his eyes and recognized the author. The wart, this time to the left, swelled up like a vein of anger; he asked me, as though it were an examination question, and yet intimately: "What do you think of this?" I sensed his annoyance, but I didn't want to admit he was right, for the book also greatly attracted me. So I said, conciliatorily: "It is too polite."

"Polite?" he said. "It's bad. It's nothing! One doesn't need to read it!" A condemnation from the depths of his voice. I gave in and pitifully closed the book, and then read on later, having been made properly curious now. That was how shakily my passion for Robert Walser began; perhaps, if it hadn't been for Professor Walder, I might have forgotten Walser at that time.

The antipode to this man, yet whom I liked because of his rawness, was young Friedrich Witz. He may have been twenty-three; we were his first class, he was fresh from the university and taught history class. I still hadn't gotten over Eugen Müller, "Greek Müller," as I called him privately. I had lost him as my teacher more than a year ago, and no comparable man had followed. I couldn't even say whom we got for history after him—a protest of the memory against that heavy loss. And now came Friedrich Witz, the second love of my school years, a man whom I never forgot and whom I found again much later, almost unchanged.

What a school that was, how varied its atmosphere! There were teachers for whom discipline was something unforced, it prevailed, as in Karl Beck's class, with no rebelling against it. There were other teachers who tried to train the pupils for the practice of subsequent life, sobriety, caution, reflectiveness. Fritz Hunziker was the epitome of such a teacher, and I waged a tenacious fight against the sobriety that he tried to inculcate in me too. There were richly talented men of imagination who stimulated us and gladdened us, Eugen Müller and Friedrich Witz.

Witz set no store by the raised podium position of a teacher. Sometimes he spoke from up there, with so much enthusiasm and fantasy that you forgot where he was standing and you felt as if you were outdoors with him. Then he would sit down among us, on one of the desks, and it was as if we were all together on a promenade. He never discriminated, he related to each pupil, he spoke incessantly, and whatever he said appeared new to me. All divisions in the world were wiped out; instead of fear, he inspired pure love, no one was put above the others anymore, no one was stupid, he skirted authority, he renounced it without attacking it, he was eight years older than we and treated us as if we were all his age. It was not a regulated instruction, he gave us what he was filled with himself. In history, we had gotten to the Hohenstaufens; instead of dates, we got people from him. It was not only because of his youth that power meant little to him, he was preoccupied with the inner effect it had on those who wielded it. Basically, he was interested only in writers, and he confronted us with them every chance he got. He spoke very well, vividly, movingly, but without prophetic overtones. I sensed the process of expansion at work, a process I would not have been able to name at that time; but, in an early, in an incipient stage, it was my own process. No wonder that Witz promptly became my ideal, in a different way from Eugen Müller, less sharply outlined, but closer, as attainable as a friend.

Instead of listing the deeds of an emperor and binding them to their respective dates, he acted him out, preferably in the words of a recent writer. It was he who convinced me of the existence of a living literature. I had closed myself off to it, dazzled by the wealth of earlier literature, in thrall to Mother's early theater experiences, and how could I have ever managed to exhaust what she brought to me from all literary cultures? I followed her memories, I was prey to her judgments. Whatever I discovered by myself crumbled if it didn't stand up in her eyes; and now I discovered that Wedekind wasn't merely an *épater-le-bourgeois* terror or a juicy item for the yellow press. When we got to Henry the Sixth, Witz didn't bother with his own words. He didn't feel adequate to this hubris, which was utterly alien to his nature. Instead, he opened a volume of Liliencron and read "Henry at Triefels" to us. He read it from start to finish, in our very midst, his right foot on my bench, his elbow propped on his knee, the book at a certain height. When he reached the passage about Henry's passionate courtship, "Irene of Greece, I love thee!", his forelock fell across the book—always a sign of his excitement—and I, who had never felt such love, felt icy shivers up and down my spine. He read with what the Germans call *Pathos*, an intensity almost verging on pomposity, today I would call it the *Pathos* of Expressionism, it was different from the *Pathos* of the 1880's and 1890's in Vienna, which I was used to hearing at home; yet his exaggeration wasn't alien to me, it was actually familiar. Watching him, as he shook the forelock off to the side with an impatient gesture, so that it wouldn't interfere with his reading, he made me feel as if I, who had always been the eldest in the family, suddenly had an older brother.

One can imagine that Witz's position did not go unchallenged. Some considered him a bad teacher because he made no effort to maintain a distance and did not regard external authority as absolute and ever-lasting. Compared with any other class, his had a kind of intentional disorder. In his presence, we lived in the middle of a force field of emotions. Perhaps what gave me breath and wings was, for others, a sort of chaos. At times, everything got all muddled up, as though no one cared about his presence anymore, and he was incapable then of creating the usual dead order with words of command. He balked at being feared; perhaps there are truly blessed people who are unable to inspire fear. At unpropitious moments there were inspections by older teachers. We didn't care to picture these reports to their superiors.

The wonderful time—it was one for me—did not last. He came to us in the spring, he left in October. Athough we had no facts to go by, the rumors among us, even among those who didn't care for him, were that he had been dismissed from the school.

Witz was so young that he couldn't act any differently: he tried to infect us with his youth. It is really not at all true that the road through the years has the same character for everyone. Some pupils come to school old, perhaps they were old previously, perhaps they were old from birth, and whatever now happens to them in school, they never get younger. Others gradually get rid of the age they have brought along and they make up for the lost years. For such pupils, Witz would have made an ideal teacher, but, by nature, they are in a minority. Then there are some who find school so difficult that they only start aging under its impact, and the pressure bearing upon them is so heavy, and they advance so slowly, that with all their force they clutch their newly gained age, never giving up any of it. But there are also some who are both old and young at once; in their tenacity at holding on to all they have come to understand, they are old; in the eagerness for all that's new, without discrimination, they are young. I may have belonged to this latter group at that time, and that must have been why I was receptive to very opposite teachers. Karl Beck, through the tenacious and disciplined manner of his teaching, gave me a sense of security. The mathematics that I learned in his class became a deeper part of my nature, as resolute consistency and something like mental courage. From a possibly very small area, which is not to be doubted, you keep on going in one and the same direction, never asking yourself where you might end up, refusing to look right or left, as though heading towards some goal without knowing which, and so long as you make no false step and maintain the connection of the steps, nothing will happen to you, you progress into the unknown—the only way to conquer the unknown *gradually*.

It was exactly the opposite that happened to me through Witz. Many dark points in me were touched at the same time and they lit up, to no purpose. You didn't advance, you were here, you were there, you had no goal, not even an unknown goal, you certainly learned a great deal; but more than what you discovered, you mastered a sensibility for things that are neglected or still concealed. Above all, he strengthened the delight in transformation: there was so much there that you hadn't suspected, all you had to do was hear about it in order to *become* it. It was the same thing that the fairy tales had done to me earlier, but now it concerned different, less simple objects—figures, to be sure, but now these figures were writers.

I have already said that Witz opened my eyes to modern, to living literature. Any name he mentioned, I never forgot; it turned into a specific atmosphere, to which he took me, and the wings he buckled on to me for such flights, without my noticing it, remained with me even after he left me, and now I flew there myself and looked about in amazement.

I am reluctant to speak of the individual names that first went into me through him. I had certainly heard some of them before, like Spitteler; others had aroused a merely passive curiousity, as if it sufficed to keep them in readiness for a later time, like Wedekind. Most of them are now so taken for granted as a part of traditional literature that it seems ridiculous to make any fuss over them. But the majority, which I will not list here, greatly contrasted with what I had gotten at home, and even though I made very few of them my own at that time, the prejudice against all writers who had just died or were still alive was broken once and for all.

Witz took us on two outings in the bare four or five months that we had him as our teacher. One outing was a fruit-wine ramble to the Trichtenhaus Mill, the other a historical excursion to Kyburg Castle. The fruit-wine ramble had been discussed far in advance, and he considered a downright revolutionary plan: he promised to take along a cousin, a violinist, she would play for us.

That made him truly popular in the class. Even those who had no rapport with his literary intoxications, even those who despised him for his lack of discipline and his refusal to inflict punishments, were captivated by the prospect of a creature of the female gender, a real cousin.

The class had been talking more and more about girls, relations had developed with a private school for girls, but consisted mainly of wishes and boastful announcements. Some classmates were already vehemently in action, there were big and physically mature boys among them who scarcely talked about anything else. Yet they couldn't do it without giggles and risqué comments. It was hard not to get drawn into such conversations. In all these things, I was truly retarded, my Mother's balcony taboo in Vienna still operated in me, and long after suffering the passion of jealousy in full force and even emerging as "victor" from the struggles I had gotten involved in, I still had no concept of what really went on between a man and a woman. In Fenner's natural-history class, I learned a good deal about animals, I drew their sexual organs in my notebook with my own hand, but it never occurred to me to relate any of that to human beings. Human love took place at altitudes that could only be expressed in blank-verse scenes, all events of love were a matter for iambs. I understood nothing in my schoolmates' off-color talk, they couldn't get anything out of me, no matter how encouragingly they grinned; I always stayed earnest amid titters and bragging and boasting, and so what was chiefly lack of understanding may have seemed like disapproval.

At bottom, it was a grotesque situation, for while others would have given their souls for a few words with a real, live girl, I went home daily to the Yalta, to a dozen girls, all older than I and secretly occupied with the same problem as my classmates, some of these girls more beautiful than any of the ones adored at the fancy girls' school. Two Swedish girls, Hettie and Gulli, whom I would find irresistible today, endlessly giggled and laughed with each other in Swedish, and even I could guess that they were carrying on about young men. There were some like Angèle, who came from Nyon on Lake Geneva, as lovely as she was timid, perhaps in the same frame of mind as I, but two years older. There was Nita, from Geneva, mentally the most mature of all, a trained dancer, who had studied with Dalcroze and who performed for us on some evenings in the Yalta. There was Pia, from Lugano, a dark, voluptuous beauty, bursting with something that I recognize as sensuality only in memory. And all these creatures, even the less attractive among them, nevertheless young girls, always with me in the hall, for hours on end, or playing with me in the tennis court, where we frolicked about heftily, and also got physically close during violent scuffles; all of them competing for my ear and my interest, for there was always something to ask about in their homework, and I could answer, since it mostly involved rules of German grammar; some of them, by no means all, conferring with me about private things too, such as reproaches in letters from parents. I, however, at the peak of this all-round delight, spoiled by these creatures like no boy of my age, anxious to prevent my comrades from finding out anything about this domestic life, for I was convinced they would have to despise me for such an exclusively feminine atmosphere, whereas they would actually have envied me for it. I used all my cunning to keep them away from the Yalta; I don't believe I ever permitted a single one of them to visit me here. Hans Wehrli, who lived in Tiefenbrunnen himself, must have been the only schoolmate of mine with any notion of the way I lived, but he was also the only one never to talk about girls in all our discussions, he always remained serious and maintained his dignity in this point too: perhaps—I cannot say positively—he was under a taboo similar to mine, perhaps he did not yet suffer from the compelling need of the others.

And now Witz made his violinist cousin a topic of discussion in class; from that moment on, she was a much more frequent topic than Witz himself; he was asked about her, he answered patiently. However, the fruit-wine ramble was put off from week to week, that must have been because of the cousin that Witz was trying to get, perhaps he wished to encourage her as a violinist and put an audience instead of flowers at her feet, a public that would welcome her in triumph. First she was busy, then she got sick, the expectations of the class reached a fever pitch. "Irene of Greece" became less interesting, I was infected by the general mood, we had no violinist at the Yalta and the violin, as my father's instrument, was transfigured for me—like the others, I stormed Witz with questions and sensed him growing more and more reticent and finally embarrassed. He was no longer positive that the cousin would come, she was about to take examinations, and when we finally met for the ramble, he appeared without her, she had begged off and sent us her regrets. With an incomprehensible instinct for these things, which I knew absolutely nothing about, I felt that something had gone awry for Witz. He seemed disappointed, he was dejected, he didn't act as cheerful and chatty as during his classes. But then, perhaps recalling his loss, he started talking about music. His cousin had dared to tackle Beethoven's violin concerto, I was glad that he intoxicated himself with a composer instead of a poet this time, and when the obligatory adjective for Beethoven cropped up, "tremendous," and was repeated several times, I was happy.

I wondered what it would have been like if the cousin *had* shown up. I had never doubted her virtuosity. But she would have had to play very well and always the right pieces to get the ardent interest of the class under control. Perhaps she wouldn't have dared to put the instrument down again and would have led us back to town through the forest, playing all the while. Witz would have been silent and followed at her heels, as a kind of forefront-admirer, to make room for her. But ultimately, our enthusiasm would have raised her to our shoulders, from where, still playing, she would have made her royal entrance into the city.

Actually, it did prove disappointing without her. The disappointment was made up for by the excursion to Kyburg Castle; Witz no longer spoke about her, instead he talked about history, which he made us familiar with in his lively and colorful way, by showing us the well-preserved castle. The high point was the train ride home; I was in the same compartment as Witz, directly opposite him and reading a guide-book I had bought in the castle. He lightly nudged my arm with his finger and said: "Now that's a young historian." His noticing something I was doing, his addressing me personally, was the thing I had most deeply wished for; but now that it happened, it contained the bitter injury of his seeing a future historian in me and not a writer. How could he have known, since I had never breathed a word about it, and his conjecturing a historian in me, something he couldn't have thought much about then, was the just punishment for my know-it-all attitude, which I exhibited in his classes too. I was quite taken aback, and to get him off history, I asked him about a writer who was being talked about and whom I hadn't yet read: Franz Werfel.

He spoke about his poetry, which was nourished by love for human-ity. He said there was no one with whom he couldn't feel empathy. No serving-girl was too lowly for him, no child, and indeed no animal; he was a sort of St. Francis, as though that name had shown him the way. He was no preacher, said Witz, but a man who had the ability to turn into any living creature so that his example might teach us love for that creature.

I credulously accepted this like everything that came from him (forming my own and very different opinion in this matter only later). But that was not the crucial event of the train ride. Touched by my timid, uncertain, and venerating questions, he began talking about himself, and he spoke so veraciously, so unheeding of any shield against other people's opinions, that, not without confusion, I got the picture of a man who was still in the process of forming, completely uncertain about his path, still truly open, without contempt or condemnations, such as I was so familiar with at home. His words, which I may not have even properly understood, have remained with me as the procla-mation of an enigmatic religion: He said he was full of zest for action and then again in utter despair. He was always looking and never finding. He didn't know what to do, how to live. This man, who sat before me, who inspired me with such love, whom I would blindly have followed anywhere, didn't even know where he was going and kept turning now to one thing, now to another; all that was certain about him was that he wanted to be uncertain, and much as it attracted me, for it came in his words, from his lips, it was wonderfully confusing—where in the world was I to follow him?

History and Melancholy

"Freedom" had become an important word around this time. What the Greeks had sown came up; since I had lost the teacher who had given us the Greeks, the peculiar structure emerging from Greece and Switzerland inside me had solidified. The mountains played a special role here. I never thought of the Greeks without seeing mountains before me, and, strangest of all, they were the same mountains that were in front of my eyes every day. They looked closer or further away depending on the atmosphere, one was delighted when they weren't covered up, one spoke and sang about them, they were the object of a cult. It was nicest to view them over a sea of fog from Mount Ütli near by; at such times, the mountains changed into islands, glistening, almost palpable, presented for veneration in all peaks. They had names and were named, some of them sounded lapidary and signified nothing but themselves, like the Tödi; others, like the Jungfrau (Virgin) or the Mönch (Monk), signified too much; I would have preferred a new and unique word for each mountain, a word employed for nothing else. No two were equally high. Their rock was hard, it was inconceivable that they ever changed. I had a powerful notion of this changelessness, I thought of them as untouchable; if anyone spoke of their conquest, I felt a malaise, and if I planned to climb them myself, I had a sense of something forbidden.

All the more life took place right by the lakes, the most exciting things had happened there, I wanted these lakes to be like the Greek ocean, and they all flowed into one when I lived close to Lake Zurich. It was not so much that anything changed its form, every place had its meaning and retained its individuality: bays, slopes, trees, houses. But in my dream, everything was "the lake," anything happening to one of them belonged to the others as well, the Helvetic Confederation created by an oath was a confederation of lakes for me. When I heard about the pile dwellings that had been discovered here and there, I was preoccupied with the thought that the inhabitants hadn't known about one another. At that distance from their own kind, without communication, it made no difference where they lived, they only needed a tiny patch of water, it could be anywhere; no one would ever know who they were; no matter how many shards of theirs were found, how many arrowheads, how many bones—they were not Swiss.

Now *that* was history for me: the alliance of the lakes, there was no previous history whatsoever, and even history itself came up to me only because I had found out about its true pre-history, the Greeks. In between, little counted; I distrusted the Romans, I was bored by Walter Scott's knights, who struck me as their descendants, jointed dolls made of armor; they got interesting only when they were beaten by peasants.

In this time of my enchantment by lakes, *Hutten's Last Days* fell into my hands, and I am not surprised that this earliest work of Conrad Ferdinand Meyer's so infallibly struck me. To be sure, Hutten was a knight, but he was also a poet, and he was depicted as a man who had fought against the false powers. He was ill and ostracized, abandoned by all, he lived alone in Ufenau by Zwingli's grace. The deeds he had performed in his rebelliousness arose in his memory, and as ardently as one felt their fire, one never forgot his present condition in Ufenau. The author saw to it that Hutten was always shown in the struggle against a superior power; and thus the thing that was so irritating about knights was omitted: the fact that even the bravest of them felt stronger because of their armor.

I was swept away by Loyola's visit to the island, this was a Loyola that no one, not even Hutten, knew: a pilgrim whom he puts up in his small dwelling during a storm, whom he covers with his own blanket, his own cloak to sleep in. In the night, Hutten is aroused by a thunderstroke, and in the brightness of the lightning he sees the pilgrim scourging his back bloody, and he also catches the words of his prayer, in which he dedicates himself to the service of the Virgin. In the morning, the pilgrim's place is empty, and Hutten realizes that now, when his day is squandered, his worst enemy has shown up. This confrontation with the opponent at the end of his life, this unawareness of unknown eavesdroppers, the insight into the futility of his own struggle, for the true foe has appeared only now, the subsequent response when it is too late—"Had I but killed the Spaniard!"—how could I help but feel that I was close to "reality" precisely here, in the midst of poetic fiction?

The lake on which Ufenau lay reached all the way down to me; Meyer had lived in Kilchberg, on the opposite bank. I felt enclosed in this long narrative poem, the landscape was illuminated by the poet, two lines most simply designated the extent to which I had by then become capable of insight into human matters: "I'm not an artful piece of fiction,/I'm human with human contradiction." The contrast between fiction and man, between what is made with prior knowledge and what is given by nature, between the graspability of a book and the incomprehensibility of man had started tormenting me. I had experienced enmity where I had not expected any, hostility forced from the outside, which did not spring from personal stirrings, whose roots I did not understand, and which I thought about a great deal. Since I had no solution, I accepted the temporary solution of viewing man as a contradiction. I seized that solution greedily and quoted Meyer's lines over and over again, until Mother demolished them in an annihilatory attack.

But beforehand, I had a year's time in which she left me alone. I followed Meyer to St. Bartholomew's Night and the Thirty Years' War. Through him, I met Dante in person, and the poet's image, as he spoke from his exile, was stamped in my mind. I had already gotten to know the Grisons mountains during hikes; two summers in a row, my first in Switzerland, I had been on Mount Heinzen in Domleschg, "the most beautiful mountain in Europe," as Duke Rohan called it. Nearby, at Rietberg Castle, I had gazed at a blood stain associated with Jürg Jenatsch, it hadn't impressed me very much. But now, reading about him, I felt like an expert tracking him down. I met Pescara's wife, Vittoria Colonna, sanctified by Michelangelo; I came to Ferrara, how dreadful, how sinister this Italy was, a land which I had heard nothing but idyllic things about. There were always exciting events, standing out in their "significance" against my daily surroundings. I didn't see the costume, I saw the variety of times and places. I noticed nothing about the varnish created by the costuming; since the ending was always gloomy, I accepted it as the truth.

In the unswerving, in the furious thirst for knowledge during those years, I was of the opinion that this varied animation of history was what captivated me in Meyer. I seriously thought I was learning something from him. No doubts assailed me, I willingly yielded to his presentation, I didn't sense what lay behind it, everything was in the open, so much was happening—what could there be behind it that, measured by this wealth, was not irrelevant and unworthy of mention?

Today, when I can no longer endure shaped history, when I only seek the sources themselves, naive accounts or hard thoughts about them, I believe it was something else in Meyer that had a deeper impact on me: a sense of harvest and fruit-laden trees, "enough is not enough," and the melancholy of his lake poems. One of them began with the lines:

Drearily wanes the sultry summer's day,
Dull and sad, my oars now plod their way.

. . . .

Far the heavens, and the depths so near—
Stars, you stars, why do you not appear?
Now, a cherished voice is calling me
From the watery grave so steadily.

I didn't know whose voice it was, but I felt it was a dead person, someone he had been close to, and the calls from the water moved me as though it had been my father who was calling. In those last Zurich years, I didn't think of him often, but his return from this poem was all the more unexpected, all the more mysterious. It was as if he had hidden in the lake because I loved it so dearly.

At that point, I hadn't yet found out anything about Meyer's life, about his mother's suicide by drowning in the lake. Never—had I known it—would it have occurred to me that I could hear my father's voice while rowing on the lake at twilight. I seldom rowed alone, and it was only then that I recited the lines, breaking off and listening: for the sake of the lines, I wished to be alone on the lake; no one learned of this poem and how much it meant to me. Its melancholy seized hold of me, it was a new feeling for me, tied to the lake, I felt the melancholy even if the time wasn't sultry and dreary, the melancholy dripped from the words. I sensed that it was drawing the poet into the lake, and although my melancholy was merely taken over from someone else, I felt the lure and waited impatiently for the first stars. I greeted them, in accordance with my age, not with relief but with jubilation. The urge to relate to the stars, which were unreachable and untouchable, began then, I believe, and increased into an astral religion during the next few years. I held them too high to grant them any effect on my life, I turned to them purely for the sight of them, I was fearful when they withdrew from me, and I felt strong when they reappeared where I could hope for them. I awaited nothing from them but the regularity of their return, the same place and the consistent relationship to their fellow stars, with which they formed constellations, that had wondrous names.

The Collection

Of the town, I knew the parts facing the lake, as well as the road to school and back. I had been to few public buildings, the music hall, the art house, the theater, and very rarely at the university for lectures. The anthropological lectures took place in one of the guild houses on the Limmat. Otherwise, the old part of town consisted, for me, of bookshops, where I browsed through the "scholarly and scientific" books that were next on the program. Then, near the railroad station, there were the hotels, where relatives stayed when visiting Zurich. *Scheuchzerstrasse* in Oberstrass, where we had lived for three years, almost passed into oblivion; it had too little to offer, it was fairly remote from the lake, and if ever I did think of it, it was as if I had lived in some other town.

In regard to some districts, I knew no more than the name and gave in, unresistingly, to the prejudices associated with them; I had no idea what the people there looked like, how they moved or acted towards each other. Everything that was distant laid claim to me, anything less than half an hour away and in an undesirable direction was like the other side of the moon, invisible, nonexistent. You think you're opening up to the world and you pay for it with blindness towards what's close by. Incomprehensible is the arrogance with which you decide what concerns you and what doesn't. All lines of experience are prescribed without your realizing it; anything not to be grasped without letters remains unseen, and the wolfish appetite that styles itself a thirst for knowledge doesn't notice what escapes it.

Only once did I find out what I was passing up; I wandered into areas of the city that I knew only from hearsay. The reason was a collection for a charitable purpose, they had asked who would be willing to do it. Every volunteer was accompanied by a pupil from the private school for girls. Mine was taller and older than I, but it didn't seem to bother her. She carried the money box, I carried what we were to sell, big bars of chocolate. She looked down at me with soothing eyes and had an intelligent way of speaking. She wore a white, pleated skirt, which seemed very elegant; I had never seen one so up close and I noticed that others were also eyeing it.

The collection began badly, the town was teeming with collector couples. People asked how much it cost and then whirled off in a huff. We weren't cheap; in one hour, we only got rid of one single bar. My companion felt insulted, but wouldn't admit defeat. She felt we ought to try apartment buildings and taverns, especially in Aussersihl. That was a working-class neighborhood, I had never been there, it struck me as absurd that she expected the poorer people to give what the rich had so far been refusing. She disagreed and grounded her opinion with no attack of emotions: "They never save," she said, "they spend everything right away. The best places are taverns, they spend all the money in their pockets on drink."

We took off towards that neighborhood. Now and then, we entered a building and knocked on every door. The tenants were still people with middle-class professions. Under one name on the second landing, the word "bank-director" was written. We rang, a gentleman with a luxuriant red face and an emotional moustache opened. He was both suspicious and jovial and asked first if we were Swiss. I held my tongue, the girl replied all the more charmingly, drawing me into her reply without exactly saying anything untrue. The man enjoyed examining her, he asked about her father's profession, and the fact that her father was a physician fitted in nicely with the purpose of our charity. He wasn't interested in my father's profession, he concentrated on the girl, who knew how to speak with intelligent airs, holding the money box at the proper height, not pushily, and making sure not to rattle the almost empty box. It took fairly long, but the smile on the man's face changed into a satisfied grin, he accepted the bar of chocolate, weighed it in his hand to see whether it wasn't too light, and tossed the coin into the box, not without adding: "It's for a good cause. We've got enough chocolate." But he did keep the bar, dismissing us in full cognizance of his good deed; when he shut the door, we were stunned by all that goodness and reeled shakily down to the first landing, where we rang without heeding the nameplate. The door opened, the man from upstairs stood before us, crimson and furious: "What, again! Of all the nerve!" With his doubly thick finger, he pointed to his name-plate, it was the same name: "You obviously can't read! Get out of here or I'll call the police. Or should I confiscate the money box?" He slammed the door in our faces, we made our woeful getaway. There must have been a staircase between the two floors inside the apartment. Who could have known; in the blissful daze of our successful sale, we had paid no attention to any name.

My companion had enough of apartments and said: "Now we'll go to the taverns." We kept walking morosely until we reached Aussersihl proper. At a corner, we saw a huge tavern; she didn't even ask me to go in first and she entered calmly. A stifling cloud of tobacco smoke came surging over us. The place was full, every table was occupied, workers of all ages, recognizable by their caps, sat before their glasses, we heard a lot of Italian. The girl threaded her way fearlessly through the tables, there wasn't a single woman whom she could have addressed, but that merely seemed to heighten her assurance; she held the money box up close to the men's faces, which was easy for her, since the men were seated. I hurried after her to be ready with the bars of chocolate on the spot, but I soon noticed how unimportant they were. Only the girl was important, and most important of all was her pleated skirt, which shone brightly in these dark surroundings. All eyes were on it, everyone gaped at it; a young boy, who actually seemed shy, reached for a pleat in the skirt and let it glide slowly through his fingers as he admired it. It was as if his touch were for the fine material and not the girl. He didn't smile, he regarded her solemnly, the girl paused in front of him, he said *"bellissima,"* she accepted the homage for the pleated skirt; he already had the coin in his hand, threw it, as though it were nothing, into the box, and didn't ask about the chocolate, which I somewhat belatedly held out to him; he carelessly placed it next to himself on the table, he was embarrassed to be taking something for his donation. Meanwhile, the girl had passed along, a gray-haired man was next. He gave her a friendly smile, reached for his money without asking, threw all the coins he had in his pocket on the table, picked out a two-frank piece, and, slightly hiding it with his fingers, he quickly threw it into the money box. Then he imperiously waved me over, pulled the chocolate from my hand, and presented it to the girl with a compelling sweep. He said it belonged to her, it was for her, she was to keep it for herself, and then he added that the chocolate was not to be sold.

Thus it began, thus it went on, whoever had money gave her some, but now they kept their bars of chocolate. Anyone without money apologized, a warm politeness prevailed, the noise at every table diminished as soon as the girl stepped up; I had feared insolent words, instead there was nothing but admiring glances and sometimes an exclamation of astonishment. I sensed I was totally superfluous, but that didn't bother me; infected by the men's mood of veneration, I told myself that my companion was beautiful. When we left the tavern, she shook the money box and weighed it, saying it was now more than half full. One or two more taverns like that, and nothing else would get into it. She was quite aware of the homage she had been paid, but she had her practical side and never forgot for an instant what was at stake.

The Appearance of the Sorcerer

I could tell how much I had changed by my grandfather's visits. He
came to Zurich only when he knew I was alone. The tension between
him and Mother must have grown; for several years he avoided her,
but they corresponded regularly. During the war, he received postcards
telling him our new addresses; later, they exchanged formal and im-
personal letters.

No sooner did he know that I was at the Yalta than he showed up
in Zurich. He got a room at the Hotel Central and asked me to come
by. His hotel rooms, whether in Vienna or Zurich, all looked alike, the
same smell prevailed in all of them. He was wrapped up in his phy-
lacteries, reciting the evening prayers, when I arrived; while kissing me
and bathed in tears, he continued praying. He pointed to a drawer,
which I was to open in his stead; inside lay a thick envelope of stamps,
which he had gathered for me. I emptied the envelope on the lower
bureau and examined them, some I had, some I didn't have, he kept a
watchful eye on the expressions of my face, which revealed delight or
disappointment to him in rapid alternation. Unwilling to interrupt his
prayer, I said nothing, he couldn't stand it and interrupted the solemn
tone of his Hebrew words himself with an interrogative: "Well?" I
emitted a few inarticulate, enthusiastic sounds; that satisfied him, and
he went on with his prayers. They took a fairly long time, everything
was established, he skipped nothing and shortened nothing; since it
proceeded at maximum speed anyhow, nothing could be accelerated.
Then he was done, he tested me to see whether I knew the countries
from which the stamps came, and he showered me with praise for every
right answer. It was as if I were still in Vienna and only ten years old,
I found it as bothersome as his tears of joy, which were flowing again.
He wept as he spoke to me, he was overwhelmed at finding me still
alive, his grandson and namesake, grown a bit more, and perhaps he
was also overwhelmed at being still alive himself and being able to
have this experience.

As soon as he was done testing me and had wept himself out, he
took me to a non-alcoholic restaurant, where "restaurant daughters"
waited on tables. He had an eager eye for them and it was impossible
for him to order anything without a detailed conversation. He began
by pointing to me and saying: "My little grandson." Then he totted
up all the languages he knew, there were still seventeen. The "restaurant daughter," who had things to do, listened impatiently to the tally,

which didn't include Swiss German; as soon as she tried to get away, he put a propitiating hand on her hip and let it lie there. I was embarrassed for him, but the girl stood still; when he was done with his languages and I raised my bowed head again, his hand was still in the same place. He took it away only when he started ordering, he had to confer with the "restaurant daughter," which required both hands; after a long procedure, he wound up ordering the same as always, a yogurt for himself and coffee for me. When the waitress was gone, I tried talking to him: I said this wasn't Vienna, Switzerland was different, he couldn't act like that, some day a waitress might slap him. He didn't answer, he felt he knew better. When the waitress returned with yogurt and coffee, she gave him a friendly smile, he thanked her emphatically, put his hand on her hip again, and promised to stop by on his next visit to Zurich. I wolfed down my coffee just to get away as fast as possible, convinced, all appearances notwithstanding, that he had insulted her.

I was incautious enough to tell him about the Yalta, he insisted on visiting me there and announced his coming. Fräulein Mina wasn't at home, Fräulein Rosy received him. She took him through the house and the garden, he was interested in everything and asked countless questions. At every fruit tree, he asked how much it yielded. He asked about the girls who lived here, their names, backgrounds, and ages. He counted them up, there were nine, and he said that more could be put up in the house. Fräulein Rosy said that almost each one had her own room, and now he wanted to see the rooms. She, carried away by his cheeriness and his questions, innocently took him into each room. The girls were in town or in the hall, Fräulein Rosy saw nothing wrong with showing him the empty bedrooms, which I had never seen. He admired the view and tested the beds. He estimated the size of each room and felt that a second bed could easily be added. He had retained the countries of the girls and he wanted to know where the French girl, the Dutch girl, the Brazilian girl, and especially the two Swedish girls slept. Finally he asked about the sparrow's nest, Fräulein Mina's studio. I had forewarned him that he would have to look at the paintings very carefully and praise some of them. He did that in his way: like a connoisseur, he first halted at some distance from a picture, then approached it and attentively studied the brush strokes. He shook his head at so much expertise and then broke into enthusiastic superlatives, while having enough cunning to use Italian words, which Fräulein Rosy understood, instead of Ladino words. He knew some of the flowers from his garden at home, tulips, carnations, and roses, and he asked Fräulein Rosy to convey his congratulations to the painter on her expertise: he had never seen anything like it before, he said, which was true, and he asked whether she also painted fruit trees and fruit. He regretted that none were to be seen and he ardently recommended an expansion of her repertoire. He thus stunned both of us, neither Fräulein Rosy nor I had ever thought of it. When he began asking about the cost of the paintings, I glared at him, but futilely. He stuck to his guns, Fräulein Rosy drew out a list from the last exhibition and informed him of the prices. There were a few that had been sold for several hundred francs, smaller ones were less, he had her give him all the prices in a row, instantly added them up in his head, and surprised us with the handsome sum, which neither of us had known. Then he grandly threw in that it didn't matter, the important thing was the beauty, *la hermosura*, of the paintings, and when Fräulein Rosy shook her head because she didn't understand the word, he swiftly interrupted me before I could translate it and he said in Italian: "*La bellezza, la bellezza, la bellezza!*"

Then he wanted to see the garden again, this time more thoroughly. In the tennis court, he asked how large the grounds belonging to the house were. Fräulein Rosy was embarrassed, for she didn't know; he was already measuring the tennis court with his paces, the length and the width, he had already computed the number of square meters, blurted it out, and reflected a bit. He compared the size of the tennis court with the size of the garden and also with the size of the adjacent meadow, made a shrewd face, and told us how big the lot was. Fräulein Rosy was overwhelmed; the visit, which I had so feared, was a triumph. For the early evening, he took me to a performance in the *Waldtheater* over the Dolder. When I came home, the ladies were waiting for me in their room. Fräulein Mina couldn't forgive herself for being away, for an hour I heard them sing Grandfather's praises. He had even figured out the size of the grounds correctly, a true sorcerer.

The Black Spider

The valley of valleys, for me, was Wallis; this was partly due to the name, the Latin word for "valley" had become the name of the canton, it *consisted* of the Rhône valley and its side valleys. On the map, no canton was as compact as this one, it had nothing that didn't belong to it naturally. I was impressed by everything I read about Wallis: its bilinguality, there were German and French parts, and both languages were spoken there as in the past; they appeared in their most ancient forms, a very old French in the Val d'Anni-vers, a very old German in the Lötschental.

Mother spent the summer of 1920 with all three of us in Kandersteg again. I often pored over the map: All my wishes now concentrated on Lötschen Valley, that was the most interesting part to see, and it was easily accessible. You rode through the Mount Lötsch Tunnel, the third biggest tunnel in the world, until Goppenstein, the first station after the tunnel. From there, you hiked through Lötschen Valley until the last village, Blatten. I pursued this plan zealously, gathered the group that I wanted to join, and insisted that the little brothers stay home this time. "You know what you want," said Mother; my ruthless way of leaving out the brothers didn't put her off, she liked it. She lived in the fear that books and conversation would turn me into an unmanly, indecisive creature. Although theoretically favoring consideration for smaller and weaker people, it enervated her in practice, especially if such consideration kept one from making towards a goal. She supported me by thinking up something else for the brothers to do, the day of the undertaking was scheduled, we would take the earliest morning train through the tunnel.

Goppenstein was even more inhospitable and more deserted than I had expected. Using the mule trail, its only connection to the outside world, we climbed up to Lötschen Valley. I found out how narrow the trail had been until just recently; only single animals could negotiate it with their burdens on their backs. Less than a century ago, there had been bears in the area, too bad you couldn't run into one now. I was mourning the vanished bears when all at once the valley opened up, drenched in sunlight, radiantly bright, high in the white mountains, ending in a glacier. You could get to the end in a reasonable length of time, but first the path, from Ferden to Blatten, wound through four villages. Everything was antiquated and different. All the women had their heads covered, black straw hats, but not just the women, very little girls too. Even the three- or four-year-olds had something solemn about them, as if they had been aware of the special character of their valley since birth and had to prove to us intruders that they didn't belong to us. These children stuck close to the old women with weathered faces who accompanied them. The first sentence I heard sounded a thousand years old. A very small, enterprising boy took a few paces towards us, but an old woman, who wanted to keep him away from us, pulled him back, and the two words she used sounded so lovely that I couldn't believe my ears. "*Chuom, Buobilu!*" (Come, boy) she said. What vowels those were! Instead of *Büebli*, which I was accustomed to hearing for "little boy," she said *Buobilu*, a rich dark structure of *u*, *o*, and *i*; I recalled the Old High German verses we read at school. I knew how close the Swiss German dialects were to Middle High German, but I hadn't expected anything sounding like Old High German, and I regarded it as my discovery. It bulked all the more powerfully in my mind, being the only thing that I heard. The people were taciturn and seemed to avoid us. Throughout our entire hike, we didn't get into a single conversation. We saw the old wooden houses, the women in black, the flowering pot plants in front of the windows, the meadows. I pricked up my ears for further sentences, all the people were mute; it may have been sheer chance, but "*Chuom Buobilu*" was the only piece of language to stay in my ears from the valley.

We were a rather motley crew, there were Englishmen among us, Dutchmen, Frenchmen, Germans; we heard lively exclamations in all languages, even the Englishmen seemed talkative compared with the silence of the valley. All were moved, all were amazed, I felt no shame for the blasé guests of our hotel, about whom I ordinarily made biting remarks; the unity of life here, in which everything fitted together, the hush, the slowness, the restraint, overcame their blaséness, and they reacted to the incomprehensible, to which they didn't feel superior, with admiration and envy. We passed through the four villages as though we had come from another star, without the possibility of any contact with the inhabitants, without any of them expecting anything whatsoever from us, they didn't even hint at a stirring of curiousity, and the only thing to occur during this hike was that an old woman called back a tiny boy, who hadn't even gotten quite close to us.

I have never been back to this valley; it must have changed a great deal in half a century, especially this last half. I made sure never to touch the image I have preserved of it. I owe it, in consequence of its very strangeness, the feeling of intimacy with antiquated living conditions. I can't say how many people lived in the valley at that time, there may have been five hundred. I saw them only as individuals, not more than two or three at a time. Their hard life was obvious. I didn't consider that some of them sought their livelihood on the outside, they seemed never to have dreamt of leaving their valley for even a while. Had I found out more from them, the image would have dissolved, and they would have become, they too, people of our time for me, people such as I knew everywhere. Luckily, there are experiences that draw their power from their unicity and isolation. Later on, when I read about tiny tribes and nations that lived in seclusion from all others, the memory of Lötschen Valley arose in me, and no matter how bizarre the things I read, I regarded them as possible and accepted them.

However, my admiration for mono- or rather quadrisyllabics, as I experienced them in that valley, was something rare at that time. It was around the same period that I succumbed to Gotthelf's eloquence. I read "The Black Spider," and I felt haunted by it, as though it had dug into my own face. Up in my garret, I tolerated no mirror, but now I shamefacedly asked Trudi for one, retreated upstairs with it, locked the door behind me, which wasn't customary in the house, and combed both my cheeks for traces of the black spider. I found none, how could I have, the devil hadn't kissed me, but I nevertheless felt a swarming as though from the spider's feet, and I washed frequently during the day to make sure it hadn't attached itself to me. I saw it where it was least expected, it once shone for me in lieu of the rising sun up on the footbridge. I plunged into the train, it had settled down opposite me, next to an old lady, who didn't notice it. "She's blind, I have to warn her," but I let it go at that; when I stood up in Stadelhofen to get off the train, the spider had decamped, and the old lady sat alone; it was a good thing I hadn't warned her, she would have died of fright.

The spider could vanish for days, it avoided some places, it never appeared in school, nor were the girls bothered by it in the hall. As for the Herder ladies—in their simple innocence, they weren't even worthy of the spider. It stuck to me, although I was not aware of having done any bad deed, and it stuck to my trail when I was alone.

I had resolved not to say anything to Mother about the black spider; I was worried about the effect it might have on her, as though it were especially dangerous for sick people, and some things might have turned out differently had I had the strength to keep my resolution. For at her very next visit I blurted the entire story out in detail, blow by dreadful blow. I omitted the pleasant baptism of the baby and all the comforting moral elements with which Gotthelf tries to soften the effect. She listened, not once interrupting me, I had never succeeded in fascinating her so totally. As though our roles were reversed, she asked about Gotthelf as soon as I was finished: just who he was and how come she had never before heard anything of such a fantastic story. I had narrated myself into terror and attempted to conceal it by going off into an old dispute between us about the worth or unworth of dialects. He was actually a Bern writer, I said, his language was that of Emmental, you couldn't understand some of it, without the dialect Gotthelf would be unthinkable, he drew all his strength from it. I hinted that "The Black Spider" would have escaped me, that I would never have gained access to it if I hadn't always been open to the dialect.

We were both in a state of excitement generated by the thing itself, even the hostility we felt towards each other had something to do with the story, but anything we *articulated* moved in the sphere of superficial obstinacy. She didn't want to hear about Emmental at all, she claimed the story was biblical and came straight from the Bible. The black spider was an eleventh Egyptian plague, and it was the fault of the dialect that the story was so unknown. It would be good to translate it into a literary German so that it would be accessible to everybody.

As soon as she was back in the sanatorium, she asked her acquaintances about Gotthelf, most of them came from northern Germany and they told her he had written nothing but unpalatable, long-winded novels about peasants, consisting mainly of sermons. "The Black Spider" was the only exception, they said, but it too was awkwardly written, full of long, superfluous passages; nobody with any understanding took Gotthelf seriously today. In her letter telling me all this, she added a derisive question: What did I want to become now, a preacher or a peasant, why not both at once, I really ought to make up my mind.

But I clung to my opinion, and at her next visit, I attacked the aesthetic ladies and gentlemen whom she allowed to influence her. "Aesthete" had always been a term of abuse in her mouth, the worst thing on God's earth were "Viennese aesthetes." The word hit her severely, I had picked it carefully, she defended herself, revealing a concern for the lives of her friends, and so earnestly that I felt as if it came right out of "The Black Spider." People threatened by death, she said, could not be called aesthetes. They didn't know how much longer they had to live. Did I believe that people in such a condition didn't think very carefully about what they read? There were stories that ran off you like water, she went on, and stories that you remembered better with every passing day. That said something about *our* condition and nothing about the writer. She was positive, she said, that despite "The Black Spider," she would never read a line of Gotthelf. She was determined to be right and win out against this dialect sinner, and she cited authorities. She spoke of Theodore Däubler, who had given a reading in the forest sanatorium, a number of writers gave readings there, she had become a bit friendly with Däubler on that occasion, even though he had recited poetry, which wasn't her thing, and she claimed he had a low opinion of Gotthelf. "That's not possible!" I said, I was so indignant that I doubted the truth of her words. She became unsure of herself and toned down her statement: in any event, others had made such comments in his presence, and he hadn't contradicted them, so he must have agreed. Our dialogue degenerated into a squabble, with each one insisting he or she was right and insisting, almost venomously, on his or her viewpoint. I sensed she was beginning to view my passion for everything that was Swiss as dangerous. "You're getting narrow-minded," she said, "no wonder, we see too little of each other. You're becoming too conceited. You live among old maids and young girls. You let them worship you. Narrow-minded and conceited, that's not what I sacrificed my life for."

Michelangelo

In September 1920, one and half years after we lost Eugen Müller as our history teacher, he announced a series of lectures on Florentine art. They were given in an auditorium at the university, I missed none of them. The very loftiness of the place—I was a long way from being a student—spelled a certain distancing of the lecturer. I did, of course, sit in the front, and he noticed me, but there were a lot more listeners than in school; people of all ages, even adults, sat among us, and I took that as a mark of popularity for the man who had meant more to me than any other teacher. There was the same enthusiastic roaring and quaffing that I had done without for so long—interrupted only by the slides he pointed at. His respect for works of art was so great that he would go mute at such times. The instant a slide was flashed, he uttered only two or three more sentences, which were as modest as could be, and then he fell silent to avoid disturbing the absorption he expected from us. I didn't care for that at all, I regretted every moment in which the roaring stopped, and whatever went into me and whatever I liked depended solely on his words.

In the very first lecture, he showed us the doors of the Battisterio; and the fact that Ghiberti had worked on them for twenty-one and twenty-eight years moved me more deeply than what I saw on the doors. Now I realized that one can devote a whole lifetime to one or two works, and patience, which I had always admired, acquired something monumental for me. Less than five years later, I found the work to which I wanted to devote *my* life. The ability to articulate it, not only to myself, and to tell other people about it later on, without embarrassment, people whose respect I cared about—that ability is something I owe to Eugen Müller's information about Ghiberti.

In the third lecture, we came to the Medici Chapel; the entire hour was spent on it. The melancholy of the reclining female figures seized hold of me, the dark slumber of one, the painful struggle of barely awakening in the other. Beauty that was nothing but beauty seemed empty to me, Raphael meant little to me; but beauty that had something to carry, that was burdened by passion, misfortune, and dark forebodings fascinated me. It was as though it weren't abstract, for itself, independent of the whims of time, but as though, on the contrary, it had to prove itself in misfortune, as though it had to be exposed to great pressure, and it was only by not being consumed in this struggle, by remaining strong and restrained, that it had the right to be called beautiful.

But it wasn't only those two female figures that excited me, it was also what Eugen Müller said about Michelangelo personally. He must have been reading the biographies by Condivi and Vasari shortly before his lecture; he mentioned several concrete features, which I came upon and recognized in these books a few years later. They lived in his memory with such freshness and immediacy that one might think he had only just learned those details by word of mouth. Nothing seemed diminished by the time that had passed since then, much less by cold historical research. Even the nose, smashed in Michelangelo's youth, appealed to me, as though he had been thus made a sculptor. Then his love for Savonarola, whose sermons he still read as an old man, even though the preacher had so violently attacked the idolatry of art, even though he was an enemy of Lorenzo Medici. Lorenzo had discovered the boy Michelangelo, he had brought him up in his home and at his table, his death had shaken the almost twenty-year-old. But that didn't mean that he didn't recognize the vileness of his successor; and his friend's dream, prompting him to leave Florence, was the first in a long series of reported dreams that I collected and thought about. I made a note of it during the lecture, rereading it frequently, and I recall the moment ten years later, while writing *Auto-da-Fé*, when I stumbled upon this same dream in Condivi.

I loved Michelangelo's pride, the struggle he dared to wage against Julius II, when he, an offended man, fled from Rome. A true republican, he also defended himself against the pope, there were moments when he faced him as though they were equals. I have never forgotten the eight lonely months near Carrara, when he had blocks hewn out for the pope's tomb, and the sudden temptation that came over him there to carve huge sculptures right in the landscape, visible to distant ships at sea. Then the ceiling of the Sistine Chapel, with which his enemies, who refused to consider him a painter, wanted to destroy him: he worked on it for four years, and what a work came forth! The impatient pope's threat to have him flung off the scaffold, his refusal to decorate the frescoes with gold. Here too, I was impressed by the years, but this time the work itself also went into me, and never has anything been so determining for me as the ceiling of the Sistine

Chapel. It taught me how creative a defiance can be if it is tied to patience. The labor on *The Last Judgment* took eight years, and even though I didn't understand the greatness of this opus till later, I was burnt by the shame that the artist experienced at eighty, when the figures were painted over because of their nakedness.

Thus arose in me the legend of the man who endures torment and overcomes it for the greatest thing that he invents. Prometheus, whom I loved, was transferred for me into the world of human beings. What the demigod had done, he had done *without fear*; only when it was over did he become the master of the torment. Michelangelo, however, had labored in fear, the figures of the Medici Chapel were created when he was regarded as a foe by the Medici who ruled Florence. His fear of him was well founded, bad things could have happened to the artist, the pressure weighing down upon the figures was his own. But it would not be correct to say that this feeling was crucial for the impression of those other creations that began to accompany me for years: the figures of the Sistine Chapel.

It was not only the image of Michelangelo that was set up in me at that time. I admired him as I had admired no one since the explorers. He was the first to give me a sense of pain that is not exhausted in itself, that becomes something, that then exists for others, and lasts. It is a special kind of pain, not the bodily pain which all men profess. When he fell off the scaffold while working on *The Last Judgment* and was seriously injured, he locked himself in his house, not admitting any attendant or any physician, and lay there alone. He would not acknowledge the pain, he excluded everybody from it, and would have perished because of it. A friend who was a doctor found the arduous way up back stairs to the artist's room, where he lay in misery, and the friend stayed with him day and night until the danger was past. It was a totally different kind of torment that entered his work and determined the tremendousness of his figures. His sensitivity to humiliation drove him to undertake the most difficult things. He could not be a model for me, because he was more: the god of pride.

It was he who led me to the prophets: Ezekiel, Jeremiah, and Isaiah. Since I strove for everything that wasn't close to me, the only book that I never read in those days, that I avoided, was the Bible. Grandfather's prayers, bound to their periodic times, filled me with repugnance. He reeled them off in a language that I didn't understand, I didn't care to know that they meant. What could they mean anyhow if he broke off to make comical gestures at stamps that he had brought along for me. I encountered the prophets not as a Jew, not in their words. They came to me in Michelangelo's figures. A few months after the lectures that

I have told about, I received the present I most desired: a folder of huge reproductions of the Sistine paintings, they happened to be the prophets and sibyls.

I lived on an intimate footing with them for ten years, one knows how long these young years are. I got to know the pictures better than people. I soon hung them up, I always had them before me, but it was not habituation that attached me to them; I stood spellbound in front of Isaiah's half-open mouth, puzzling over the bitter words he spoke to God, and I felt the reproach of his raised finger. I tried to think his words before knowing them; his new creator prepared me for them.

Perhaps it was arrogant of me to think such words, they sprang from his gesture, I did not feel the need to experience them in their precise form, I did not seek the correct wording where it could easily have been learned: the image, the gesture contained the words so powerfully that I had to keep turning to them yet again, that was the compulsion, the true value, the inexhaustibility of the Sistine Chapel. Jeremiah's grief, Ezekiel's vehemence and fieriness also attracted me; I never gazed at Isaiah without seeing them. It was the *old* prophets who would not let me go; even though Isaiah was not really depicted as old, I nevertheless included him among them. The young prophets meant as little to me as the sibyls. I had heard of the bold foreshortenings admired in some of these figures, I had heard about the beauty of the sibyls, the Delphic, the Libyan Sybil, but I merely took in that admiration like things I read, I knew it through the words in which it was described for me, but they remained paintings, they did not stand before me like exaggerated human beings, I didn't think I heard them like the old prophets, the latter had a life for me such as I had never experienced, I can only— very inadequately—call it a life of obsession, next to which nothing else existed. It is important to observe that they did not become gods for me. I did not perceive them as a power established over me; when they spoke to me or I even tried speaking to them, when I faced them, I did not fear them, I admired them, I dared to ask them questions. Perhaps I was prepared for them by my early habituation to the dramatic characters in the Vienna period. What I had felt back then as a raging torrent, in which I swam in a kind of confused daze, amid so many things that I did not know how to distinguish, was now articulated for me in sharply differentiated, overwhelming, but lucid figures.

Paradise Rejected

In May 1921, my mother came to visit me. I led her through the garden and showed her all the blossoming. I sensed that she was in a dark mood, and I tried to soothe her with fragrances. But she did not inhale them, she maintained a stubborn silence, it was bizarre to see how quiet her nostrils remained. At the end of the tennis court, where no one could hear us, she said "Sit down!" and she sat down herself. "This is over!" she said abruptly, and I knew the time had come. "You have to leave here. Your mind's deteriorating!"

"I don't want to leave Zurich. Let's stay here, here I know why I'm in the world."

"Why you're in the world! Masaccio and Michelangelo! Do you believe this is the world? Little flowers to paint, Fräulein Mina's sparrow's nest. These young girls, the way they fuss over you. Each more respectful and more devoted than the next. Your notebooks chockfull of the phylogeny of spinach. The Pestalozzi Calendar, that's your world! The famous men you leaf through. Did you ever ask yourself whether you had any right to it? You know the pleasant part, their fame; did you ever ask yourself how they lived? Do you believe they sat in a garden, like you now, among flowers and trees? Do you believe their life was a fragrance? The books you read! Your Conrad Ferdinand Meyer! These historical tales! What relation do they have to the way things are today? You believe that if you read something about St. Bartholomew's Night or the Thirty Years' War, then you know it! You know nothing! Nothing! Everything is different. It's awful!"

Now it all came out. Her dislike of science: I had waxed enthusiastic about the structure of the world as revealed in plants and animals; and in letters to her, I had said it was good to detect a purpose behind it, and I was of the still unshaken opinion that this purpose was a good one.

But she didn't believe the structure of the world was good. She had never been religious and never resigned herself to the way things were. She never got over her shock at the war. It passed into the experiences of her sanatorium period, she knew people there who were virtually dying before her eyes. She never discussed that with me, it was a part of her experience that remained concealed from me, but it did exist within her and exerted its effect.

She cared even less for my sympathy with animals. Her dislike was so great that she indulged in the cruelest jokes with me. In Kandersteg,

on the street in front of our hotel, I saw a very young calf being yanked
along. It resisted every step; the slaughterer, whom I knew by sight,
was having no end of trouble with it; I didn't understand what was
happening; she stood next to this scene and explained quite coolly that
it was being dragged off to slaughter. Right after that, it was time for
the *table d'hôte*, we sat down to dine, I refused to have any meat. I
stuck to my resolve for several days. She was annoyed; I put mustard
on my vegetables, she smiled and said: "Do you know how they make
mustard? They use chicken blood." That confused me, I didn't see
through her derision; by the time I understood, she had broken my
resistance, and she said: "That's the way it is. You're like the calf, it
has to give in too in the end." She wasn't picky about her methods. But
she was also convinced that humane feelings are meant for human
beings alone; if they were related to all forms of life, they would have
to lose their strength and become vague and ineffective.

Her distrust of poetry was a different matter. The only interest she
had ever shown in poetry was in Baudelaire's *Les Fleurs du Mal;* that
came from the special constellation of her relationship to Herr Professor. She was bothered by the smallness of the form in poems, they
ended too quickly for her. She sometimes said that poems lulled you
them shakento sleep, basically they were lullabies. Adults ought to
watch out for lullabies, it was despicable remaining devoted to them.
I believe that the measure of passion in verses was too low for her. She
set great store by passion, she found it plausible only in drama. For
her, Shakespeare was the expression of the true nature of man, nothing
here was diminished or alleviated.

I must recall that the shock of death had struck her with the same
force as myself. She was twenty-seven when Father suddenly died. This
event haunted her for the rest of her life, twenty-five more years, in
many forms, whose root was always the same, however. Without my
realizing it, she was an emotional model for me in that. War was the
multiplication of that death, absurdity intensified to massiveness.

More recently, she had also begun fearing the overwhelmingly feminine influences in my life. How was I to become a man through mere
knowledge, which kept attracting me more and more intensely? She
despised her sex. Her hero was not some woman, it was Coriolanus.

"It was a mistake leaving Vienna," she said. "I've made life too easy
for you. I saw Vienna after the war, *I* know how it looked then."

This was one of those scenes in which she tried to demolish everything
she had built up in me through years of patient efforts. In her own way,
she was a revolutionary. She believed in sudden changes, breaking in

and ruthlessly altering all constellations, even in individual men.

Her special anger focused on my account of the two seaplanes that had crashed into Lake Zurich very close to us. The crashes had occurred a week apart, in autumn of 1920, and I had written about them, shaken and terrified. The connection with the lake, which meant so much to me, infuriated her. She said those deaths had been something lyrical for me. She scornfully asked whether I had also written poems about them. "I would have shown them to you, if I had," I said; the reproach was unfair, I talked to her about everything.

"I thought," she then said, "that your Mörike inspired you." And she reminded me of his poem "Reflect, Oh Soul!" which I had read to her. "You're trapped in the idyll of Lake Zurich. I want to take you away from here. You like everything so much. You're as soft and sentimental as your old maids. You probably want to end up as a flower painter?"

"No, I only like Michelangelo's prophets."

"Isaiah, I know. You told me. What do you think he was like, this Isaiah?"

"He strove against God," I said.

"And do you know what that means? Do you have any idea what that's all about?"

No, I didn't know. I held my tongue. I was suddenly mortified.

"You think it consists of holding the mouth half-open and glowering. That's the danger of pictures. They become frozen poses for something that occurs incessantly, constantly, on and on."

"And is Jeremiah also a pose?"

"No, neither is a pose, not Isaiah and not Jeremiah. But they turn into poses for you. You're satisfied if you can look at them. That saves you the trouble of having your own experiences. That's the danger of art. Tolstoy knew it. You're nothing as yet and you think you're every-thing you know from books or pictures. I should never have led you to books. Now, paintings have come to you through the Yalta. That's all you needed. You've become a bookworm and everything is equally important to you. The phylogeny of spinach and Michelangelo. You haven't earned a single day of your livelihood yourself. You've got a word for everything connected with that: business. You despise money. You despise the work it's earned with. Do you realize that you're the parasite and not the people you despise?"

Perhaps that dreadful conversation was the start of our falling-out. At the time, I didn't perceive it as that. I only had one thought, to justify myself to her. I didn't want to leave Zurich. I sensed that during this conversation she had made up her mind to take me away from Zurich and put me in a "harder" environment, which she had some control over as well.

"You'll see I'm no parasite. I'm too proud for that. I want to be a human being."

"I'm human with human contradiction! You really chose that carefully. You should hear yourself quoting it. As though you had discovered America. As though you had done God knows what and had to repent it now. You've done *nothing*. You haven't earned a single night in your garret yourself. The books you read there were written by others for you. You select what you find pleasant and you despise everything else. Do you really think you're a human being? A human being is someone who's struggled through life. Have you ever been in any danger? Has anyone ever threatened you? No one's ever smashed your nose. You hear something you like and you simply take it, but you have no right to it. I'm human with human contradiction! You're not a human being yet. You're nothing. A chatterbox is no human being."

"I'm not a chatterbox. I mean what I say."

"How can you mean anything? You don't know anything. You've just read it all. Business, you say, and you don't even know what that is. You think business consists of raking in money. But before a man gets that far, he has to have some ideas. He has to have ideas that you haven't the foggiest notion about. He has to know what people are like and convince them of something. No one gives you anything for nothing. Do you think it's enough just putting on some sham for people? You wouldn't get very far like that!"

"You never told me you admire that."

"Maybe I don't admire it, maybe there are things I admire more. But I'm talking about you now. You have absolutely no right to despise or admire anything. You first have to know what's really going on in the world. You have to experience it personally. You have to be buffeted around and prove you can defend yourself."

"I am doing that. I'm doing it with you."

"Well, then you've got an easy time of it. I'm a woman. Things are different among men. They won't let you off so easily."

"What about the teachers? Aren't they men?"

"Yes, yes, but that's an artificial situation. In school, you're protected. They don't take you seriously. They see you as a boy that has to be helped. School doesn't count."

"I defended myself against my uncle. He couldn't win me over."

"That was a short conversation. How long did you see him? You'd have to be with him, in his business, day after day, hour after hour, then you'd see whether you can hold your own. You drank his chocolate in Sprüngli and ran away from him: That was your entire achievement."

"He'd be the stronger one in his business. He could order me around and push me around. I'd have his vileness in front of my eyes all the time. He certainly wouldn't win me over. That much I can tell you."

"Maybe. But that's just talk now. You haven't proven anything."

"I can't help it that I haven't proven anything yet. What could I have proven at sixteen?"

"Not much, that's true. But other boys are put to work at your age. If things were right, you'd have been an apprentice for two years by now. I saved you from that. I don't notice your being grateful to me. You're just arrogant and you're getting more arrogant from month to month. I've got to tell you the truth; your arrogance irritates me. Your arrogance gets on my nerves."

"You always wanted me to take everything seriously. Is that arrogance?"

"Yes, for you look down on others who don't think as you do. You're cunning too and you make things comfortable for yourself in your easy life. Your only real concern is that there are enough books left to read!"

"That was the way it *used* to be, when we lived on *Scheuchzerstrasse*. I don't even think of that anymore. Now I want to learn everything."

"Learn everything! Learn everything! No one could do that. One has to stop learning and do something. That's why you have to get away from here."

"But what can I do before I finish school?"

"You'll never do anything! You'll finish school, then you'll want to go to the university. Do you know why you want to go? Just so that you can keep on learning. That way, you'll turn into a monster and not a human being. Learning isn't an end in itself. One learns in order to prove oneself among other people."

"I want to keep on learning all the time. Whether or not I prove myself, I want to keep on learning. I want to learn."

"But how? But how? Who'll give you the money?"

"I'll earn it."

"And what will you do with what you learn? You'll choke on it. There's nothing more awful than dead knowledge."

"My knowledge won't be dead. It's not dead now either."

"Because you haven't got it yet. It becomes something dead only when you get it."

"But I'm going to do something with it, not for myself."

"Yes, yes, I know. You're going to give it away because you haven't got anything yet. So long as you've got nothing, it's easy to say that. Once you really have something, then we'll see whether you give anything away. Everything else is claptrap. Would you give your books away now?"

"No. I need them. I didn't say 'give away,' I said I'd do something, not for myself."

"But you don't know what yet. That's all airs, empty talk, and you indulge in it because it sounds noble. But all that counts is what a person *really* does, nothing else matters. There'll hardly be anything left that you could do, you're so contented with everything around you. A contented person does nothing, a contented person is lazy, a contented person has retired before he has begun doing anything. A contented person keeps on doing the same thing over and over again, like a bureaucrat. You're so contented that you'd rather stay in Switzerland forever. You know nothing of the world and you'd like to retire here at the age of sixteen. That's why you've got to get out of here."

I felt that something must have embittered her particularly strongly. Was it still "The Black Spider"? She was thrusting away so violently at me that I didn't dare bring it up right away. I had told her about the generosity of the Italian workers when I was collecting money with the girl, she had liked that. "They have to work hard," she had said, "and yet they're still not hardened."

"Why don't we go to Italy?" I wasn't serious, it was an attempt to change the subject.

"No, you'd like to amble around museums and read old histories on every town. There's no hurry. You can do that later. I'm not talking about pleasure junkets. You have to go to a place which won't be pleasurable for you. I want to take you to Germany. The people are badly off there now. You ought to see what happens when people lose a war."

"But you wanted them to lose the war. You said they started the war. If people start a war, they ought to lose it, I learned that from you."

"You've learned nothing! Otherwise you'd know one doesn't think of that any more when the people have met with disaster. I saw it in Vienna, and I can't forget it, I can see it all the time."

"Why do you want me to see it? I can imagine it, after all."

"Like in a book, isn't that so! You think it's enough to *read* about something in order to know what it's like. But it's not enough. Reality is something else. Reality is everything. Anybody who tries to avoid reality doesn't deserve to live."

"I'm not trying to avoid it. I told you about 'The Black Spider.' "

"That's the worst example you could pick. That's when my eyes opened about you. The story absorbed you because it belongs to Emmentwl. All you think about is valleys. Ever since you visited Lötschen Valley, your mind's been degenerating. You heard two words, and what were those words? 'Come, little boy,' or however they pronounce it there. Those people can't speak to save themselves, they never talk. What can they say, cut off from the world and ignorant of everything. They'll never talk there; but you made up for it by talking all the more about them. They would have been flabbergasted if they'd heard you! You came back from your excursion and spoke about Old High German for days on end. Old High German! Today! They may not even have enough to eat, but why should you care! You hear two words, you think they're Old High German because they remind you of something you read. That gets you more excited that what you see with your own eyes. The old woman knew perfectly well why she was suspicious, she's had her experiences with people like yourselves. But you people chattered away as you hiked through the valley, happy and elevated by *their* poverty, you left them there, they have to struggle on with their lives, and you people show up at the hotel as conquerors. There's dancing in the evening, but you're not interested, you've brought something better along, you learned something. And what? Two words of Old High German, allegedly, you're not even sure if that's right. And I'm supposed to watch you creep away into nothing! I'm going to take you to the inflation in Germany, then you'll forget all about the Old High German little boy."

Nothing I had ever told her was forgotten. Everything was brought up. She twisted every single one of my words around, I couldn't find any new word to make her waver. She had never struck away at me like that. It was a matter of life and death, and yet I greatly admired her; if she had known how seriously I took it, she would have stopped; each of her words lashed me like a whip, I sensed that she was being unjust to me and I sensed how right she was.

She kept coming back to "The Black Spider," she had taken it altogether differently from me, our earlier conversations about it had been *untrue*, she hadn't wanted to deny it, she wanted to get *me* away from it. What she had said about Gotthelf had been a skirmish, he didn't interest her at all. She wanted to deny in him what she perceived as her own truth, it was her story, not his, the setting of the spider was not Emmental, it was the *Waldsanatorium*. Of the people with whom she had discussed it, two had died in the meantime. She had previously spared me the deaths, which were not infrequent there, and she didn't even let me guess what had happened when we saw each other again.

I knew what it meant when she didn't bring up a name anymore, but I took care not to ask. Her dislike of "valleys" was only seemingly due to the confinement. What she reproached me for—the propensity for idylls, the innocence and self-complacence—was nourished by *her* fear: the danger from which she wanted to save me was a greater one, it was the danger with which our lives had always been marked, and the word "inflation," which she used in connection with Germany, a word I had never heard her use, sounded like a penitence. I wouldn't have been able to state it so clearly, but she had never spoken so much about poverty, that made a big impression on me; and even though I had to muster all my strength in order to save my skin, I liked the fact that she rationalized her attack by pointing out how badly off other people were.

But that was only part of it, and the threat to take me away from Zurich struck me more deeply. There had been peace in school for over a year. I had started understanding the other pupils and I thought about them. I felt I belonged with them and many of the teachers. I now realized that my position in Tiefenbrunnen was a usurped position. My reigning there as the sole male was a bit ridiculous, but it was pleasant to feel safe and not always be challenged. Besides, the process of learning had become more and more lavish under these circumstances, not a day passed on which nothing was added, it looked as if it would never end, I imagined it would go on like that for the rest of my life, and no attack in the world could have gotten me away from that. It was a time *without fear*; this was due to the expansion, I was expanding everywhere, but I wasn't conscious of any injustice, the same experiences were accessible to anyone, after all; and now she confounded and confused me by trying to put me in the wrong because of my enthusiasm for Lötschen Valley and trying to make me seem unjust towards its inhabitants.

This time, her derision didn't break off suddenly, it kept intensifying with every sentence. Never before had she treated me as a parasite, never before had there been any talk about my having to earn my own keep. The word "apprentice," which she threw at me, was something I associated with practical or mechanical activity, the last thing in the world she had ever impressed on me. I was smitten with letters and words, and if that was arrogance, then she had stubbornly raised me in that way. Now she was suddenly carrying on about "reality," by which she meant everything that I hadn't as yet experienced and couldn't know anything about. It was as though she were trying to roll a tremendous burden off on me and crush me underneath. When she said "You're nothing," I really felt as if I had become nothing.

These leaps, these raging contradictions in her character, were not alien to me, I had often witnessed them with amazement and admiration, those very things stood for the reality which she reproached me for not knowing. Perhaps I had banked on that too strongly. Even in the period of our separation, I had always referred to her in everything. I was never certain how she would react to my accounts, all initiative remained with her, I desired her contradicting me and I wanted it to be fierce; it was only in regard to acknowledged weaknesses of hers that I could deceive her with inventions like the dancing mice in the moonlight. But even then I always had the feeling that it was up to her, that she wanted to be deceived. She was a marvelously lively ultimate authority, her verdicts were so unexpected, so fantastic, and yet so detailed that they inevitably triggered counter-emotions giving one the strength to appeal them. She was a higher and higher ultimate authority, and although she seemed to lay a claim to it, it was never the final authority.

But this time I had the feeling that she wanted to annihilate me. She said things that couldn't be quibbled with. I agreed with some of them on the spot and my defense was lamed. If some objection did occur to me, she jumped over to something entirely different. She raged through the life of the past two years as though she had only just learned about all the events, and things she had once apparently accepted with either approval or bored silence now suddenly turned out to be crimes. She had forgotten nothing, she had her own way of remembering, as though she had concealed from herself and from me the things she was now condemning me for.

It lasted a good long time. I was filled with terror. I began fearing her. I no longer wondered why she was saying all those things. So long as I had sought her presumable motives and retorted to them, I had felt less disconcerted, as though we were facing each other as equals, each leaning on his reason, two free people. Gradually, this self-assurance crumbled, I found nothing more within me to use with sufficient strength, I consisted only of ruins now and I admitted defeat.

She wasn't the least bit exhausted after this conversation, as she normally was following conversations about her illnesses, her bodily weakness, her physical despair. On the contrary, she seemed strong and wild and as implacable as I liked her best on other occasions. From that moment on, she never let go. She busied herself with the move to Germany, a country that, she said, was marked by the war. She had the notion that I would enter a harder school there, among men who had been in the war and knew the worst.

I fought against this move in any way I could, but she wouldn't listen and she took me away. The only perfectly happy years, the paradise in Zurich, were over. Perhaps I would have remained happy if she hadn't torn me away. But it is true that I experienced different things from the ones I knew in paradise. It is true that I, like the earliest man, came into being only by an expulsion from Paradise.

Printed in the USA
CPSIA information can be obtained
at www.ICGtesting.com
LVHW091131150724
785511LV00001B/72

9 780374 518028